THE
STRANGER
IN MY BED

THE
STRANGER
IN MY BED

and other

Real Life Stories of Hope and Change

Marvin H. Berenson, M.D.

Cove Books
Beverly Hills, California

Cove Books
P.O. Box 11688
Beverly Hills, CA 90213-4688

The Stranger in My Bed
and other
Real Live Stories of Hope and Change

Cover design: Robert Aulicino

Publisher's Cataloging-in-Publication
(Provided by Quality Books, Inc.)

Berenson, Marvin
    The stranger in my bed : and other real life stories of hope and change / Marvin H. Berenson. -- 1st ed.
    p. cm.
    LCCN 2002093184
    ISBN 0-9700885-3-1
    1. Eating disorders--Treatment--Case studies.
2. Compulsive behavior--Case studies. 3. Depression, Mental. I. Title

RC552.E18B47 2002   616.85'26
                                        QBI02-701894

ACKNOWLEDGMENTS

My gratitude is extended to the many people who helped make this book possible, especially to the eight patients whose case histories I am presenting. Their courage to overcome formidable obstacles in their lives inspired me to write their stories.

I want to thank my literary editor Mary Embree for her consistently helpful editing and direction as the book took form.

Doug Berenson, my son, greatly contributed to the editing and helped in the book's overall development. His advice and overview were consistently useful.

Irene Cole, a literary friend, reviewed and commented openly on needed corrections or changes and was always ready with advice and suggestions.

Also contributing ideas, critiquing the book, and offering invaluable editing were Patricia Rosenburg, Kelly McCool, Jean Berenson, Joe Tilem, and David Bordeaux.

Special thanks to John Kremer for his astute guidance and encouragement in the writing of this book.

CONTENTS

INTRODUCTION

CHAPTER ONE   1
SARAH: The Awakening

CHAPTER TWO   26
HAROLD: Your Children Can Save Your Life

CHAPTER THREE   58
ANGELA: The Artist's Model

CHAPTER FOUR   94
CARL: The Yo-Yo Man

CHAPTER FIVE   122
JUDY: Taking Control

CHAPTER SIX   149
SCOTT AND MARILYN: The Stranger in My Bed

CHAPTER SEVEN   199
NANCY: Twelve More Pounds and I'll Be Perfect

CHAPTER EIGHT   222
JEFFREY: The 375-Pound Man

APPENDIX 1   265
SUMMARY: The Five Keys to Permanent Weight Control

APPENDIX 2   271
GUIDED IMAGERY THERAPY

ABOUT THE AUTHOR   273

INTRODUCTION

"I don't believe anyone can help me. I've tried many times in the past year to overcome this terrible affliction. Yes, I call it an affliction. I can no longer blame my parents or my sister. I can only blame myself. I now want to live but I believe I'm dying. Doctor, look into my eyes. Tell me truthfully, do you see my death?"

When I first met Sarah, at the age of forty-three, she had reached the lowest point of her life. She felt that death was close. During the years that I knew her she would find a way to rise from the painful depths of her despair and for the first time would feel what it meant to be fully alive and to be loved.

The eight patients who fill the pages of this book are like Sarah. All had extraordinary qualities, histories, relationships or problems. Some felt overwhelmed by defeat or by a persistent helplessness. Yet all faced their conflicts with hope and courage and ultimately rose above their desperation to move into a world of renewed faith to find success in changing their lives. All affirmed the belief that we have within us a great power that can be tapped to guide us toward health and true fulfillment. All would reveal some of the intricacies of the process of inner discovery and provide new insights into self-growth. In this group were many of my most complex, challenging and inspirational patients.

These eight patients initially sought therapy to be helped with unusual compulsive eating disorders. All eventually gained insight into their compulsive behavior and used strikingly creative methods to improve their life and belief in themselves. They fought valiantly to overcome great obstacles and many found success in surprising ways.

They were patients whose beliefs, attitudes and body images were often distorted by events from early periods of their lives. Memories were often hidden from awareness. One man, Jeff, who weighed 375 pounds, was convinced that he was doomed by his genetic make-up to always be obese. He faced incredible problems from his past that had become imbedded in his body.

Angela never weighed more than 124 pounds. When she entered my office for her first session she was consumed by terror. She fully believed that if she left my office, she would be unable to stop eating the small amount of food that would make her weigh 125 pounds. At that precise moment she would no longer exist and destroying her body was necessary to conform to that belief. Her first visit extended many hours into the night. Rarely have I known anyone who faced terror as she did.

Why did I select these particular eight cases histories? Most were chosen because they illustrated how certain overweight people struggled with and overcame difficult eating compulsions. I also selected cases that I hoped would be inspirational to readers. They offered exceptional examples of how optimism about life and especially about ourselves created the power to rise above major obstacles.

I understood the barriers each of these eight people confronted and greatly admired their ability to bring meaning and eventual happiness into their lives. Each endured untold anguish, yet did not give up. All were able to face disturbing insights that at times caused a temporary increase in their pain. I learned again and again that those who claim the bounty of life will find it no matter what odds appear against them.

I wanted to find among my patients those who could truly awaken our souls.

They would be patients who had the ability to articulate their struggle and bring the reader into the passion of their recovery. They would be people that we could come to know. Each would exist in a world that anyone could understand no matter how strange and bizarre that world was.

Like many therapists, I reach deeply into the hearts and mind of my patients. When patients tell me something highly disturbing and I feel their suffering deeply I often cry with them.

I used to think that it would embarrass my patients if they noticed my tears. I never allude to my reaction since it just seems that it's part of what happens between two people who feel closeness. Despite such emotion, I don't believe I lose my objectivity. Perhaps in a way it's a measure of my understanding and thus ultimately helps me be objective. I mention this because you will find my tears in the pages that follow.

To assure confidentiality I have modified names, situations, circumstantial factors and other elements. However, the essential facts are completely unchanged. To make the case histories more vivid and alive to the reader, I have presented them in narrative form. Dialogue is used whenever possible. I hope that this approach facilitates your understanding of how these eight patients found solutions to what had initially been presented as insurmountable problems.

Exploring and facing oneself is not easy. I use imagery techniques to uncover the past when I believe that it is the only way a person will ever truly overcome the serious problems they carry with them. Most of us do not need to re-experience early traumas so intensely or attempt to recover the past. Yet we all want to live better. How does one find a comfortable and happy life? There's no magic formula. But there are some guidelines.

In the eight case histories presented here, I allude to and sometimes briefly describe pertinent parts of The Five Keys Diet. A description of the diet program, which includes the rag doll relaxation technique, can be found in Appendix 1. The Guided Imagery Technique is explained in Appendix 2.

I also address the value of mental imagery. In the diet book I encourage the use of imagery exercises and describe how to use them to enhance one's life. Most of my patients found them to be an important part of their success. Many also found other uses for mental imagery, including discovering new ways to stimulate creativity, becoming more efficient, improving concentration, and enhancing athletic and artistic abilities. The eight patients in this book created many imagery exercises that I share with you.

These case histories are the testimonies of courageous people who fought long and hard to overcome tenacious eating disorders and to develop control over their lives. The stories of their struggles can be understood by each of us. To varying degrees we have all experienced hardship and despair. Most of us can realize the great effort that is needed to overcome personal difficulties and unacceptable habits that limit our happiness. I believe that by sharing in the extraordinary journeys and ultimate success achieved by these eight persons, you will be stimulated to make your own life more satisfying and fulfilling.

CHAPTER ONE

SARAH: The Awakening

As I opened the door to the waiting room I saw Sarah sitting slumped over, staring at the floor. She was sobbing quietly. She was as obese as I had been led to believe from our brief telephone conversation when she called for an appointment. "I'm so heavy I can hardly walk," she had murmured as I carefully questioned her on the telephone. "No, I don't know how much I weigh. I don't own a scale," ended the discussion about her weight.

As I looked at her it was her face and clothes that drew my attention. Her dark gray dress, already too small for her, was covered with bits of many meals and seemed to accent her sad appearance. But it was her face, framed by gnarled, stringy hair that mainly struck me. Her tear-streaked face and eyes that only looked downward was one of torment and deep depression. Had I misunderstood her reason to see me? The referring physician said she was depressed and wanted to lose weight, but gave me little information about the state of her deterioration. My first thought was the possibility of an organic brain disorder, perhaps early Alzheimer's, but the referring doctor certainly would have told me if that were the case. Was her appearance strictly due to a profound depression?

I walked over to her and held out my hand as I introduced myself. She made no attempt to respond, but continued looking down at the floor. Tears ran unheeded down her face.

"Please come into my office," I suggested, offering my hand to assist her. She didn't move.

"I realize that this is a very difficult moment for you but coming into the office will give us an opportunity to talk. I would like to know why you're so unhappy." She still didn't move. "You don't have to talk in the office if you don't want to."

Shyly, Sarah raised her head and looked into my eyes sadly. She seemed so alone and frightened as she slowly took my hand. I led her into the office.

That was the beginning of my long relationship with Sarah. What followed was a voyage into the profound desperation that had overwhelmed her for so many years and the path that we both followed as she slowly rose from the depths of her depression.

Sarah was forty-three, born and raised in a small town on the eastern seacoast. Her only sibling, Maggie, three years her senior, was found to be mentally retarded when Sarah was around three. Unaccountably, her parents devoted all their energy and what love they had to try to make Maggie normal, relegating Sarah to the periphery of the family. When Maggie became tyrannical and brutalized Sarah it was ignored by her mother and father. When Sarah fought back she was criticized or punished. Slowly, inexorably, she slid into depression and shied away from contact with anyone.

In school she became known as weird and a loner. "Don't mess with Sarah" was the word that went around the school. She was known to lash out suddenly and violently at anyone who came too close. Her teachers almost despaired but held out hope that someday Sarah would "grow up." After all, they reasoned, although she never talked, she managed to get the highest grades in her classes and knew answers that other children did not. By the third grade, when she had become almost totally alienated from her family and classmates, Sarah began to gain weight. "I would have died back then," she once whispered to me, "if I couldn't eat chocolate cookies. I used to steal money from my mother and buy boxes of cookies and hide them in the basement where I would go to eat. I needed to eat. Eating kept me alive."

My first session with Sarah moved me profoundly. During the first fifteen minutes she sat quietly crying. I moved my chair a bit closer and waited. I told her that there was no need to speak until she was ready to do so. "More important is to feel comfortable with me and know that in this office you can just sit and be and not talk if it's too painful."

What I learned during that first session was the horror that she carried with her since early childhood. I sat and listened, unable to move, unable to stem the tears that slowly came into my eyes, and barely able to maintain the emotional objectivity needed to help her. In that first hour I became immersed in a vortex of emotions that would occupy me for the next three years. But I also sensed that behind the horror and desperation was a soul waiting to be born.

"When I first began to eat, hidden in the dark basement, I felt life come into me. I was no longer alone. No longer afraid that I would hurt Maggie or my mother and father. I hated them and I hated myself. I was filled with frightening thoughts of cutting them up and flushing them down the toilet. The more I ate, the more I began to revel in those evil thoughts. Back then I didn't think my thoughts were evil. I thought they deserved to die. I hated them."

Sarah spoke of living in total isolation for the past ten years. She made no friends and saw no one. When she went out people avoided her. She rarely bathed and knew that her body odor kept people away. At first she did it deliberately but as the years progressed she just forgot to bathe as she slipped further and further into a bizarre mental state. As I heard her story I wondered if she had been going through a period of psychosis. I probed her thoughts and listened to my inner reactions to discover if indeed she was even now psychotic and needed hospitalization. But when she described her inner world, it was with intense feeling and eloquence and free of the disorganized language of psychosis. Sarah was residing in the deepest throes of depression and aloneness. She had come to see me at the time when her life had almost ceased and outside nurturance had long since ended.

"When I look at my body and feel my horrible puffy skin and feel the endless torment in my mind I wonder why I came to see you," she said, now looking directly at me. "I don't believe anyone can help me. I've tried at times in the past year or so to overcome this terrible affliction. Yes, I call it an affliction. I can no longer blame my parents or my sister. I can only blame myself. I now want to live but I believe I'm dying. Doctor, look into my eyes. Tell me truthfully, do you see my death?"

I didn't know what to say. "Do I see your death?" I asked, not wanting to place the burden of an answer upon her but not really understanding what she was asking.

"I feel such bleakness, such emptiness, such a lack of being, that I believe that the look of death is already inside me and soon death will come and bear me away." Her voice was so soft I could hardly hear her. She cried silently now and waited.

"No, Sarah," I finally responded, "I don't see death when I look into your eyes. I do see your deep despair, but not death. If it were death inside you, you would never have sought me out."

"I don't want to die," she said, her voice filled with anguish. "I don't know if I can ever come back to living again, but I don't want to die. Today, knowing I was coming here I bathed for the first time in over a month. I didn't want you to be as repulsed by me as I am to myself. I wanted you to help me. I need to find a way to come alive again. I need to lose this terrible covering of atrocious fat that has kept me imprisoned for much of my life. I came to you because I need someone to help me extricate myself from my fatness. I know that I'm fat because of my feelings, but I also know that my fatness has been my jail. I will only be free when I no longer carry my own prison."

She became silent. I looked long and intensely at her. Where did those words come from? She speaks like a poet, I thought. How overwhelming her life must be, struggling so desperately to get free. And her body has become her battleground.

By the time Sarah reached adolescence she was the fattest person in her class. No one criticized or made fun of her to her face. They were afraid of her. "I knew how to make everyone avoid me," she told me one day. "I knew that if I was tormented, I might kill someone. I really felt back then that I would do it.

"On the first day of high school I carried a large scissors with me. I was in the hall when a small runty kid came over and taunted me. 'You don't belong here, fatty. Get out of here before I kick the shit out of you.'

"I looked at him a long time. Others had now gathered around us. I calmly reached into the large purse I carried and brought out the scissors. Screaming, 'I'll kill you,' I raised it over my head with the apparent intent of trying to kill him. My timing was perfect. I was more terrified of what I was doing than he was but he was convinced I was about to kill him. Without a sound he ran from me, and I chased him for a few yards. Then I turned the knife upon the others who were watching and everyone ran. No one ever bothered me after that. No one reported me. I was free to suffer in silence." Sarah cried when she ended the story. I stifled my own tears as I felt the horror of that moment in her life.

Sarah's brilliance as a student shone even more brightly in high school. Despite weighing over 225 pounds then, she found her way into the hearts of a number of students and teachers. She became the editor of the school newspaper. Her written words struck deep chords in those who read them. In college she rose to the top of her class and was respected for her intelligence and contributions to various student activities. But Sarah always felt alone. No close friends entered her world. Only the sharing of ideas brought her into the company of others. After class she would return home and bury herself in books and her writings. She graduated from college as valedictorian of her class.

She told me what she said on that fateful day of her graduation from college. "I decided that all the other students and parents and professors lived in a fantasy world, believing that the world was good and our time on earth was a blessing from God. I stood before them and quoted from *Dante's Inferno and Purgatory* but rephrased his words to fit what I felt was the nature of life. I talked about the Hell that everyone goes through, the disasters that await us, the torture and torments of living, the descent we all take into endless pain and suffering.

"I told them how we dissemble, pretend anything to believe we're alive and have others love us. None of us is truly alive, I remember saying, and most of us live desperate, lonely, and impoverished lives. Our pretenses will ultimately fail and in our attempt to make our lives better we do all sorts of devious and horrible things leading us to the inferno that awaits us.

"I think everyone in that audience was horror stricken that I would give such a depressing commencement speech. But the final blow came at the end of my speech when I said that all of them have witnessed such emotions. They have seen a person living in the deadly embrace of total alienation. I saw heads shake as though they could not imagine such a person. I then stood as tall as I could and said that 'I am such a person.'

"When the gasps died down I said, 'and today is the last time any of you will ever see me again.' Then I sat down. The audience was silent not knowing what to do or what to think. I knew they were thinking that I was going to kill myself. And for a time I thought that's what I would do. Instead, on that very day I returned to my parent's home and closed myself in my room. Under the threat of suicide I made my mother do everything for me.

"It was in that room that I began to write my poetry under a pseudonym. Many poems were published and I became somewhat famous. People claimed to have met me. But no one ever did. For ten years I never left my room until the day came when I moved to Los Angeles. I stopped writing under that pseudonym and people wondered what happened to me. They will never know that on that day another part of me died and joined the rest of me in my living death.

"For over five years I made no attempt to contact my parents. It was as though they had died. I hardly thought of them. Then on impulse I wrote to my mother and told her where I was. I didn't hear back from her until two years later when I received a short note saying my father had died several months earlier. Nothing more. Not even how he died. Just that he died. I tore up the letter. I felt nothing."

At the beginning of Sarah's treatment I had some doubts abut how much I could help her. She had inextricably tied getting well with losing weight. Her state of mind was so negative about life, her depression so deep, and her anguish so overwhelming that I feared she would be unable to reclaim her life. Her work with me would extend far beyond weight control. We decided to work together twice a week.

On her fourth session I told her about my diet program (see appendix). I decided to postpone using imagery at this time, believing that she would benefit by gaining some conscious control over her compulsive eating first. Without any questions she absorbed what I told her and simply said, "I'll do what you tell me." Although she made no attempt to hide her continuing depression, inside her another force had awakened. This force initially allied itself to me. Soon Sarah and what we came to call her life force were one. That is when Sarah essentially took control of her treatment.

She bought a large bathroom scale and we both learned that her weight was 251 pounds. She began to walk; at first, just a few minutes a day. Within three months, now weighing 237 pounds, she was walking five miles a day and joined a gym. The first time I heard her laugh occurred when she described asking the gym instructor whether she would be responsible if she broke a machine in the gym because she weighed a ton. "The instructor responded," she said, "with just the slightest wink, 'If you break any machines we give you a year free membership. That's the rule.'" I saw Sarah smile for the first time. Her smile was beautiful.

During her fourth month, a stabilization month, she became acutely disturbed and her depression deepened as she spoke of her childhood relationship to her sister. She regained eight pounds. Her compulsion to eat chocolate cookies reasserted itself. That was the month I introduced the use of mental imagery and we truly joined forces to help her overcome her depression and obesity.

After describing how imagery worked and how it could become an important part of her diet program, Sarah immediately claimed her need to create her own imagery. As a writer and the creator of poetic images, imagery was not foreign to her. When I said we could develop the imagery together she informed me that she needed to do it for herself, although she would listen to my suggestions.

Almost as though I wasn't in the room, she expressed her thoughts out loud. "I don't need any imagery to prevent me from binging, raiding the refrigerator or going to a market. I only need to focus on why I eat. It's because I'm so empty inside that unless I put food in there I know I'll die—not from starvation but from the lack of love."

"Sarah," I replied, "you wanted to stay alive and found your only way to survive. Now you are on the verge of finding another way not just to survive, but to become more alive."

From the first imagery that Sarah created I felt an unknown force had risen within her. Her imagery was like no others in my long practice. From the first imagery exercise, her source of love began to change. From food it gradually moved toward self-love.

Following is how Sarah related her first imagery experience on that pivotal day that initiated the remarkable changes in her life. She closed her eyes, took several slow, deep breaths, and quickly went into a state of relaxation. She spoke, intoned is the better word, of what she was then suffering and let it infuse her mind. "I feel so empty. I feel like nothing can fill me. I'm so horrible inside. Even my mommy (her voice began to grow childlike) didn't love me. No matter what I would do she was always angry with me. I was a bad, bad child. That's what she always said, 'If you don't behave, no one will ever love you. Do you hear me? No one will ever love you.'" Sarah cried, her chest heaving as she tried to regain control.

Her sobbing slowly ebbed and again she spoke. "I feel so empty. I need to fill myself. What can ever fill me? What can I put inside me so that I won't feel so alone?"

Several minutes passed. Sarah was no longer crying. A determined look had come to her face. "I know what I can fill myself with and not feel empty anymore," she said, as much to herself as to me. "I can imagine that I'm filled with everything that I loved when I was a little girl. I know that once inside me no one can take them away and the emptiness will disappear."

"What sort of things do you remember?" I asked, wondering what might have given her some feeling of being loved.

"I remember hugging a little Raggedy Ann doll that I loved very much. And I had a little rubber dog, and flowers, many flowers that grew wild where we lived. There was a bath towel that mommy used to dry me after a bath, and my high chair where mommy fed me, and a pair of mommy's shoes I found in the trash, and my birthday dress, the only new one I ever had that I wore on three different birthdays until it became too small. How I loved that dress." She stopped and for a few moments remained silent. Then she cried. "That's all I remember that I loved. They're the only things that made me feel good inside. I want to fill myself with them. I know they'll make me feel better. Do you understand?"

I looked at Sarah, her head still bowed, crying through closed eyes. Yes, I thought, I do understand. The memories of those few objects are all she has from a past when she felt no love from her mother, father or sister. Her sadness was overwhelming because she understood with a deadening finality that her love came from a small doll, a rubber dog, and a dress but not from those she desperately needed to love her.

"Yes, Sarah, I do understand you. You need to feel filled with those few objects that you loved as a child. For now it will do."

"No, don't say that." She screamed at me.

For the first time I discovered the dormant anger that once fed her belief she could kill someone. Inwardly, I rejoiced for she would surely need anger and assertiveness if she were to forge a path from the abyss she was in.

"It's not for now. It's for all time unless I decide to change it. You have nothing to do with what I fill myself. You don't know how empty I feel. Words like empty, unfilled, mean nothing. You think those words describe how I really feel. I'd rather have those things inside me forever than nothing. Do you understand?"

Shaken by her response I was slow to reply. "Yes, I think I understand you. I won't interfere with your choice of imagery again. Your wish to get well is now motivating you and I understand your judgment here is not to be questioned."

For several weeks Sarah used the imagery to put other things that she loved as a child into herself. Books, crayons, paints, brushes, balls, neighborhood dogs and cats, a small chain bracelet she had found, even crickets. But not once did anything human come into her. Sarah's first imagery experiences had described the nature of the problem confronting her. She was a person devoid of any sense of human love.

In the weeks that followed, she created other imagery exercises that she could practice at home. They included a wide range of subjects indicating the breadth of her disturbances. One was seeing herself as huge in size, far fatter than she was, and then with this grotesque body approaching strangers and having them embrace her.

Another imagery was coming up to people holding the body of a dead animal, sometimes a cat or dog, but usually a squirrel or raccoon, and telling them she had killed it. Instead of moving away from her in disgust, they moved closer and embraced her saying, "It's all right. You must have been very, very angry to do that but we understand why you did it. And we still care for you very much."

Another very bizarre imagery had her moving into a crowd of people and suddenly taking a knife and ripping open her abdomen out of which poured tiny misshapen creatures of all kinds. Instead of people gasping in horror they came forward to comfort her saying it's good she could show what she felt like inside and they still loved her.

Her creativity and courage in revealing her inner world were endless. Each excursion into the desolation and pain of her past gave rise to new imagery, bringing her closer to areas of her tortured upbringing that had remained buried. Her search was relentless.

Toward the end of the first year of therapy much of her imagery involved her mother. Her imagery is among the most devastatingly honest and expressive of what it means to a child not to be loved that I've ever encountered. Yet, no matter how devastating her feelings of rejection by her mother felt, the imagery always ended with Sarah's being loved. She was determined to bring love into her life.

In one visualization she sat on her mother's lap as a small child. Then to her mother's horror Sarah began to dissolve until she was only a puddle of water that had soaked her dress. Her mother cried desperately and said, "Sarah, Sarah, you must come back to me, I love you. You must come back to me. I love you." Over and over her mother chanted that refrain and slowly from the puddle of water Sarah reemerged. Her mother said, "Sarah, you must never go away again. I love you."

Another showed Sarah, again as a child, beating her fists against her mother's body, harder and harder. Her mother at first tried to defend herself and then whispered, "Sarah, please don't hit me anymore. I love you. I love you." This refrain was repeated dozens of times. Sarah's imagery involved many examples of her desperate need for love. No matter what she would do to her mother and later to her father and sister, they would respond with love for Sarah.

In another of her endless grotesque imagery, Sarah appears as a horrible gargoyle, spewing forth fire at her mother until she was being consumed. Even as her mother was reeling with horror and dying, she finally screamed, "Sarah kill me, kill me, I deserve to die for what I did to you, but I love you. I die, knowing I love you." With those words, Sarah became her self and threw her arms around her mother's charred body and said, "I will heal both you and myself. I will stop hating you."

One extremely cruel version of testing her mother's love was of Sarah repeatedly stabbing her mother with a large knife. Even as her mother was being killed, she protested, "but Sarah I love you. I know you are angry with me but I love you. If you need to kill me, I'll still love you." Before her mother's final breath, Sarah began to nurse her back to health. As each cut was treated and healed Sarah said those magical words that began to transform her, "Mother, I love you, too. I love you, too."

Shortly after the imagery when she first uttered the words "I love you," to her mother, a series of events furthered the rapid changes Sarah was making. She had lost over 50 pounds and was able to jog three miles. Until now she had never bought any new clothes, only taken in her old ones. Then a chance meeting with a middle-aged man catapulted her into a reexamination of her life and appearance.

For several months Sarah had frequented several coffeehouses near her home. She had decided to venture forth and try to overcome her shyness and fear of rejection. One afternoon with book in hand she sat down at the outside patio of a neighborhood coffeehouse and buried her head in her book, while slowly sipping coffee. A friendly voice startled her. "Do you mind if I sit here with you?"

Quickly looking up she stared into the kind eyes of a pleasant looking man holding a cup of coffee and blushed. "Why no, I guess not," she said hesitantly.

"What are you reading?" he asked, as he sat down.

"Why, uh, just a book of poetry," Sarah stammered, flustered and uncomfortable.

"I don't often see people reading poetry when they're drinking coffee," the man responded warmly.

"Oh, I read other things too," Sarah said, somewhat defensively.

"I see. You must enjoy books. My name is Charles."

"I'm Sarah." Her voice may have sounded faint and cautious, but from that moment onward Sarah walked a new path.

During the next few months, as she continued to lose weight, Sarah began to buy new clothes. Because her savings were dwindling, she began to write poetry and short stories under her old pseudonym. Former venues for her work quickly heralded her return to the literary scene and her new work began to appear in major papers and magazines. Only then did I realize that I had once read her work and was, in fact, one of her fans.

Charles became her first friend, followed by others. As she gained more confidence in herself, people gathered around her. Her newfound friends sought out her insight and wisdom. She learned that even though she was still overweight people accepted her. More important, she began to like herself.

In the latter part of her second year with me Sarah had lost about seventy-five pounds and had maintained her rigorous exercise and imagery schedule. She fully believed that she would continue to lose weight until she reached her desired body. By now she had filled many books as she wrote voluminously in her journal. She had begun to write a novel based loosely on her life. Her short stories had received considerable recognition. In addition to her continuing relationship with Charles, she had developed several new important friendships, including a woman who would become her best friend. Although she had not yet visited her mother, she had reestablished contact with her.

Sarah's imagery delved deeper and deeper into her childhood. Memories and fantasies flooded her mind. Night dreams offered new ideas and frequently were developed into imagery. Then began a series of imagery exercises she created over a period of a month that let to a major breakthrough in gaining the long sought freedom from her deep-seated fears.

Everything up to that time had been preparation for what now unfolded. She was about to begin the final climb out of the abyss that had imprisoned her for so long. Her thoughts became darker and more penetrating. Her imagery followed, as she began to visualize going into caves, under water or into deep pits. At times, I guided her to pursue the deeper and more unconscious elements in her mind. At other times she guided herself. The imagery was stimulated by a deep belief that something terrible had once happened to her and the memory was hidden inside her.

During an imagery session at home alone she entered into the deep recesses of a vast cave. Going deeper than ever before, she came into a large room with a high platform supporting a throne. The skeleton of a long dead adult lay slumped against the back of the throne. Unable to move she stared at it for many minutes. And although it hadn't stirred she felt it wanted to speak to her. A rising sense of horror began to grip her and she ended the imagery session shaken and frightened.

When she told me what had happened she again became frightened and felt she mustn't probe any further in that cave. "Sarah," I said cautiously. "You have felt there is something missing in your understanding of yourself. Perhaps this imagery is revealing something that may help you."

Sarah began to cry softly at first, then more loudly and her body rocked back and forth, almost as though someone were shaking her. I had learned not to intrude into areas of her evolving imagery but conditions were changing. Some deeply entrenched dormant memories were beginning to awaken and she was terribly frightened. Sarah had come too far to stop now and I had complete faith in her ability to handle any conflict. I suggested she reenter the cave and told her I would guide the imagery.

Guided imagery differs somewhat from the mental imagery she had used up to this time. Instead of having Sarah create her own imagery, I would guide her through a changing panorama of images attempting to bring unconscious conflicts into consciousness.

Sarah agreed to my suggestion that I guide her back into the cave to once again face the skeleton on the throne. Sarah was about to take a trip into her unconscious mind through the power of guided imagery. Going into a state of deep relaxation Sarah again entered the cave. She looked closely at the walls and ceilings searching for clues about herself in the interior of her mind. The cave symbolically represented her inner world. No animate objects were seen. She became hesitant and anxious as she approached the throne room. But this time something had changed. The skeleton was sitting up and gazing directly at her as she neared the throne. It raised a bony arm and pointing a finger at her, began to speak.

"Sarah, you are evil, an abomination, a vicious murderer. You are not fit to live." The voice coming from Sarah was deep and menacing. What was I hearing? I was shocked at the words of hate that came from the skeleton. Where did this come from? Sarah seemed too dazed and horrified to re-act.

"Sarah," I directed, "ask the skeleton why it makes such accusations."

"No. No. I can't. I'm afraid." Sarah had become a little child, her voice filled with fear. "Why does it say that to me?"

"Ask the skeleton why." I said, more firmly.

In a timid, hesitant voice Sarah asked. "Why did you say that to me?"

"You know why." The skeleton intoned. A deep silence followed.

"Ask the skeleton who it is." I finally directed, knowing how painful this dialogue between two parts of herself had become.

"Who are you?" Sarah asked in a subdued voice. "Who are you?"

"You know who I am," the skeleton retorted. "You thought you could hide from what you did. But I saw you try to kill your sister."

"No, No, I didn't try to kill her. It was an accident," Sarah cried shrilly.

"No. It was no accident. You wanted to kill Maggie. You always wanted to kill her."

"Maggie hated me. She always hated me. I was smarter than her. She was so dumb."

"But you didn't have to taunt her, make fun of her," the skeleton hissed.

"It wasn't me who did that. It was Mommy and Daddy. They made fun of Maggie because she was so dumb. I heard them say it. And they'd say it to her face in front of me. And made me say things to show Maggie how smart I was. It made Maggie mad at me. She always wanted to hurt me."

"Sarah, You tried to kill her. You're the one who did it to her."

"Now I remember," Sarah shouted, almost frenzied, her head shaking violently. "I remember. I remember it, I remember it."

I became alarmed, as Sarah seemed out of contact, her face bright red as she continued to roll her head back and forth. "Sarah, are you all right," I asked. "Do you want to go on?"

"Yes," she screamed. "Don't stop me now. I want to know what happened."

"Go on," I said quietly.

"Don't come near me. Sit back down," Sarah shrieked at the skeleton that had now risen.

But the skeleton advanced and now towered above her, intoning, "Sarah, you are evil, an abomination, a murderer."

"No, No, No. I'm not. I'm not. I'll tell you what happened."

Sarah appeared to be in a trance. Her eyes remained closed as she spoke to the skeleton, a part of her aroused from its deadly sleep to finally confront her with a deed that had deeply scarred her mind. "Mommy and Daddy always made fun of Maggie, and Maggie hated them and hated me, because they made it seem I was so much better than she. One day when Mommy was in her room talking on the phone Maggie grabbed me in the kitchen and tried to smash my head against the door. My nose began to bleed. I thought I was going to die. She hated me so much. I broke free and grabbed the only thing I could find, a big frying pan and I hit her on the head and she fell to the ground." Sarah wailed as the memories of that painful moment assailed her.

"No, Sarah, that's not what happened," the skeleton screeched. "You hit her and hit her again and again until her head was bloody and you though she was dead. You wanted her dead."

"No, I didn't." Sarah was crying hysterically. "I didn't. I hit her because she was trying to hurt me."

"And then the doctors came and took her away in an ambulance," the skeleton taunted. "She didn't come home for almost three weeks. They didn't think she would live, don't you remember that, Sarah?"

Sarah continued to cry as memories of her past returned. "I remember that," her voice was almost inaudible. "I know, because Mommy said she didn't open her eyes for two weeks. Everyone thought she would die. And they said I did it. But it was Mommy and Daddy who made it happen. They made Maggie mad at me and made Maggie want to hurt me."

"No, Sarah, you're lying," the skeleton sneered. "You know that your mommy and daddy loved Maggie much more than you. They hated you and never showed you any love. Don't you remember when they called you evil, a murderer, an abomination?"

Sarah stopped crying, although her chest continued to heave. "Yes, now I remember everything. When Maggie came home from the hospital they made it seem like they only loved her. They gave her everything and told me I was a bad, bad girl. They stopped loving me and never even held me again. They gave everything to Maggie. They said I had destroyed her brain and made her into a child who would never be able to live alone. She would always need to be taken care of because of what I had done. They never loved me again." Her anguished words tore at me. Her voice was so low it seemed to fade away even as she spoke, "I was only a little girl. I was only three years old."

The picture was almost complete. I now understood what Sarah had suppressed all her life. She had come to believe she had almost killed her sister. Her parents had resented Maggie, probably when they must have become aware that she was mentally retarded and long before the birth of Sarah. They constantly taunted her with Sarah's greater intelligence. Finally, Maggie, feeling totally rejected attacked Sarah, who she considered the source of her rejection. And in that brief struggle, as Sarah tried to defend herself against her much bigger sister, the accident that profoundly changed Sarah's life happened.

From her parent's guilt over their own anger and resentment of Maggie came the total rejection of Sarah who they now blamed for Maggie's mental condition. By making Sarah the scapegoat and seeing her as the evil and aggressive one attacking the innocent and loving Maggie, they absolved themselves of blame for the attack. Her parents now turned their hate against Sarah. Her parents, internalized and represented by the skeleton in her mind and totally devoid of any humanity, were the constant reminder that Sarah was an evil and abominable killer.

On the following session the final piece of the puzzle fell into place. Although no specific imagery was created to deal with this new information Sarah spent the week in reflection and finally decided to confront her mother with these newly remembered facts. Sarah described her long and painful telephone conversation and how her memories and suspicions had been substantiated. Her mother admitted that Maggie had been diagnosed as mentally retarded about six months before Sarah had been born. Due to increasing abnormal behavior and slow mental development Maggie had been hospitalized and carefully evaluated. Besides having an IQ of 75 she had other unspecified brain abnormalities. At the time, her mother was pregnant with Sarah.

When Sarah was born apparently healthy and bright they placed their hopes and love upon her. Maggie was shunned and ridiculed and constantly compared unfavorably with her much younger sister. Sarah remarked how sad she felt as her mother revealed the true facts of the past and realized that her mother was completely devoid of compassion for Maggie. Her mother seemed unaware of Maggie's struggle to survive both before the accident and after.

The accident turned out to be a composite of memories. Under Sarah's close questioning her mother admitted that Sarah had only hit Maggie once according to the doctor's report. Her mother had not seen the struggle and came to the kitchen only when she heard Sarah screaming. The blow smashed in the frontal area of Maggie's skull and she did re-

main in a coma for almost two weeks. When Maggie re-
turned home, still not fully recovered, her parents needing to
make amends for their own guilt, gave all their love to
Maggie. Her mother, still not admitting the extent of her re-
jection, only said that Sarah had become impossible and
withdrawn and they just decided to leave her alone.

The final piece snapped into place when Sarah told me
that she had lied when she said that Maggie lived in their
home in a separate room and they managed to get along. She
had been afraid to tell me the truth. In actuality, Maggie
moved out to a group care home where she lived and did
simple tasks, but had considerable freedom to move about if
she desired. When she returned home to see her parents once
a month the sisters rarely talked.

When Sarah was thirty-two, Maggie had been killed in a
brutal murder in a sleazy hotel where she had gone with a
man she had met at a bar. On the day after the murder the
local paper carried the story emphasizing the loneliness of
this poor unfortunate girl who had been essentially aban-
doned by her parents. The accusation burned deeply, and her
mother resenting the need to constantly take care of Sarah,
once again attacked her.

In a vindictive voice she screamed at Sarah. "You're a
murderer. You killed your sister. You're the one who did it."

Three days later Sarah left home and moved to Los An-
geles.

Sarah needed to assimilate this new information and in-
sight. I believed that she needed one more confrontation with
the skeleton. Now was her opportunity to finally extricate
herself from her death-like existence. I told this to Sarah. I
watched as her eyes widened and she stared momentarily at
me. Her eyes glazed over and she seemed to leave me. I did
not speak knowing Sarah was in her own mind deciding
whether to take this final journey knowing that it would be
for me as well as herself.

I wanted to help Sarah find that elusive road to inner

peace for rarely had I met someone so submerged in pain and suffering and yet so determined to come alive. I was now offering Sarah an opportunity to shed the last vestiges of her past that had so destructively tied her to her parents. Almost five minutes passed without a word being spoken. I waited.

"I will go back with you to talk to the skeleton," was all she said.

Sarah closed her eyes and breathed deeply. I watched as her body relaxed and wondered what lay ahead. In journeys of the mind there are no barriers to discoveries and frequently nothing that prepares you for revelations

"Sarah, enter the cave where you will meet the skeleton again." I said.

Sarah's eyes, under her closed lids, darted side to side and I knew she was scanning the cave. "There's strange writing on the wall," she finally said.

"Can you make out the words?"

"I don't think so," she responded frowning. "Wait a moment. I can see some of the words. One is blood, another is dying. I'm afraid."

"Sarah, there's something that's unfinished and you need to confront it." I said reassuringly. "You've come so far. This next step may be the most important of all."

"I'm not stopping. But I am afraid," she whispered. "I see a fallen angel painted on the wall."

"Does it mean anything to you?"

"I don't think so. It's a kind of Renaissance painting like you might see in a painting of Titian or Rubens. It looks ancient."

"Perhaps it represents some old memory or fantasy that you've had." I suggested. "Do you have any ideas about the words or picture you described?"

"No, I don't think so."

"All right. We won't dwell on them now. Their meaning may become clear later. Continue going forward."

Sarah became quite still.

After a few minutes I again addressed her. "Sarah, I presume you are still in the first part of the cave. Is something stopping you from going to the throne room?"

"My feet won't move. I'm afraid of what the skeleton will say to me."

On a hunch I added. "No, Sarah, I think that you're afraid of what you will say to the skeleton."

Sarah appeared startled. "Yes, that is what is stopping me," she said. "My mind is racing and I don't know what will come out. But I'm going into the throne room."

I now waited. My words no longer mattered. Sarah was about to come, once more, face to face with a frightening part of herself. She had learned many things since the last meeting. She knew that she would finally confront the hatred of her internal parents. I had faith that she would know what to do.

"Well, Sarah, you decided to return," the skeleton said sarcastically. "Just keep in mind that no matter what you now believe, you did try to kill your sister. And that deed will be with you forever."

"No, Mother, you're wrong." Sarah said strongly.

"Don't call me mother," the skeleton screamed. "I'm not your mother. I'm you. Understand me. I'm you and I tell it as it is."

"No, Mother, I now know you put those terrible thoughts into my head with your crazy...."

"How dare you call me crazy," the skeleton angrily interrupted her.

"Because, Mother, you were crazy. I didn't realize that till this minute, but you and father were crazy. But it was mainly you. You turned Maggie against me. You hated her and you taught me to hate her. And you really hated me from the moment I was born. No mother who loved her child would have done what you did to me. You never tried to help me through that terrible ordeal when I thought I might have killed Maggie. You made me think I tried to kill her because I hated her. But, Mother you were the one who hated, hated, hated everyone," Sarah cried loudly, as she uttered those searing words.

"Stop it this instant. You have no right to talk to me that way," the skeleton shrieked. "I am your mother and I deserve respect. Do you hear me?"

Sarah laughed, a deep sarcastic laugh. "So now you've become my mother. Yes, I can call you that even though you hardly deserve to be called anyone's mother. All these years I suffered believing I was evil like you said I was. But Mother you were the evil one. I wanted to believe you once loved me. I thought you loved me even when you turned me against Maggie. Maggie was sick and unable to help herself. And you hated her and it was you that wanted her to die. Wasn't it? Tell me that isn't true."

The skeleton began to wail and then to scream. I watched almost with horror as I saw Sarah's face contort into one of hate and fear as the screams of her skeleton-self tore through her. Sarah was reliving her past facing terrifying feelings she had suffered as a child. Everything inside her was now coming unglued and flooding her mind. This must be like an exorcism, I thought, as I watched, not daring to speak. Slowly the fear left Sarah's face and was replaced by a grim determination.

"Yes, you can't speak, can you?" Sarah taunted. "You evil witch. You hateful person. You don't deserve anyone's love. It was your blood that I should have shed on that day I struck poor Maggie down. You lied to me all those years. And now I know it. You poisoned my mind. You deserve to die."

I felt the energy exuding from Sarah's body. Her passion and triumph were palpable. I shared her exultation. But I knew she could not rest while such hate flowed through her.

Sarah, I thought, take the final step. Try to hear my thoughts. Such hatred comes from the love you once held for your mother. Your mother was not the angel you wanted as a tiny child. You must accept the fact that your mother is the fallen angel. Sarah, I silently, but fervently implored, take the next step.

And she did.

The skeleton's screams slowly waned and became silent. In a subdued voice Sarah began to describe the demise of the skeleton, the demise of her internal mother. Even as she spoke Sarah seemed to grow. How does one explain such a feeling when, of course, Sarah physically remained the same. But I knew as surely as I'm writing her story that on that fateful afternoon Sarah grew up.

"Mother, I know how you suffered. I know because I felt you inside me all my life and I suffered for both of us. You had become a victim of your hate and your lack of compassion. If you loved yourself more, you would have loved Maggie and you would have been able to love me too. You suffered because you could not love. No greater suffering could befall anyone."

Holding herself tightly by arms that stretched across her chest, Sarah began to cry. She now sat alone with her slowly disappearing mother. Many minutes passed before she spoke again. "Mother, I can't let you die inside me believing that I only hate you. I know now how great my hate was and now it's gone. I've given it to God who can accept it and forgive me for hating you as I did.

"For now I can only forgive you for what you did to Maggie and me. I cry, even now, when I think how much Maggie suffered because of you and also because of me. When she lived I reduced myself to living in death just so she would have nothing to envy. When she died I also wanted to die. The words of murderer, your words to me, rang in my soul. But something stopped me from dying and now I have found a way to live. I have found a person who believes in me and I know in my heart that he truly loves me. For him and most of all for myself I want to live and give my love to others. I want to spend my remaining years atoning for my sins of hate. Mother, I now know that I can love. Someday I will tell you that I love you too."

Sarah left therapy almost a year later, but she has maintained contact with me over the years. She had fully awakened the spirit that had lain dormant in her for so long. She had reached her desired body weight but most important she had overcome the deep depression that had imprisoned her for so long.

I often remember her words spoken on that pivotal day when she had forgiven her mother. She was right. I did love her and I know how much she loved me. We had shared a journey together. Sarah was filled with the kind of love that can only be felt as God-given. Her love was given freely to all she touched. In the years that followed, her love nurtured those who came to know her. Sarah was truly an angel of life that brought love to her world.

Some months after her therapy had ended Sarah returned to see her mother and without any restraint or hesitation took her in her arms and said in a warm and soft voice, "I love you."

CHAPTER TWO

HAROLD:
Your Children Can Save Your Life

"You have to find a way to get into his head quickly. His diabetes is rapidly worsening. His wife says that he won't take his anti-depressive medication unless she feeds it to him. I can't seem to get through to him." These words spoken by his referring doctor echoed in my mind as I opened the door to the waiting room to meet Harold for the first time.

The man I saw before me appeared to be in a trance, barely moving. I could hear his slow labored breathing. With great effort he rose from his chair. When our handshake ended, his hand dropped to his side as though it were dead. The unspoken message was clear. Harold was extremely depressed and had withdrawn into a world where he was nearly inaccessible.

I wondered how he had gotten to my office. As he slowly walked to the consultation room my question was answered. A woman entered the waiting room. Her red eyes told of suffering and crying. "I'm sorry I'm late," she said, "but I had to use the bathroom. I see you've already met Harold."

For the first twenty minutes Harold was unresponsive. The story that unfolded from Claire, his wife, attested to her unspoken fear that he might die at any time. Throughout the session she frequently turned to look at her silent husband.

Claire began, "Although Harold was always heavy he was in good health until about six or seven years ago, when he turned fifty. He was about the same weight as he is now, about 250 pounds, which I guess at his height of 5' 7" made him quite obese. But he didn't mind and I loved him and his weight didn't bother me most of the time.

"I noticed that he was drinking a lot more water and getting up to go to the bathroom frequently at night. He shrugged it off saying it was just a sign of getting older. He did go for a check up and was told his prostate was normal. But at that time he never told the doctor of his thirst and frequent urination.

"About three years ago he began to slow down. He stopped going out to play golf or tennis. He even stopped walking, which we used to do together. He said he was just out of shape. His breathing became labored on the slightest exertion. I became scared it was his heart and he finally agreed to see our doctor. That was when he was told he had Type 2 diabetes and had to go on a diet and an exercise program. Otherwise his diabetes could worsen and he might require insulin injections.

"Things went from bad to worse. He began to feel fatigued all day. He had trouble getting up to go to the office. He's an accountant and his staff took over most of his work. He became very depressed. Some days he couldn't even leave our house. The doctor tried to prescribe drugs to help his depression but Harold wouldn't take them. He rarely followed his diet.

"Last year an infection on his right leg turned into an ulcer. The doctor became alarmed, especially when it was clear that his diabetes was out of control. The doctor finally prescribed insulin but Harold frequently refused to take it. I watched him like a hawk but couldn't be with him all the time. He began to talk strangely, muttering to himself and saying that life was a dead end. I became afraid he would kill himself and the doctor prescribed a different anti-depressive drug. I don't believe he realized that Harold had hardly taken the previous one. He would never take his pills by himself. I hand fed him. He literally became like a child.

"What was so difficult for me and the children was that before the diabetes came he was the most wonderful, outgoing and loving father and husband. He was always ready to help people and everyone loved him. It's like his whole personality had changed. And now he's so withdrawn that he not only doesn't take care of himself, but also doesn't seem to care if he even lives. He needs me around all the time and sometimes I can't be there for him."

During Claire's description of Harold's medical and psychological condition I detected no change in his demeanor that would suggest that he had heard what she said. I needed to find a way to make contact with him. He seemed behind an impenetrable wall. What would open him up?

"Claire, what are the most important things or people in Harold's life?" I asked her.

"No doubts here," she replied. "Our family. The four children and me. There was nothing he wouldn't do for any of us. He used to be the best father. The kids adored him and so did I."

"You're speaking as though those feelings were in the past." I remarked.

"I can't help but feel that way," Claire said, as tears came to her eyes. "In the past three or four months he has hardly stirred even when the kids come into the room. Even though I encourage them to spend time with him, they mostly leave him alone."

"Tell me about the children," I said. "I want Harold to know how much the children miss him." I was searching for my opening. Often small children can open the doors to a closed mind. I directed my next comment to Harold.

"Harold," I said. "Please listen closely to what Claire is about to say. She's talking out of love for you and about your love for your children."

"We have four wonderful children," Claire began. "The apple of Harold's eye is our youngest one, Mitzy, who just turned nine. She loves to dance and Harold used to whirl her around the house dancing to her favorite music. Next youngest is Bobby, who is twelve, very scholarly for a kid. Sometimes he would help Harold with his accounting. Next is Jimmy who just turned fourteen and used to give Harold a hard time with his smart-alecky ways. Sometimes he pushed his father too far and Harold would lose his temper. But Harold was always good-natured and they'd make up quickly. Our oldest is Linda, who is a freshman in college and wants to become a lawyer. She and Harold have always had wonderful times together. She's especially upset by her father's illness."

"Harold," I said turning to him. "I am certain you heard Claire as she told me about your children. You obviously still love them. Not being able to show your love adds enormously to your suffering. You're here to get well. I want to help you. But you need to help me do it. Do you understand me?"

He gave no verbal response but I saw a slight change in his posture and a tightening around his eyes. "Harold, you need to get better because your four children and Claire are depending on you." I watched carefully. There was no doubt he was listening. What's stopping him from talking? Hopelessness? Fear that he can't get well? He needs to be shocked out of this state. He needs to know his condition is not hopeless.

"Harold," I said. "Your children need your love. You are depriving them of it. Harold, in the same way that you feel hopeless, your children feel the same. They have grown up feeling your love. You loved them deeply. They still need it. They are still children. You love them. They need to know it. You don't want to harm them by remaining ill. You can get better. You need to do it for them. Do you understand? Harold, I want you to nod your head if you do understand that you need to get well for them? Do it now."

And so he did. Anguish spread across his face and he began to cry. Claire went and knelt at his feet and took his hands and pressed them to her lips. They cried together.

I waited a few minutes. But I knew the time for active intervention was now. An opportunity like this is precious and must be used.

"Harold," I said. "Stand up and take Claire in your arms. She has waited for you to do that for a long time. She loves you and will help you. She needs to know that you can rise up for her and for yourself. Now, Harold. Now."

Slowly I watched as he struggled and slowly rose to his feet and took his wife in his arms. The crying intensified. I cried with them. I recognized a breakthrough had occurred. From long experience I knew that a very depressed person must know that he can reach out to me and know that I'm there for him completely and without restraint. I knew that when he held Claire he had acknowledged that I had entered his life. I did not hide my own tears. He needed to know that I felt love for him also.

Many minutes passed. As he stood and cried and held his wife, Harold was changing. No words were needed. Love was my ally. It is not easy for a deeply depressed person to break through his wall of helplessness. But Harold responded and took his first step out of his depression.

Now all that mattered was to make this first and fragile change into something that would last and grow and become the impetus for his recovery.

"Harold," I said, "I know how good it feels to hold Claire, but now I want you to sit down and tell me everything you can about Mitzy. Everything you can think of. I want to know why you love her so much and why she loves you. Can you do that for me?"

Harold looked directly at me for the first time. With a brief smile, he nodded. He saw my tears and heard my muted thank you. He needed to know that his smile was important to me. When he sat down Harold told me about his love for his young daughter.

"Mitzy is my little angel," he began. "I hate myself for

making her suffer. I have been so weak and sick." His voice was halting, even hesitant, as he struggled to shape his thoughts.

"Harold, you are now taking the first step to getting well. You must begin to love yourself for soon you will again give your love to Mitzy and all your children. I don't want you to dwell on your self-hate. It is now time to change your thinking." My words were definite and needed to be heard. He would hear this refrain over and over as the weeks and months passed. He needed to become free of the excessive guilt that ensnared his mind.

"Go on, Harold," I urged. "Why is Mitzy your little angel?"

"I love all my children but Mitzy is different."

"How is she different?" I asked.

"Almost from the time she could speak she sounded like a little poet. Isn't that so, Claire?"

Claire could hardly believe her ears as Harold for the first time in months directed a question at her. "Yes, dearest," she replied. "She is a little poet. Tell the doctor about all the poems she had written just for you."

For a few moments Harold didn't speak. Finally he recited, "Daddy, daddy, I love you so. You bring me joy and so much fun. We dance and play and laugh so much. I think I'll burst for loving you."

Claire went over to hold her husband. "Dearest, isn't that the very first poem that Mitzy wrote for you. It's years ago. I didn't know you remembered it."

How does one stop tears when a man who seemed almost dead not many minutes earlier had found his voice and it was a voice of love?

"Yes, I remember it," he said softly. "I would never forget that poem."

"Do you remember other poems of Mitzy?' I asked.

"I remember many of them," Harold responded and proceeded to recite poem after poem written by his daughter.

After each one his wife laughed or cried or sometimes both. Harold joined her. His laughter filled the room. Sometimes I laughed with them, but mostly I was quiet, absorbing the scene before me.

Harold recited Mitzy's poems for nearly a half hour. Not all spoke of love. Some dwelled on other aspects of family life or nature. All showed a precocious understanding of life beyond his daughter's age. I could understand his strong connection with her. I learned later that he tried not to show favoritism to any of the children, although the other children knew that Mitzy was special in their father's eyes. They also loved her. Mitzy had become the pet of the entire family. And because Harold had so much love to give no one felt deprived.

Although I was encouraged by the rapid change in Harold I did not have any illusion that his problems were solved. We needed to determine why he became depressed and resisted getting help for so long. Was the diabetes intensifying the depression as happens frequently in diabetics? Did Harold get depressed because he could not tolerate the idea of becoming incapacitated and even dying at an early age?

Certainly it would appear that a man with his happy family life would want to do everything possible to get well. What was missing in the equation? He had many opportunities to improve his diabetic condition before he became severely depressed. There were many puzzling elements that needed to be solved to enable Harold to overcome his depression and control his Type 2 diabetes.

By the end of our first meeting Harold had removed the barriers that had kept him apart from his wife. I felt his gratitude and believed he had the strength to go forward. However, I would soon learn of other obstacles that would take much courage to overcome. His path to recovery would not be smooth or easy.

I saw Harold and Claire the following afternoon. Although he walked in rather briskly and smiled I immediately perceived the pain on his face. Claire also looked worried. I waited.

Claire spoke first. "Harold just told me something on the way to see you that scares me and he's reluctant to tell you, but he promised to do it."

Harold took a deep breath. "I've been having chest pains whenever I exert myself. It's been going on for several months and I haven't told anyone. I think it's partly why I became so withdrawn. I was afraid to move. I know this sounds crazy, but I was afraid I was going to die and I just kind of curled up inside, until one day I no longer had the energy to move. It's like a powerful force inside told me to stop everything. I watched everyone around me suffering. I wanted to say something. I wanted to go to our family doctor and tell him but somehow I couldn't even get myself to call him.

"Before I had become so petrified I had looked up angina and heart disease and knew that diabetics are much more prone to getting heart problems than non-diabetics. Another symptom that I've been having even longer and I also haven't told anyone is numbness and tingling sensations in my hands. Recently it has started in my feet. I also seem to have lost strength in my hands. I read all about neuropathy that diabetics get and I felt it was another warning that I would soon die. At the same time I knew that diabetics don't die of neuropathy.

"I also felt that there was no reason to eat right despite knowing that my blood sugar fluctuated like crazy. And although I was taking insulin, I was out of control. It was a sign from God that my time was up and I think I was just waiting to die. Until yesterday when I came to see you I had become convinced death was right around the corner. I saw no purpose in seeing a psychiatrist and avoided talking to anyone about my problems until yesterday. Actually my family doctor and Claire forced me to see you. I thought you could do nothing, except confirm that my death was near.

"Do you have any idea how overwhelming my feelings were?" He looked directly into my eyes. "I felt hopeless and desperate and resigned all at the same time. When my children came into the room to say hello or kiss me or even try to hug me I just sat there and cried inwardly. I wanted to tell them how much I loved them and how frightened and sad I felt about leaving them. I wanted to tell them that they had given me more love and pleasure than they could ever know. But all I did was feel their lips touch my cheek and their hands trying to crawl into mine. I saw their tears and I also saw and felt their anger.

"I had left them and they were confused and knew that I had abandoned them. Yet, I could do nothing. I waited to die. How could this have happened to me? What you did yesterday made me suddenly feel I want to live, and that maybe I could live a little longer and help my children understand that I love them. Even when I'm dead they will really know my love is with them."

I was deeply disturbed by Harold's words and his belief that he was soon to die. I had no idea how severe his heart disease was but I had no doubt that he had been in a profound depression. What could have caused it? Certainly not diabetes alone, although diabetes apparently was a major contributing factor. Without a history of any previous depression the picture was unclear.

The fortuitous circumstances of his first meeting with me had literally shocked him out of his depression. I realized that this could be very temporary unless he changed his thinking about his impending death. Fear of dying from a heart attack usually impels a person to seek medical treatment. Harold did the opposite. He withdrew and kept his symptoms from everyone and waited to die.

Although angina indicated heart disease, it did not determine the severity of his condition. This needed immediate evaluation. His neuropathy was not life threatening but it was clear that he was rapidly developing many of the secondary symptoms of diabetics. He needed to gain control over his diabetes as quickly as possible.

Claire assured me that as soon as they left my office she would call their family doctor and immediately arrange for a complete cardiac and neurological workup.

I told Harold that his physical condition might not be as severe as he thought. Believing that he was dying caused his thinking to become radically negative. He was convinced, even now, that he was near death. Although I was tempted to strongly reassure him I knew that such reassurances would not ring true. Until he was carefully examined none of us could know for certain the extent of his heart disease.

However, no matter how serious his condition, he needed to focus on his negative beliefs and attitudes and eliminate them quickly. It was important that he loses weight, starts exercising, returns to a healthy diet, and overcomes his depression. For the time being I would not modify his anti-depressive medication.

Claire assured me that I would receive the reports of his cardiac and neurological evaluations. I scheduled another session in two days. In the meantime, I strongly urged Harold and Claire to look up information about diabetes from the American Diabetes Association and read about diet, depression, secondary illnesses, and exercise.

"Harold," I said as the session came to an end, "You need realistic information, a new diet and exercise program, and a new belief in yourself that you can fight your diabetes and depression. At our next session we'll begin our exploration of all these areas."

During the following two days his cardiovascular and nervous systems were thoroughly evaluated. He had significant cardiac disease that had not appeared on earlier routine EKG's but not imminently life threatening. He had no need of heart surgery or angioplasty at this time. He was prescribed nitroglycerin for his angina. The heart specialist felt that he needed to lose a hundred pounds as quickly as possible. I consulted with his family doctor and we decided that I would handle his diet and exercise programs as part of his therapy. The family doctor would monitor medical needs, including regulating his insulin requirements.

At his next visit Harold seemed upbeat, apparently reassured by the exhaustive examination that he was not in any immediate danger. However, it was imperative that his diet and exercise program begin immediately.

I carefully described all the components of the Five Keys diet, including the use of mental imagery. Surprisingly, he had never attempted any diet despite being overweight most of his life. Determining the proper diet for diabetics differs somewhat from other overweight people. Besides losing weight it is important to diminish, if not eliminate, dependency on insulin. Most Type 2 diabetics find that with proper dieting and exercise, blood sugar decreases and can be effectively controlled without insulin.

Harold generally ate a small breakfast and a large lunch and dinner. He was always hungry before it was mealtime. I suggested that he eat six meals a day and divide his calories equally among them. He would go on a low fat diet and give up sweets, cake, white bread and other refined sugars. He expressed some resistance but agreed.

Due to the urgency to lose weight quickly it was decided that he would reduce his caloric intake by 750 to 1,000 calories a day leading to a weight loss of one and a half to two pounds a week. I told him to expect greater weight loss during the first month due to water excretion.

"Taking into consideration using your stabilization period it will take me two to three years to lose a hundred pounds," Harold exclaimed.

"That's correct," I agreed. "You've never been on a diet and may not know that most people who diet too rapidly gain it all back in a year or two. By following a sensible weight loss program and learning to adjust to the gradual weight loss on a monthly basis you should never gain it back.

Also, you will definitely feel better and may even be off insulin long before you have lost 100 pounds. Much of the blood sugar control comes from changing to a healthy diet and establishing a good exercise program."

"Okay," he agreed. "I can understand that. I think I was reacting to the fact that I don't expect to be around three years from now."

I glanced at Claire who was visibly alarmed by his pronouncement. "Harold," I said, "there is no way of knowing if that is true or not. But one thing is certain. If you don't undergo a major revision in your lifestyle through diet and exercise your condition is apt to worsen and indeed you might not be here in three years. By controlling your weight and reaching a weight of 150 pounds, you could conceivably live for many years."

Claire took Harold's hand. "Darling, you have fought this for years and only a week ago you were certain you were on the verge of death. Now everything seems different. Look how much the children responded when you came home a few days ago and gave each of them a big hug and kiss. I know that Mitzy cried with joy when she just heard your old voice. We had all been so afraid of what was happening to you. I heard her crying after she had gone to bed and you were resting. I went in to be with her and all she could say over and over again. "Mom, is daddy going to be all right? He won't die will he? He's going to get better, isn't he?"

Tears appeared in Harold's eyes. "Doctor, I won't fight you again."

"Harold, it's okay if you do," I said. "I much prefer you to voice your objections and reactions here so we can examine them, rather then take them home and find some way of sabotaging your diet and exercise programs."

During the remainder of the session I clarified how he would use the Five Keys diet. He would check with his family doctor to determine any changes in his insulin usage with the lower calorie input and the division of his food intake into six equal meals. Also he needed to discuss the use of water with his meals. With diabetics I always suggest starting the use of water with meals slowly and build up to the full amount over a period of time—usually one to two months.

He quickly agreed to the daily use of a bathroom scale and when necessary using the special one-day water diet. He also understood the value of the stabilization period. In addition to adapting to his new monthly weight he would be able to determine the effect on his blood sugar as well as his cardiac and neurological symptoms.

He agreed to start a journal and record changes in weight, feelings about his diet and anything else that might be impinging on his motivation.

Exercise would initially be very simple. Only walking. Since he had not been active for months and suffered from angina he would start out with short walks. One hundred yards was a good beginning. He laughed when I suggested such a short distance and I cautioned him not to overdo it. We needed to find out if and when he needed to use nitroglycerin. I praised his desire to exercise more vigorously but told him, like his diet, slow is better. If he is able to handle the 100 yards then he could increase his walking about 100 yards every second day. He would reach one mile in about a month.

The first month is crucial for a diabetic with cardiac disease. It helps establish his capacity for control and reveals how the gradual increase in his exercising would affect his heart. My suggestions were to be discussed with his doctor before he started. If there were objections or other recommendations then he needed to tell me and I would consult with his family doctor. The need for collaboration with the physician who is overseeing the diabetic patient is essential.

I went over the dietary program. Besides reducing his calories and eating six small meals a day, his weight loss would be governed by the daily use of the scale. I encouraged him to learn about calories and portion sizes. Also saturated fats were to be reduced as much as possible and total fat kept under thirty percent of calories, preferably much less. Complex carbohydrates would comprise fifty to sixty percent of his calories. Refined grains and sugars were to be sharply reduced, if not eliminated.

Now I told him that we needed to find out why his response to the increasing symptoms of his diabetes led to depression and withdrawal rather than a more proactive approach to treat his disease.

"Is that necessary?" he asked.

"Yes," I answered. "It's necessary to prevent you from slipping back into a depression. Although it appears that you're over your depression it's not uncommon that one goes into a remission for a short time and then resumes the depression. We need to face that possibility."

"Isn't that discouraging me?" he asked.

I smiled. "No, Harold, truth is better. There's no point in denying what you inwardly know anyway. However, if you can change your thinking and behavior without seeking the reasons why you became so depressed, perhaps there will be no need to probe into underlying issues. I suggest that we see how things go."

"I'll do anything to get better," he said emphatically.

"Let's see what you do with the rest of the program," I said. "Be very alert to any negative ideas and resistances. We'll examine what happens during the coming weeks and determine how to bring in mental imagery. It can be used to change many things about your life, including any tendency to become depressed again."

In the following month Harold followed the program dutifully and lost eleven pounds in weight. Although he was elated, I cautioned him that half of that was water and now he must stabilize his weight for one month. During the very first week he had his first relapse and regained three pounds, which he quickly lost by using the special one-day water diet.

During his weekly sessions he had shown no inclination

to probe into his past although he briefly talked about his mother having repeated depressive episodes during his childhood. He understood that his family background might have increased his vulnerability to depression but showed little interest in examining his relationship with his mother or other members of his family. I did not push it.

He had taken control of his life once again and was encouraged by the gradual reduction of his insulin dosages. During the month his use of nitroglycerin also diminished slightly. He was on his way to health.

For the stabilization month we decided that he would increase his walking distance approximately ¼ to ½ mile each week. He walked each day usually accompanied by Claire and often by one or more of their children. The old family unity had been reestablished.

I had now seen Harold for two months and the pattern of his new life had been established. Claire no longer accompanied him to his weekly sessions. He had developed a healthy dietary program and was now walking two-and-a-half miles daily. The goal was five miles a day. Sporadic angina still occurred. Although I had no further clues about why he had succumbed to such severe depression I now wondered whether such knowledge was necessary to forestall any recurrence. The answer to my question would soon appear.

"Harold, although everything seems to be going well," I said, as he began his third month of treatment, "we need to address certain issues that affect your overall health."

"I'm all ears," was his jovial reply.

"You still require insulin and nitroglycerin. You need to find a way to stop using the two drugs. I'm suggesting that we now establish a mental imagery program to facilitate your overcoming these needs and also help your cardiovascular system."

"Maybe it's only a matter of losing more weight and building up my body through exercise," he suggested.

"I think you definitely have to do that but since time is

also a factor, you have nothing to lose and everything to gain by using imagery. We mustn't ignore the fact that you do have significant cardiac disease."

"I'll do anything to help myself," he said. In previous hours I had explained how mental imagery worked and how it influenced thinking and behavior.

"First we need to determine what elements in your eating habits are still causing you problems."

"Nothing that I can think of."

"Nevertheless, let's examine how you eat. Almost all dieters have hidden agendas that can lead to trouble when they finally reach their ideal weight and start to eat normally."

"I'm eating six small meals a day, although some days it's only five meals."

"That's okay and some day you may be able to go back to three meals a day, if you prefer. Do you still get hungry despite the six meals?"

Harold thought for a moment. "Yes, I do feel hungry often but I know that one of my meals is coming soon enough, so I wait. The only time I failed was at the beginning of the month, which you know. That was the day I binged."

"Let's develop some imagery to help you control your hunger." I suggested. "You already know that diabetics are prone to bouts of hunger due to the fluctuations in blood sugar. So part of this problem will be overcome as you get better control over your blood sugar. Nevertheless, I think imagery can also help you."

"Okay," he said. "It would be great not to feel hungry so often, even get rid of it. Is that possible?"

"Yes, absolutely," I said. "I've had many patients who have learned to eliminate any feelings of hunger without it interfering with their desire and love of good food."

"I'd like to learn how to do that," Harold said enthusiastically.

"We'll include it in your imagery exercises," I said. "Now for some other questions. Do you ever feel you want to binge but control it through will power?"

"Yeah, lots of times, But I look at that as normal."

"You have to change your concept of normal," I said. "From now on you need to look at any unusual impulse to eat as something to change. Changing your beliefs about eating is necessary to change your eating habits and behavior permanently. Impulsive eating can lead to rapid weight gain especially if triggered by stress of any kind. It's important to make you stress-resistant and also help you get rid of any tendency to binge or overeat."

"Okay, that all makes sense. Can we set up imagery to help me in those areas?"

"We can," I responded. "Imagery is a win-win mental activity. It's almost always helpful and many times you will discover new ways to use it that go beyond your use in weight control. It often leads to new insights about yourself.

"What else might affect your dieting?" I asked. "Think of particular habits that involve your eating. How about raiding the refrigerator? What makes you overeat at home or when eating out? How about feeling down, or being anxious? Do those feelings make you overeat?"

Harold reflected on my questions. "In a way all those things you mentioned may affect me at times but never to the extent that they interfere with my determination to stay on my diet."

"All right," I said. "Let's start. Keep in mind that whatever imagery we create can be changed or modified at any time. You will also be adding other imagery later. There's no limit to how often you can use them or when. The more you use imagery the better."

"I'm ready," Harold said.

"A few final words first," I said. "Like other dieters you will want to create imagery to control overeating. However, I also establish imagery for all diabetics to foster improved health in all bodily organs, but especially those prone to be affected by diabetes. In your case your heart and neurological system will be a focus of your imagery."

"That sounds good to me," Harold said. "Let's start with trying to help me stop being hungry between meals. Can we tackle that with imagery?"

"Yes, and that would be a good place to start. Most dieters profit from this kind of control but having diabetes makes it almost imperative that you overcome normal hunger and separate it from hunger that might arise if your blood sugar drops too much. If your hunger is accompanied with nervousness, palpitations, or faintness you may be having a hypoglycemic episode. We'll create the imagery from your personal experiences. What do you feel when hungry?"

"My stomach begins to grumble. It's not quite painful but definitely makes me uncomfortable and I want to eat."

"Anything else?"

"I think I actually salivate thinking of food," he replied, after some moments of reflection. "I sometimes get absolutely ravenous and will eat anything in sight."

"All right," I said. "Now, as in all imagery, exaggerate your feelings so your need to eat is overwhelming. That is the imagery setting. You are suffering from excessive hunger. Now to combat the hunger we need a counter force. How would you like to do it?"

"Of course I could stuff my mouth with food," he laughed.

I also laughed, but quickly took on a serious tone. "You can even do that if stuffing your mouth would make you totally uncomfortable, such as throwing up or making the food burn your mouth or having it turn into something noxious."

"I could use any of those images," he said reflectively, "but why can't I just wish the hunger away?"

"You can," I affirmed. "You are then in effect saying that the power of your mind can change negative beliefs."

"I like that approach," Harold said decisively.

Following this line of reasoning and self-appraisal, he experimented with different imagery settings and ways to fight his negative beliefs. During the remainder of the session Harold created his first group of imagery exercises.

> He imagined feeling incredibly hungry. Saliva poured out of his mouth and his stomach contracted violently causing him to double over with pain. He was ravenous. Then with an inner surge of power he ordered the pain and salivation to stop. "I will never feel hunger again," he declared, as his symptoms totally disappeared. He exulted in his newfound ability to control his hunger. He added, at my suggestion. "I believe in the power of my mind. I can change any bad habits or thought that I want to."

> He imagined feeling the urge to binge on food even without feeling hungry. The urge became overwhelming and he visualized going to the refrigerator. Standing guard was a giant who blocked his way and told him he will no longer use the refrigerator for binging. He ended the imagery by saying, "I will never binge again."

> To further control his ravenous hunger he visualized opening the refrigerator and finding the food inside was completely spoiled and inedible. As an alternative exercise he would visualize seeing piles of food on a dining table that he would approach and with a sweep of his arms shove it all to the ground where it immediately decayed.

> He visualized becoming terrified over the fear of having a heart attack and dying. At the height of his terror he stated loud and clear that he is not having a heart attack and that he is not dying. He proclaimed that he will never fear having a heart attack even when he experiences actual angina. He imagined

feeling complete relief from his fear.

> Harold's final exercise in this series was an end-state imagery exercise. He visualized weighing 150 pounds, looking trim and fit and being admired by Claire and all others that he meets. He imagined that he looked younger, walked with a quick step, and was able to do whatever exercises he wanted. His diabetes is completely under control and his blood sugar is normal. He is healthy in all ways, including his heart, blood vessels, and nervous system. There is no evidence of angina or any other symptoms. He feels more alive and exults in his newfound body and state of mind.

All diabetics would benefit using similar imagery. End-state imagery facilitates developing a sense of well-being and helps to overcome doubts about getting well. It encourages a positive attitude toward self-healing, which would be constructive in helping to heal any disease that he had.

We ended the session by my briefly reinforcing his motivation to do the imagery and to believe in its power even when there is no clear evidence that it is helping. "Remember that you do the imagery exercises six to twenty times a day. More frequent practice is better. The mind and eventually behavior change with repetition."

Ultimately, blood sugar control comes from losing weight, exercise, a healthy diet, and eventual stabilization. Unless these areas are adequately managed the imagery will not benefit the diabetic. The imagery encourages and stimulates the diabetic's desire and motivation to do everything possible to overcome the diabetes. Type 2 diabetes can be managed by consistently following a proper program.

During the following months Harold continued to lose weight. He had occasional relapses which he corrected using the one-day water diet. Eight months into the program he weighed 224 pounds. He walked five miles a day, six days a week. Although he still experienced angina at times when exercising the condition was effectively treated by nitroglycerin. Claire and he had reestablished an active sex life. He was now enjoying his new low fat and moderate carbohydrate diet. He had finally become free of the need of insulin.

Harold still lived with premonitions of dying young. Due to the moderate degree of hardening of his coronary arteries his fear of a heart attack was not groundless. We decided to add imagery exercises to address these issues.

> He visualized himself the size of a red blood cell traveling through his bloodstream to all body organs armed with a powerful laser beam that completely cleared away any plaque or arteriosclerosis. He then imagined all the blood vessels of his heart, brain, kidneys, genitals, liver and extremities glistening and smooth and without any sign of plaque formation. He felt healthy and free of arterial disease.

> In addition to visualizing all the coronary arteries free of plaque or hardening, he imagined his heart becoming stronger, able to pump more blood to the body and being free of angina. He saw his heart beating steadily and powerfully into the distant future when he would be 100 years old. He exulted both as a middle-aged man with a vibrant heart and as a 100-year-old man fully alive with a heart as strong as ever.

Initially, Harold had questioned how imagery could affect real coronary disease. It was important for him to understand that the body tries to cure itself if the conditions are right. The only thing that has been shown to reverse hardening of the coronaries is an extremely low fat diet, too low for most people to adhere to. However, losing weight, exercising, and eating a low fat diet helps by slowing up plaque formation and allowing collateral circulation to develop to increase blood flow to the heart muscle. When the arteries become too narrow for adequate blood flow then by-pass surgery or angioplasty might be indicated.

Two months later Harold suffered a mild heart attack during one of his daily walks. He was successfully treated by angioplasty. His premonition had come true and had been anticipated by his continuing need of nitroglycerin. When I saw him two weeks after his angioplasty he was once again depressed though without the profound withdrawal that had brought him into therapy initially. Though depression after a heart attack is not uncommon, he agreed that he needed to investigate the underlying cause of his depression. It could be affecting him unconsciously and undermining the progress he was making in dieting and exercising.

Harold's mother was a loving and caring person who devoted herself unstintingly to the welfare of her three children. "Mom put herself out all the time," he said with evident affection. "She was just that kind of person. Everyone knew it and looking back I think everyone, including me, took advantage of her. She never complained. She was just a wonderful mother. I don't think I ever felt the slightest bit of anger toward her."

"When we first met, you briefly described your mother as depressed a lot of the time," I said. "How does that fit in with your telling me she was so loving and giving?"

"I don't know," Harold said, perplexed. "It's true she was depressed and often cried by herself. She would always say, 'don't fret over me. I'll get over it.' Although we never knew what she was getting over."

"Was she depressed frequently?" I asked.

"I don't remember very well when I was a kid, although I don't think she was depressed all the time. When she died about eight or nine years ago she wasn't depressed at all.

"However, I do remember something that made her cry. When I was about ten I found a little kitten that was all dirty and really thin. I took it home and mom immediately gave it a bath and fed it milk. I remember how excited she was as the kitten lapped up the milk.

"For several days she took really good care of it and then one day it just disappeared. When I came home from school she greeted me with tears in her eyes saying the kitten had run away and she didn't know why. She had taken such good care of it. I hadn't thought of that for years but what was striking was she didn't get over losing the cat for days."

"I agree," I said. "Your mother's extended reaction is rather unusual. Was she always so reactive if someone left her or possibly didn't do what she wanted? "

"I don't know," he replied.

"Your comment before that you never felt the slightest bit of anger toward her seems equally unusual. No matter how wonderful a mother is, children do feel anger at times."

"I guess you're right. My kids get angry often enough."

"Harold, I believe it would be helpful to examine the relationship with your mother to see if it contributes to your depression."

Harold was silent a few moments. "I really doubt there's much that will be helpful. My depression is tied to my diabetes and heart disease."

"Yes, I think that's true, but we have never understood why you became so profoundly depressed and withdrawn instead of doing everything possible to treat your illness and try to get well."

He thought for a moment, and then said. "That's true. Okay. What do you suggest I do?"

"Tell me everything you remember about her and let's see what we learn. Over the coming weeks we can focus on your past and that includes your dad and two sisters."

"I got along great with my sisters. I was the baby of the family. Lillian was seven years older than me and Gladys was four years older. I think they both felt I was their baby. My dad was a good guy but he worked most of the time in construction and sometimes he was a bartender at his friend's bar. He died in an accident when I was nineteen. But I know he also had heart disease. He smoked a lot and was also heavy. I was lucky having such a great childhood." Harold became quiet.

"You said your mother was very caring and did everything for you." I said. "What are the things she did for you?"

"Why all the usual things," he replied, puzzled by my question.

"Well, if she did all the usual things why would that make her so giving and different from other mothers."

"Well, that's a good point. I think it was the way she did things. She wanted to do things for everybody. I think if people didn't ask her to help them she was upset. I remember once that one of my teachers actually came to our house to find out why my homework was not in my handwriting and if I was really doing the work.

"The funny thing was mom insisted that she write out things in her handwriting to make it easier for the teacher to read, but I did do my own work. The teacher told my mother that I needed the practice in writing and should do all my own work. I think that really upset mom but she stopped doing so much," he laughed. "Still she was always checking up on me to make certain everything was going okay."

He paused and then frowned. "When I went away to college she insisted on coming with me to set up my dorm room. I didn't want her to come but she insisted. Boy, I was really pissed off but I didn't say anything. She just wanted to help."

"But you were pissed off," I said cautiously. " I thought you said you were never angry with her."

"Oh, that. Well, that was different. After all I was big enough to take care of my own room."

"Was this a common occurrence?"

"What do you mean?"

"That your mother was so caring that she often helped you more than you wanted."

"Well, when you put it that way, it happened all the time. She couldn't help herself. She was such a giving person. She did it for everybody, except maybe my dad."

"How come she wasn't so helpful to your dad?"

"I don't know. Anyway, he wasn't home very much. Being a general contractor took him away from home much of the time. When he was in town he loved playing bartender and he'd be out almost all night."

"How did your mother handle his absence?"

"Oh, she didn't like it, but was afraid of saying anything most of the time. But sometimes she blew her stack when he'd come home late drunk as a skunk. They would scream so loudly at each other that we all awakened."

"Was your father an alcoholic?"

"I don't know. I never thought much about it. But come to think about it now he did drink a lot."

"How did you feel when you heard them fighting?"

"It was kind of scary hearing them scream at each other but my sisters would hold me and say that it would be okay by morning."

"So there were times when your mother became quite angry and wasn't so giving."

"Well, what would you expect? My father didn't seem to care what she felt and we hardly saw him and he never took us out to play. It was always my mother who did it. And she never said anything bad about my father either."

"So she suffered in silence," I said.

"Yeah, she suffered a lot in silence."

"Do you think this had anything to do with her frequent depressions?"

For once Harold seemed stunned. "It must have had something to do with it. Why didn't I see that before? Look,

I may as well tell you something that's really hard to talk about. One night, when I was about fourteen and already in bed, I heard my parents yelling at each other and then some loud noises. Neither of my sisters was home that night. And when the noise quieted down I went back to sleep. I think I was afraid to get up and see what happened." Tears appeared in Harold's eyes. "I always thought I should have gotten up.

"The next morning when I saw my mother she looked terrible and she had her arm in a sling. My father wasn't around. She said she had slipped and broken her arm and had gone to the emergency hospital during the night. They had fixed it. When I asked her why her face was so bruised she said it happened when she fell. That was the last I heard of it.

"My father didn't come home for nearly two weeks after that. She said he had to go on a business trip. But I remember that time because my mother stayed in bed all the time my father was away and my aunt came to take care of us. I remember hearing my mother crying every morning. I can hear it now."

How quickly the peaceful memories of his childhood had been shattered. The source of his depressions had become apparent. I waited while he dried his tears and wondered where all this was leading. Was the father's abuse only directed to his mother? Did his mother always try to hide her anger and anguish only to turn these feelings against herself? Was her depression primarily unexpressed anger? Was Harold's the same?

During the next few months, further "forgotten" memories of Harold's childhood came to light. As he recalled his past it was clear that his mother was, in fact, a giving and caring woman. She insisted on everyone succumbing to her need to be loving. Her life was taking care of others. Friends of her children would come over when they were troubled or needed support. His mother wanted no assistance from others. Her life was tied to giving. She had become a martyr to the cause of making certain her world was filled with her love. She tolerated no opposition. You had no choice but to accept her love.

Even earlier memories of his childhood returned. "It happened when I was about six or seven," Harold began. "My grandparents, my mother's folks, were visiting us. We only saw them once or twice a year but I really looked forward to seeing them. They always brought us presents and it made my mother happy. My father was late as usual.

"We were waiting for him to come home and my mom was getting nervous. Everyone was hungry. I remember in the morning his yelling at my mother that he'd be home on time and to stop screaming at him. I only remember hearing him screaming and I felt scared. He seemed so angry.

"He didn't show up and finally my mom said let's eat without him. He must be tied up with business. She always said that but on looking back at all I've learned in the last month I'd say he was mostly out getting drunk. Anyway we ate and my grandparents tried passing it off with jokes."

Harold stopped and tears again appeared in his eyes. "Goddamn my father," he exploded. "Goddamn him to Hell."

I waited.

"I remember this so clearly," he muttered, "We were quietly eating some dessert when my dad walked in drunk as could be. He walked over to my mother and without saying a word just slapped her across the face. My mother was so shocked she didn't even scream. But my grandpa rose and I think he was going to strike my father when my mom rushed between them and said to her father, 'don't do anything to him; it's all my fault.'"

Harold was no longer able to contain his tears. "My sisters and I didn't know what she was talking about. What did she mean it was all her fault? My father scowled at her and staggered out of the room. He never said anything to her parents. God, how could she have been so blind?

"When he was gone my grandfather wanted to call the police. My mother told him not to and said that my father was just upset because of something she had done that morning. She never said what it was and I now think it was all a lie. She had to suffer in silence and take all the blame for what happened. I now know that she was abused constantly and I think her parents knew it. She just wouldn't strike back and protect herself. I think this continued until my father died. I'm glad he was killed. It was the only thing that stopped him from hurting my mother."

Harold poured out his soul to me hour after hour during the following few months. His idyllic childhood had disappeared in a torrent of abuse and unhappiness. Through all of it his mother stood out as a beacon of hope and love but there was a huge price to pay. His mother had forbidden Harold from expressing anger toward his father. Nor would she blame his father for what happened to her. Instead she blamed herself for all the anguish that befell the family. And she insisted that her love, her inexhaustible love would be showered on everyone. Her love would be the antidote for his father's anger and hate. His mother never openly complained. By her extreme passivity she continued to ask for further abuse.

Harold turned away from his father and grew closer to his mother. It was understandable that he would take over her traits and not his father's. He, too, became a loving person, but not one who forced his love upon others. Instead he gave love to his family easily and freely. Nothing was expected in return. His kids grew up free to express whatever feelings they felt, including anger.

Like his mother, he kept his anger deeply buried. But, unlike his mother, who at times would explode at his father and then withdraw into depression, Harold turned any sadness or frustration he felt into a reason to overeat. This contributed to the development of his diabetes. His anger at his worsening illness was suppressed and turned against himself in the form of a deep depression. In his own way he had finally become like his long-suffering mother.

One final memory returned to Harold. It was another experience that he had "forgotten." It was a memory he needed to forget that otherwise would have shattered the myth of his all-loving mother. That would have been unbearable to him.

"I was around thirteen or fourteen," Harold began. "I'm almost embarrassed to tell you what happened because I totally closed my eyes to what I saw. It was Saturday afternoon and I had been playing baseball all morning and hadn't been home for about four hours. I was hungry and went home expecting to find lunch waiting for me. Instead no one was home, at least no one was in the kitchen. There was nothing prepared for me to eat, which was unusual.

"So I went upstairs to wash and change my clothes when I heard my mom sobbing in her bedroom. I was scared and knocked on her door. She didn't answer so I walked in. She was lying in bed on top of the covers crying, her clothes half off, now I realize they were torn off. Her face was red and there were cuts on her arms. That's when she saw me. She looked at me with such a weird look I felt like running out. But she held her arms out without saying a word and I just went to her and we just lay there for a long time crying together. I don't even know why I cried so much but that's all I did, just cried.

"Then she started kissing me. Nothing sexy, you understand, just kissed me but she couldn't stop. Kind of like she was desperate. I didn't know what to do, so I kissed her back and told her I loved her. I asked what happened and she said she had an accident. I needed to believe her. But I knew my father had hurt her again. I remember thinking why didn't she call the police or just kill him. But I didn't say anything to her. I think I needed to believe her. She kept saying 'I'll be all right; just hold me,' and kept repeating 'I love you' to me. And I said it right back to her.

"She clung to me tighter and tighter. I wanted to break away but couldn't. She rocked her body against me and cried some more. I know what you're thinking, but I tell you it wasn't sexual. She would never be sexual with me. Yet the rocking continued and I rocked back and forth with her. I couldn't help myself. She kept saying how much she loved me and would do anything for me. She was so unhappy and had to know how much I loved her.

"She loved me more than anything in the world, she said. Finally, the rocking just seemed to stop. Just like all the feeling had gone out of both of us. And she just lay there, unable to speak anymore. I think she just fell asleep. I felt so bad for her that I wished that I could take her place and let her be happy again. She stayed in her room all that day and didn't speak to anyone. My father didn't come home that night."

Harold stopped speaking and tried to stifle his tears. I agreed that what he had experienced was not sexual. It was more the desperate need of a lonely woman, abused, forsaken, and unloved by the man she had married. She had to absorb love in whatever way she could get it. Harold loved his mother and she took his love into herself, much as a hungry and empty child reaches out to be filled with food and rocked to sleep.

"Harold," I said, even as he cried, "can you see how your relationship with your mother created the underlying cause of your depression? Like her, you buried your anger at your father. You needed to become like her to maintain the belief that your father was not an abusive person."

Harold sobbed uncontrollably. "Why did she stay with him? I hated him and I wasn't allowed to say anything to him. She made my life miserable by not standing up to him. She suffered so much that I guess I couldn't tell her how I felt. I would have felt terrible if I had upset her even more. She was so unhappy."

How difficult it was for Harold as he tried to grasp the intense anguish he still felt from his past and how it colored his entire life.

"Harold," I said, "you loved your mother dearly and suffered when she was unhappy. Buried inside you was the anger that would one day cause you to become depressed and withdrawn. It was more than just anger at your father. We now know that you also felt anger toward your mother. Because you also loved her so much it was not easy to show anger toward her."

Harold nodded. "I feel so bad now thinking that maybe my mother knew how I felt toward her. That I didn't just love her. Maybe it made her feel even worse. Maybe that's why her life was so empty that she needed to make everyone feel she loved them. She made me say I loved her. Even though I really did. She must have felt so empty inside."

"You felt emptiness much as she did," I said. "But instead of reaching out and insisting that everyone loves you, you overate. You took a different path to overcome your own emptiness.

"When you developed diabetes it was as though you were destined to suffer and even to die. You saw it as your punishment for hating your father against your mother's wishes and also feeling anger toward her for not protecting herself or you. You became imprisoned by your guilt and anger much as your mother."

Harold stopped crying. "It's so strange how all these feelings and memories have been inside me all these years. I needed to remember my childhood as perfect and my mother as an unselfish and loving person. But now I see that she loved because she had no choice. Without being a loving person and having everyone respond to her in that way, her life would have been totally empty. She couldn't face that my father hated her. That would have been too devastating.

"I wonder if she believed that anyone truly loved her? Could she have known that she made us love her? When she tried to help me even when I didn't want it, I would feel terrible guilt by wanting to tell her to leave me alone. So I never did. I hid my frustration and anger. I had really become just like her."

"Not just like her," I said. "Though you also denied your anger and needed to be a loving person, you married a woman who loved you. You gave to your children, as your father never gave to you and your sisters. You were not a drunk, nor did you abuse anyone. You have a greater capacity to love without coercion or possessiveness than your mother. In a sense you actually were able to take into yourself the real love from your mother, which I believe was abundant despite her suffering.

"Your most significant problem has been overeating. You ignored that until your diabetes developed and you feared dying. The full force of the guilt and anger that had been stored in you since childhood resulted in your becoming depressed. All this happened unconsciously. Until now you had remained unaware of how your childhood had played such a fundamental part in your depression. Maybe now with your newfound knowledge you can finally overcome your depression and continue on your road toward health."

Harold continued to see me for another two years. In his last year his visits were monthly. Shortly after having his angioplasty his angina had disappeared. He continued to lose weight, slowly but inexorably. In the three years that I saw him he lost eighty pounds. A year later he reached his ideal weight of 150. He kept in contact with me for another four or five years, with occasional brief cards.

He and Claire, frequently joined by their children, went on many long and exhilarating hikes He continued using the scale and water as part of his daily weight monitoring. Above all he emphasized that he never takes for granted that maintaining weight control is automatic. He continued to use imagery techniques to foster good health and to maintain his unrelenting belief that he will live to be 100.

CHAPTER THREE

ANGELA: The Artist's Model

"You've got to stop me from killing myself," the distraught young woman said as soon as she sat down.

I had no clue of what to expect when I made the appointment to see Angela. I had received an urgent call from a former patient begging me to see her friend immediately, saying it was a matter of life and death.

"Please tell me what would make you do that," I said.

For several moments Angela stared at the floor before looking up to reply. "I know what I'm going to tell you sounds crazy, but I swear I won't be able to stop myself. I already know how I'm going to do it."

I looked closely at Angela. Except for her tear-stained face, there were no other obvious signs of a deep depression. However, I did not doubt that she felt out of control and could possibly do what she feared. Angela was a stunningly beautiful woman. She wore no jewelry or makeup. She was well groomed and her clothes were tasteful. There was no dishevelment frequently seen in acute depressions.

I waited as Angela gathered the courage to continue.

"Doctor, even I know that what I'm going to say doesn't make sense, but you have to believe me. It's absolutely true." Angela said, lowering her voice until she was almost inaudible. "If I gain one more pound of weight I won't be able to live."

With those words Angela broke down and cried uncontrollably. I have had other patients who felt threatened as they gained weight and became depressed and occasionally even suicidal. But I have rarely seen anyone with a fear as intense as Angela's.

"Can you tell me why gaining one more pound will compel you to die?" I asked.

"I don't know, but I just can't gain any more weight."

"Have you already gained some weight that has disturbed you?"

"Yes," she responded. "My normal weight is 118 pounds and I'm only 5' 5". Look at me now. Two years ago when I weighed this much I also thought I was going to die, but I locked myself in my bedroom so I wouldn't eat anything until I lost all the extra pounds."

I didn't ask what her weight was now. I didn't want her to feel that I was questioning her judgment about her body size. However, my concern about her sense of reality was growing. She didn't appear to weigh more than 120 pounds.

"Why can't you do the same now?" I asked. "If it worked before it should work now."

"I don't know why," she said. "Something is stopping me from locking myself up or even to stop eating. I bought a pair of handcuffs and wanted my best friend to handcuff me to the bed but she refused, saying the whole thing was crazy and she wouldn't have anything to do with it."

"Why not do it yourself?" I asked, groping for some clue to this strange kind of conflict.

"I don't know," she moaned. "I can't seem to do anything to stop myself. That's why you have to make me stop. You have to do something. Marcia said you would help me."

When Marcia had called she said, "Angela is like a totally different person. I've never seen her so agitated and depressed. Most of the time she's delightful to be around. I have never heard her say she was going to commit suicide before. I'm really frightened."

"Angela," I said reassuringly, "I'll do everything I can. Tell me how this fear developed and how it got tied to gaining a small amount of weight."

"It's not a small amount of weight to me," she said, obviously irritated with me. "I can see you don't understand."

The picture had suddenly become clearer. Many overweight or extremely thin people have a distorted body image that affects their eating. The anorexia nervosa patient may be convinced that she is heavy or even obese when she is thin and even dying of starvation. Overweight people have different degrees of tolerance about their body size. Some accept their weight, whatever it is. Others become troubled and often want to hide. Angela was neither anorexic nor obese, but it was evident that she had a distorted body image.

"Then please try to make me understand," I said.

"I don't think you can help me," she said despondently.

"It's not easy to continue when you feel you might not be understood," I said. "But how about giving me another chance? It will be helpful if you try to tell me exactly what is so disturbing about a small weight gain."

Angela glared at me briefly then suddenly changed and definite warmth exuded from her. "Do you really want to know?" she asked.

"Yes, I really do. Something is upsetting you and gaining weight can have a major impact on a person who is concerned about her body."

"I hate my body now," she said, grimacing as she glanced at her legs. "I look just like a Botero sculpture and if I get any fatter I won't be able to exist."

I looked at her quizzically, which must have shown for she immediately added. "You do know Botero, don't you? His women are the fattest in creation. There are no fatter women in the world."

"Yes, I know Botero's works, but aren't his sculptures of women as well as men and animals purposely distorted?"

"Of course they're distorted," she replied sharply. "I'm quite aware of that. But he has a certain image of women in his mind and thus that kind of woman can exist. And I am that kind of woman."

"How are you that kind of woman?" I asked, puzzled.

"Just look at me and imagine you are Botero and are making a sculpture of me. I exist in Botero's mind as a really fat woman. Botero would see me that way and that's who I am. Now do you understand?"

I was alarmed. Was I dealing with an unusual form of paranoia, a body distortion delusion? Something seemed peculiar in the way she described her body and self-image. But having me imagine I was the artist was certainly not what a delusional person would suggest.

"Do you always see yourself as a Botero sculpture?" I asked.

"No, of course not," she said brusquely. "Only when I weigh 124 pounds."

"Then that is your current weight," I ventured.

"Of course it is, isn't it obvious? No it's not obvious. I'm sorry since you didn't know what I weigh so how could it be obvious. I weigh 124 pounds and that turned me into a Botero sculpture. There are no fatter women in any other artist's mind. If I gain one more pound I will no longer exist. I would be fat beyond any woman's body ever conceived by an artist."

"I'm beginning to understand. If no artist can conceive of a fatter woman, then gaining that extra pound essentially means you don't exist. You only exist if you are in the mind of an artist."

"Yes that's it exactly."

"What would happen to your body?" I asked. "Would it just disappear or explode?"

"No, there just wouldn't be any more body and I could no longer be alive."

"Your body must exist in the mind of an artist?" I asked, wanting verification of her strange belief. "Is that it?"

"Yes, I've felt that way for a long time," she said. "It started in my second year in college. Since then I've always believed that I had the body that an artist had created. I felt that artists loved me. You should see me when I look like Botticelli's Venus."

"Botticelli's Venus is very beautiful," I said.

"Yes. She's the world's most beautiful woman."

"When do you see yourself as Venus?"

"When I weigh 118 pounds I am truly the Venus of Botticelli."

Is Angela the kind of person who lives with the identity of another and acts as though she is that other person? To see herself as the model of an artist and a different model depending on her weight presents a very unusual picture of her struggles to achieve her own identity.

"Who do you look like when you weigh between 118 and 124?" I asked.

"When I'm 119 I look like all the nymphs of Fragonard," she giggled. "Aren't they delightful as they frolic about?"

"Yes, Fragonard's nymphs are indeed lovely to look at." I agreed. "And who are you at 120?"

"I'm getting a bit heavy at 120 pounds," she said, frowning. "But I'm still very pretty. I look like the Venus de Milo, with her arms and body totally intact, of course."

"Venus de Milo does have a beautiful body."

"She's too heavy," Angela said.

"Yes, I can see that," I said. "And how about 121?"

Here Angela paused and looked searchingly at my face. Was she afraid I would reject her strange identification with artist's models? Did she wonder if I thought she was crazy?

"I don't like myself when I reach 121. I look fat, especially my face, like Renoir's women. I look like all his women, but it's not so bad because I understand that he loved his models. Still, I wonder if they looked like the women he painted. You probably want to know about what artist's model I look like at 122."

I smiled. "Well, this is giving me a better picture of how

you view your body as you gain weight, pound by pound."

"You still don't understand. It's not how I view my body. It's what I become when I gain weight. I really do look like those artist's models. Maybe it's hard to grasp. But it's no different from a person who believes he's a man living in a woman's body. They even give such people a name: trans-sexuals. But they can have operations to convert them into the opposite sex and they can take hormones until they look like what they feel. When I reach a certain weight I know that I'm another person.

"Anyway," she continued, "when I reach 122 I'm really beginning to hate myself and I get scared that I won't be able to stop gaining weight. At 122 I look like the models in Ruben's paintings. And at 123 it's Gaston Lachaise. His fat, big-breasted, ugly women really frighten me. I get scared when I become one of his women for it's only one more pound till I'm where I am today, a Botero woman, and then only one pound away from killing myself."

Angela looked down at her hands and touched her abdomen. A terrified look crossed her face. "You've got to help me. I don't want to die. Please let me stay with you. Just today, and don't let me eat?"

Her desperation touched me deeply. How could I let her leave my office not knowing whether she would eat and gain that last pound? Would she then actually kill herself? She was not a typically depressed person who had lost a loved one or was dying of a fatal disease. Her suicide would be the result of a perceived change in her body size.

What does Angela need to know to control her eating? Drinking two glasses of any liquid could cause her to gain a pound. How strong is her compulsion to eat? Could she control that compulsion? Would she take that irrevocable step and commit suicide? Somehow she doesn't see it as suicide but rather as the inevitable elimination of her body. Killing herself would be simply following an inner compulsion based on her strange beliefs.

"Angela, how do you know that you've gained weight? In any one day a person can fluctuate four or five pounds due to eating, fluid intake, exercise, amount of urination, or the amount of sweating."

"I know that," she answered. "I weigh myself each morning on my own scale so I know exactly what I weigh."

"So this morning you weighed 124 and became terrified."

"I've weighed 124 for two mornings. And this time I'm afraid that I won't be able to keep from gaining that extra pound. It's like there's a voice inside me that says you will become too huge to exist and you must leave this earth."

I looked at the terrified woman sitting in front of me and realized that I was baffled by her condition. I also did not know how to prevent her from eating. I needed more information to understand how such a strange malady could happen to her.

"Angela," I said softly, "I want you to remain with me until we are both certain you will not gain weight. I still have to see three more patients. Stay in my waiting room and I'll see you for a few minutes between my other patients. After that we'll have as much time as we need to figure out what to do."

Angela broke down and wept. I felt my own tension diminish as I noted the relief in her face. I now needed to find out what was causing this bizarre illness. After composing herself she went into the waiting room to wait. I was ill prepared for what was to follow in the coming hours.

When I entered the waiting room to get Angela it was just after 5 PM. As far as I knew she had never left the room.

"Do you have to use the ladies' room?" I asked.

"No, since I came here at one o'clock I haven't had anything to drink or eat. I'm feeling less afraid."

She followed me into the office.

"I'm glad you're less afraid. Now you're going to do something that will guarantee you will weigh less than 124 pounds by tomorrow morning."

"What do I have to do?" she asked.

"Nothing much, but at first it may seem odd since you're afraid of putting on weight. I'd like you to drink two glasses of water."

Seeing her shocked face I smiled and quickly told her that drinking water was for two purposes. One was to avoid dehydration. The second was to lose weight. I explained that the kidney would excrete all excess water, taking salt with it. As the body salt decreases the body needs less water. With less bodily water you would lose weight.

"I also want you to drink one full glass of water each half hour until you have had four more glasses of water," I continued. "By tomorrow morning you should be down to 122 or 123 pounds at most. That should remove your need to kill yourself."

Without warning she sprang from her chair and came over to where I was sitting and put her arms around me. She was crying. "I was so afraid when I was sitting in your waiting room. At times I thought I would have to leave and get some food but I kept thinking how sorry you would feel if I killed myself. I just waited for you."

"I'm glad you waited. I would have felt very sad if you had done anything to yourself. Together you and I are going to find a way to overcome this fear you have." I slowly disengaged her arms.

"I was so afraid you wouldn't like me or would think I was too strange to help," she whispered.

"No, Angela, I like you very much and you're not too strange to help. But now you have to help me understand you better."

"You won't send me away, will you?"

"No. Absolutely not. You may stay here until you feel certain you can return home and not overeat. And no matter what time we stop tonight, I want to see you tomorrow morning. Now here's a glass so you can have your first two glasses of water," I said, pointing to the door leading to the water cooler. When she returned she told me her strange story.

Angela was twenty-nine years old, never married, and had not dated for many years. She seldom went out except to work. For six years she has been employed as a research analyst by a large investment house

Angela's mother had been abandoned by both of her parents at an early age and was raised in an orphanage. While in high school she met Angela's father.   Angela had no memory of her father who had apparently abandoned her mother shortly after Angela's birth. Her mother never spoke about him, except to say he had just disappeared one day and was never seen again.

A few years after her father's disappearance Angela's mother moved quietly into a new neighborhood and hired a nanny who essentially raised Angela.

After moving into their new home Angela remembered three elderly men visiting her mother regularly. Angela described her mother's relationship with these men as warm and friendly. They frequently brought gifts for Angela as well as for her mother. Her mother quickly furnished the modest but elegant home and rarely left it during the week. Each of the men would visit several times each week. Although the men apparently knew each other they were never in the house at the same time. One man occupied most of her mother's time and would occasionally stay over for dinner. His name was Wallace.

Angela traced her connection to becoming Venus to a time in her junior year in high school when she was elected homecoming queen. She was also an aspiring actress and was in the drama club. She modestly stated that she was voted the most beautiful girl in her class.

At the time of the homecoming parade her picture appeared in a local newspaper. Several evenings later Wallace visited her mother and commented on how grown up and beautiful Angela was. Later her mother told Angela that Wallace liked her very much and wanted to take her to bed. For doing that favor he would set up a $50,000 fund that would be used for her college education. Angela said she was surprised at the request since Wallace had seemed to avoid her when he visited her mother.

Her mother did not push her but said she should think it over. During the next few weeks Wallace brought her gifts. One of them was a copy of the Botticelli painting of The Birth of Venus. He commented that she was as lovely as Venus, who he considered the most beautiful woman ever painted by an artist.

Several weeks later, after she had grown to love the painting of Venus, she agreed to spend one night with Wallace. On that evening Wallace came over early and brought her flowers and a beautiful negligee. They had dinner together, alone for the first time. Her mother had excused herself and had gone to her bedroom. On that night she had her first taste of champagne. Briefly she reflected on what her mother thought of her sleeping with the same man she slept with and then dismissed the thought.

In her bedroom Wallace slowly undressed her and spent the first hour merely touching and caressing her body exclaiming that she was truly the embodiment of Venus. He kissed and fondled her and then spent the remainder of the time engaging in mutually responsive oral sex. He attempted intercourse just once and immediately lost his erection.

During his final minutes with her he ran his hands over her body, again and again, whispering, "You're my Venus. You must never change. You must always be just as you are tonight." Before he left he told her he loved her.

Angela who told me the story without hesitation and certainly without conscious guilt said that was the first and only time she ever had sex with a man and to this day she has remained a virgin.

I interrupted her story by pointing to the clock on the side table. She immediately rose to get her next glass of water and then excused herself to go to the ladies' room. When she returned she resumed her tale.

"After Wallace left me that night he never again asked to be with me," she said, beginning exactly where she had left off. "Actually he kind of ignored me except to call me his Venus every now and then. A month or so after the sex he showed me a copy of the trust he had set up for my college education and again called me Venus and lightly ran his hands over my body. I was dressed at the time. He asked me how much I weighed and I said I didn't know. So he walked me over to my mom's scale and told me to undress and get weighed. I obeyed him. I weighed exactly 118 pounds.

"As I dressed he looked at my body and said, 'Angela, you are perfect, a perfect woman. You must always weigh 118 pounds. Then you will be more beautiful than Venus herself.'"

Pieces of the puzzle were beginning to come together. She never had the benefit of living with her father. Her mother's decision to become a prostitute or mistress to three men and to spend her days occupied with keeping her body beautiful began molding Angela's feelings about her body image early in her life. The role that Wallace played in her life was unclear but his telling her that she was more beautiful than Venus also contributed to the picture. However, none of this really clarified how this strange malady developed.

"Did Wallace's words that you must always weigh 118 pounds compel you to watch your weight in high school?"

"No. Although I never forgot what he said it didn't have much meaning to me at first. I dated some in high school and in my first year of college but didn't have sex with any-one. I was taking art history and hoped to become an art teacher. I dabbled in drama for a few semesters and even thought of trying to become a movie actress but I didn't like what people wanted me to do to further my career.

"In my second year of college I was almost raped by my painting instructor, Jason. He was an artist and asked me to come to his studio to pose for him. l did and he painted a large nude painting. His style was to grossly distort the woman's body. Although he disguised my face it became known all over that I was the model. I developed a kind of notoriety. The critics said his distortions were totally repulsive and unaesthetic but no one blamed the model. Even so I felt the criticism was somehow directed at me. I saw myself in the painting.

"When he completed the painting he asked me to stay and he would make dinner. He lived at his studio. I agreed and I got kind of drunk. Before long I was in bed with him and he was trying to push himself into me. I became incensed and tried to push him away. The more I fought the more he tried to force me to have intercourse. Finally he told me that I was a slut and he had made the painting look like me. I was absolutely shocked and although he later apologized for trying to rape me, I never forgot his saying that I looked like his painting. That's when I began to look at my body differently."

I still couldn't understand how even that experience could give rise to her bizarre eating problem. What made her attach her body weight to specific artist's models? I asked her that very question. All she knew was that one day, shortly after the attempted rape, she had awakened with the thought that she must make certain she weighed 118 pounds so she could be more beautiful than Venus, like Wallace said.

"At that time I only weighed about 122 pounds. But I still felt ugly, like Jason's painting. I immediately went on a diet and lost the four pounds. It was only when I reached 118 that I felt beautiful again. For weeks afterwards I would look at myself nude in the mirror and admire my body. I still had the picture of Venus and would compare myself to her.

"For several weeks I managed to remain at 118 pounds. But one day I weighed 119 pounds and I panicked. Somehow I was unable to see myself as Venus and certainly not as beautiful. I knew that one pound couldn't make that much difference but I couldn't stop thinking that I looked different. That's when I chanced on some paintings of Fragonard and Boucher and thought I was more like those paintings. I convinced myself I looked like the models painted by Fragonard.

"But I was dissatisfied. Although I wasn't yet obsessed with my eating, I began to weigh myself each morning hoping I would get back to 118. Instead one morning I was 120. I thought I looked quite heavy especially in my breasts and hips and without thinking I saw myself as Venus de Milo that I used to think was the most beautiful sculpture in the world. As I looked at photos of her body, I wondered why I had not realized that she was quite heavy and certainly not as beautiful as I had been taught.

"By now I was desperate to get back to 118 and in my desperation ate even more. Soon I weighed 121 and I knew I had become fat like Renoir's models. I began to gulp down food and the very next day I was 122 and I looked like Ruben's models. Don't ask me how I came to those artists. I just did. Remember, I had been studying art history and I liked those artists. But now I found their women repulsive and I became frantic. On the very next day I was 123 and to my horror I had a body like Lachaise's sculptures. We had been studying him in a sculpture class. The final day I weighed what I do now, 124 pounds, and I knew that I must never be any heavier than that. I was a fat pig like Botero's women.

"I stopped eating and went on a fast and as I slipped back in weight I again became the very models I had seen as I had gone up in weight. It was at that time these ideas became fixed in my mind."

"Did you believe then that you would have to kill yourself if you went over 124 pounds?" I asked.

"No. That came several years later when I again approached 124. In the meantime I had developed a very strict diet. I knew the calories of everything and always ate the same things and in the same amounts. Sometimes I cheated or went out to eat so my control was not perfect."

"Do you recall what happened the first time you felt that you would have to kill yourself if you gained one more pound?"

For a minute or more Angela sat staring into space. "I think it just happened," she finally said, "I know it's a crazy idea but I can't get it out of my mind."

Again she paused and a deep frown crossed her face. "Something is making me feel sick," she said softly. "When I see myself as Botero's model I know I exist in his mind. It's almost like I don't exist for myself. Yet part of me knows that doesn't make any sense."

I was relieved to hear that she knew her beliefs were irrational. For a while I was uncertain. I decided to probe more deeply into the causes of her bizarre body image disorder.

"Something in you is tied to this belief that you need to die if you become fatter than Botero's women," I began. "At least you're aware that your belief, as powerful as it is, is a false one. You know that you continue to exist for yourself independent of being identified with the various artists' models."

"I'm not certain I believe that," she responded.

"Well, I'm going to proceed believing that inwardly you are aware that you do exist separately from those models."

"All right."

"Can you imagine a woman fatter than Botero's?"

"I don't know."

"Try something for me," I said. "Close your eyes and imagine a very fat woman standing in front of you."

"All right. I can do that."

"Describe her to me."

"She's just a plain fat woman. Straight hair, rather ugly. Nothing special."

"How does she compare to Botero's fat woman?"

Angela squinted at the woman she was visualizing. "She's not as fat."

"Now, try to see a woman much fatter than Botero's."

"I can't," she said grimacing. "It's just blank."

How odd, I thought. Normally a person can visualize any size object desired.

"Angela, can you visualize a woman thinner than Venus?"

"Yes," she said quickly. "I can see women so thin you can hardly notice them."

"Can you imagine yourself as one of those very thin women?"

"No, absolutely not. I would never let that happen. I would never be less than 118 pounds unless I was locked up and being starved."

"Can you imagine yourself locked up and starving and weighing only 100 pounds?"

"No, no," she cried. "I would look horrible. I can't imagine being locked up and not able to eat."

"But can you visualize yourself being that thin?"

"Yes," she finally said, very frightened. "But it must never happen."

"Of course, it must never happen," I said. "But I needed to know if you could visualize it. Your inability to see yourself heavier than 124 pounds becomes all the more puzzling."

"Does that mean you're going to send me away? " she asked.

"No, Angela," I again reassured her. "I'll never send you away."

I was as baffled as ever over the intensity of her fear. She still believed something was forcing her to eat and would eventually destroy her. I decided to introduce guided imagery into our meeting. The fact that she was unable to visualize a woman fatter than Botero's indicated a major block in her ability to probe into some area of her unconscious mind.

"Angela, Are you willing to try another technique to discover what lies behind your fear?"

"I'll do anything you want," she said. "Only don't send me away."

"I won't send you away. But I would like you to consider using guided imagery."

I explained the technique and stressed its power to overcome resistances to the unconscious mind. She agreed to try it. Closing her eyes she took several deep breaths and let her body fully relax.

At my instruction, Angela visualized herself at the age of ten and slowly moved back in time until she was five years old. In the years between five and ten her recollections were spotty, although a few pertinent memories came to light. Wallace and several other men occupied her mother's life during that period. Angela's days in school seemed almost meaningless to her. She recalled very little except for praise from a few teachers for her precocious ability to draw and paint.

Noteworthy was a paucity of interactions with her mother who seemed to ignore her. At the age of eight Angela left home one afternoon. No one noticed that she had not appeared for dinner. Angela told me that she frequently ate dinner alone. Her absence was not discovered until late at night when Wallace discovered that she was missing and initiated the search. When the police brought her home she didn't recall her mother being there to welcome her. It was Wallace who had waited for her. He later insisted that her mother find a new nanny.

While listening to Angela's words I felt her utter desolation. I could not detect any sadness or even disappointment in her voice to indicate that she realized her mother had essentially abandoned her. Angela had become inured to her mother's rejection.

Angela was unable to remember why she had walked away or if she had intended to run away. She said. "Why would I run away? I was happy at home. I liked being alone and not having anyone bother me."

Apparently, Angela never felt close to anyone during that period. I was beginning to understand that from an early age Angela was alienated from the world and had come to accept her emotional isolation.

Angela's world as a small child was a world of emptiness. It became one of fantasies of playmates and imagined love. Angela had learned as a small child to exist almost entirely in her mind.

Moving farther back to a time before she went to school provided me with my first real understanding of how Angela developed her strange interaction with the artists' models.

"Angela, in a few minutes I am going to have you visualize yourself in your home at the age of four," I said. "You will try to fully describe whatever you experience. You'll be entering a period of life where your memories are often hidden and your fears and fantasies are disguised. Sometimes your thoughts will be as they actually were. At other times you may combine experiences. Your objective is to describe every image, thought and feeling as you have them without any censorship. Are you game to go ahead?"

"Yes," she whispered.

"Are you afraid?"

"Yes."

"I can understand your fear. Do you have any memory of this period of your life at all?"

"No. I don't even remember where I lived or who took care of me."

"Take a few deep breaths and let yourself relax. Now it's time to visualize yourself back in your childhood home at the age of four. Go there now."

Silence followed my words.

I waited several minutes before speaking again. "Angela, please try to describe whatever you're visualizing."

"It's all black. I don't see anything," she said. "Nothing is there."

"That sometimes happens when the forces of repression keep memories out of consciousness. Would you like to continue?"

"Yes, I want to know why I'm so afraid. I don't want to die."

Unseen tears came to my eyes as I tried to reach into the empty spaces in Angela's mind, but also saw nothing. Therapists as a group are empathic and often seek understanding by probing into the inner worlds of those they treat. I often try to put myself into the minds of my patients and attempt to feel and be with them.

I imagined the same darkness in Angela that she had found. Where was the rich world of the child that is usually so easily reached through guided imagery? Where are the symbolic forms of her memories? I knew I was tapping the same area of the mind from which dreams spring forth, an area of untold riches. But a black curtain had descended over this period of her life.

"Angela," I said softly. "You're temporarily unable to access this part of your mind but it exists even though you can't visualize it. Even though you see no clear pictures, the pictures are there. The imagery exists even in the blackness."

I watched the movement of her eyes, as she searched for those hidden images. "Angela, I want you to ignore the darkness and describe to me the room you are in. You are still four years of age. You are at home. You are in your bedroom. Describe it even though you believe you can't see it. It is there in your mind."

Again silence.

"Angela, although memories of your early childhood are hidden, they haven't totally disappeared. They're hidden because you suffered then and needed to bury those feelings. But we can reach them anyway. Do you still want to go on?"

"Yes."

"All right," I said, wondering how far I dared to reach to

get her to remember. Only my conviction that she faced a very real danger of suicide prompted me to go on.

"I want you to return to the age of six and again visualize your mother as you did before in your imagery. When you see her describe her as fully as possible."

A slight smile came to her face as she saw her visual screen filled with the image of her mother. "Mama is sitting in a chair reading a book. She's wearing a tight lavender dress. Her hair is all fluffy. She's barefoot. She's very beautiful."

"Where are you?"

"I'm sitting on the floor watching her. She doesn't seem to notice me."

"Stand up and go over to her. Look directly at her and ask her what she's reading."

"I can't do that. She'd be angry."

"Why would she be angry?"

"Because when she's reading I'm not allowed to interrupt her."

"Do it anyway," I directed.

"I can't."

"Yes you can," I said. "Do it."

"Mama, what are you reading?" Angela's voice had become very hesitant and childlike.

"Angela, I told you never to bother me when I read." Her mother's voice assaulted her. I was astonished how quickly Angela had adopted two different voices to the two persons in her childhood imagery, something I had not suggested to her.

"Angela, tell your mama that you will say what you want and she just can't go away and not be there for you."

"I can't say that," she whispered. "She'll be so angry at me."

"Nevertheless, Angela, You can say it. You need to say it. And when you do, look right at her. Keep repeating your words and then I'll tell you what to do."

"Mama, you can't go away and not talk to me. I'm your daughter. You must speak to me." Her voice got higher and louder.

"What is your mama doing?"

"She's screaming at me."

"Now Angela, reach out and grab your mother and immediately see yourself at the age of four still holding on to her."

This time Angela did not hesitate. "I've grabbed her arm."

"Now take her back to the age of four."

"I'm here," she cried. "I see her. She's different. She's not wearing anything. But I see her. I'm still holding her arm. She doesn't even notice me. She's sleeping."

"Angela, you're now in that period of your life when things seemed so black." I waited. Angela became hesitant.

"Is your mother still sleeping?" I asked.

"Yes."

"Call her name."

"Mama, Mama," she called in a scarcely audible voice.

"Your mama can't hear you. You must speak louder," I urged.

"I'm afraid she'll be angry if I wake her up."

"You need to wake her up. You must know what happened when you were a little child. We need to know why you came into this period holding onto your screaming mother and found she's asleep. Angela, it appears your mother wasn't there for you. You need to wake her now."

"No, I can't do it," Angela whispered. "Something terrible will happen."

"Angela, you can only bring forth what is already inside you. Whatever happened has already happened. We need to find out what it was."

"She seems to be fading away," she said fearfully.

"Angela, right now, shake your mother's arm and scream her name. Do it now."

Silence.

"Now," I ordered. "Now."

With a piercing scream Angela broke through her fear. "Mama, Mama, wake up. Wake up, Mama. You need to wake up. Mama, Mama."

I watched with growing apprehension as Angela began to shake and pull at her hair. I was torn between letting the experience unfold and stopping it. What would it take to overcome the blackness that covered the fears of her past?

And her mother awakened.

"Don't hit me, mama. Don't hit me." Angela cried terrified.

"Angela, don't let her strike you," I directed. "Tell her you need to talk to her."

Angela saw herself backing away and timidly saying, "Mama, I need to talk to you."

"I don't want to talk to you," Angela screeched in her mother's voice.

I shivered as I heard the harshness of her internal mother coming from Angela's mouth. Her mother's rejection that had remained buried for so long seemed total. Certainly such rejection could leave a child vulnerable to eventual suicide.

"But, you must talk to me," Angela said, feeling braver. "I need to know why you hate me."

"I'll tell you once more what I told you a long time ago. You are not my daughter even though I gave birth to you. I never wanted you. Your father raped me and you were the result. You ruined my life. You'll have to find your own way to live."

"No, you can't hate me. I am your daughter."

"Think anything you want. I am going back to sleep. Don't ever wake me again. If you do, I'll kill you. Do you understand? I'll kill you."

Even as Angela spoke those ugly words I noted a stiffening of her back and not the collapse I might have anticipated. In one brief moment the truth had come out. Even as a child

Angela had known that she was unwanted but that terrible knowledge had come under the cloak of her inner blackness. What small child could have accepted such a pronouncement? And what kind of mother would say that to a small child?

That session revealed the absence of any love during her early childhood. She had grown up believing she was unlovable. She was as empty of love as one can be and yet remain alive.

To make certain she would never again be fearful of facing her mother, I had Angela repeat her confrontation with the same results. Both saddened and enlightened Angela told her mother that she would now find a new way to be filled with love. If her mother wouldn't love her, she would learn to love herself.

Finally, I directed Angela to tell her mother she could talk to her anytime she wanted and her mother would not be able to hurt her. With this step I was attempting to reduce the potential to suicide. Later Angela would incorporate this into the imagery exercises she would practice as she slowly wiped away the belief she was unlovable.

As the guided imagery ended, Angela said to herself softly, "I love myself. I love myself." Again tears came to my eyes. Did she believe in her own love?

When Angela opened her eyes and looked at me, remembering everything that had transpired in the imagery session, she cried and came over and took my hand in her own. She sat down on the floor next to me and just held my hand. Not desperately. But rather to know that I truly existed for her. Not like her mother whose arm she had grabbed only to learn that she was not there for her. My hand was real. For many minutes we sat together in silence.

And I looked at her and thought of what she and I had gone through together. Certainly every therapist has moments that seem transcendent, where something seemingly miraculous has occurred with a patient. I have had some, but few that moved me as much as those moments when I sat in silence with Angela holding my hand.

I took Angela to dinner that night. It seemed right that her work with me would include her first meal without fear that she would gain that final pound and need to die. I knew that with the water she drank and the low calorie salad she ate her weight would be considerably less the following morning. She believed me and when we said goodnight her fear had left her.

The following morning she called as I had suggested after she weighed herself. She weighed 122 pounds. I scheduled her next appointment. We now needed to ferret out the way she brought the artist's models into her life. That they filled a deep emptiness was clear. But how they gained such a tenacious hold on her mind and why these particular artists were selected was still unknown.

When she entered my office later that day I immediately knew a profound change had taken place in her. The fear of dying had disappeared and she had already decided to quickly lose the remaining four pounds. To give her better and less obsessive control over her weight, I introduced her to the special use of water and the bathroom scale, which she agreed to adopt.

To fortify her insight and help convert it into a lasting change in her thinking and behavior I suggested mental imagery, which appealed to her. She decided on four imagery exercises based on her experiences of the day before.

She visualized herself sitting on the floor with her mother looming over her, screaming and calling her names, saying she was worthless. Angela then rose and stood before her mother and in a loud voice said, "Mama, you are a bad person. You are filled with hate and I will no longer listen to you." Angela became taller and taller as her mother shrunk away and disappeared. Angela exulted saying she would now only listen to herself.

She visualized seeing her mother in bed totally ignoring her. Angela reached down and grabbed her mother, shaking her until she acknowledged Angela's presence. Angela hollered. "You can never ignore me again. You will always listen to me when I want to talk to you." She continued to shake her mother until she agreed to never ignore her again.

For her initial imagery to eliminate her fixation on being beautiful at only 118 pounds, she visualized gaining one pound and feeling the same as though she still weighed 118. When she was comfortable at 119 she would visualize her weight at 120 pounds and imagine feeling as beautiful as at 118. I advised her not to extend her weight beyond 120 pounds at this time.

At my suggestion she added an end-state imagery exercise to overcome the need to see herself as Venus. She reluctantly agreed to use it. She visualized seeing herself at 118 pounds and, one by one, covering her naked Venus body with a variety of different outfits. She play-acted enjoying looking at her new self in the different clothes. With each change of clothes she exclaimed, "I am no longer Venus. My body is my own. I am not Venus."

During the next few weeks Angela quickly lost the four pounds and was elated as she again saw herself as Venus. Neither the insight into her childhood nor the continuing use of the mental imagery affected her belief that she looked like Venus and the other artists' models at various weights. I made no effort to change those beliefs. She needed to be certain that she had control over her weight before we tackled the task of trying to understand how these artists had penetrated her mind.

Although Angela avoided most people and never went out on a date she had developed several close friends, including Marcia. She did her work as a research analyst well and was respected for her diligence and thoroughness. When we talked of her isolated life, tears came to her eyes. She was lonely and knew that she avoided most people out of fear. Losing control of her eating was only part of the fear. The primary concern was her belief that there was something wrong with her, something irreparably defective that anyone who got to close to her would discover.

Since the attempted rape by her art teacher she didn't want to be alone with any man. Although she feared rape, she was more terrified that a man would find something terrible inside her. She couldn't reconcile her belief that she was the beautiful Venus with the contrary belief that she was ugly and empty inside.

However, she was aware that being Venus would attract men. She described how she avoided all such attraction to her. She wore no makeup, maintained a mournful expression, kept her hair tightly bound, and wore loose nondescript clothes. No man ever attempted to ask her out. I knew that it wasn't only because of her outer appearance but the signal that she was unavailable.

She lived in two separate worlds. The outer world included her work, maintaining a household, and spending some time with friends. The inner world revolved around her fantasies.

For a month after our first meeting I saw her twice a week. Although she continued to work on the newly discovered memories of her early childhood there was little new material. It appeared that she had repressed much of this very painful period of her life.

In the middle of the second month of therapy an incident happened that opened the door to her fixation on the artists' models. It started when she agreed to attend a small dinner party that Marcia was giving for a few friends. Up to then Angela avoided all events where she might be tempted to overeat and where she would have to dress in a way that might attract men. At the party she met Sheldon, a writer. He wanted to date her. And she liked him. Angela was beginning to change and for the first time she stated that she now felt "enslaved" by her obsessions. We decided to again go into her past using guided imagery.

Although her identification with the models didn't begin until after the attempted rape such a major alteration in her self-concept could not have occurred without some connection to her past. I decided to direct my interventions to her later childhood when she first knew she had artistic ability.

She immediately visualized returning to the age of seven and said, "Although I had been drawing for a while I didn't put much meaning to it. Then one day Wallace took some pictures out of his briefcase. He said that he learned from my mother that I was the one who had drawn them. He said they were beautiful.

"I learned later that after seeing the first one he had told my mother to collect any others she could find that I left around the house. Since I didn't put much store in their value I generally just drew things to keep busy and discarded them."

"To have had your mother do that knowing how much she hated you indicates he must have been quite impressed with your talent," I commented.

Angela blushed. "Oh, I don't know, but that's what happened."

She stopped talking.

"Something else came into your mind," I said. "What are you visualizing now?"

"It's so strange," she said, "but remember when I told you that Wallace said I looked like Venus after we went to bed together? Well, I guess it wasn't the first time he said that for I can recall a time that he brought me a book of art and that picture was in it. He told me that it was one of the world's most beautiful paintings. I think I was about eight years old then."

And now a flood of memories came to her that revealed the basis of her obsession with the seven artists. Wallace began to spend more and more time with her when he visited her mother. He brought her many books of art and carefully went over styles, periods, leading artists, and acknowledged masterpieces.

"I can't imagine why I ever forgot all that he did for me," she exclaimed as she marveled at the plethora of memories of her relationship with Wallace. "When he described the beauty of Botticelli's Venus he also showed me how the same beauty was captured in his painting of the Primavera. The women were so beautiful he said that they would bring tears to his eyes. I even think he cried when he showed me the paintings. I had forgotten how sensitive he was."

Going to bed with Wallace now began to have greater significance, I thought. Wallace had become more like a surrogate father than I had perceived before.

"I remember when he told me about the first time he saw the original sculpture of Venus de Milo. He said he just sat on the ground and stared at it until a guard told him to move on. He had laughed when he said that on subsequent viewings he thought that if she had all her limbs she would be a formidable wrestling foe because she looked so strong. But she was beautiful, he would always say."

"Were you always alone when he spoke to you about art. Or did some of this take place when you were having dinner?"

She paused and I knew she was scanning other images. "I think we were always alone, but I'm not certain. Something is fuzzy about some of the images." Her mood suddenly lightened.

"I remember the first time he showed me the works of

the Impressionists. He said that Monet understood light better than any artist who ever lived and he was the heart and soul of all the impressionists, but it was Renoir who brought light, rich colors and romance into his paintings of women, especially his nudes." Angela stopped and frowned.

"I distinctly recall him saying that Renoir loved flesh so much that he made all his women very fat. Wallace loved the paintings more for the color and style rather than for the individual nudes. They were all just a bit too fat for him."

She stopped, then repeated her words. "Wallace thought Renoir's nudes were too fat."

"Yes, " I said. "I understand what you're driving at. You begin to feel uncomfortable once you hit 121 pounds, the weight you imagine yourself as a Renoir nude."

"Yes, I thought of that the moment I recalled what he had said. And I now remember Wallace's feelings about Rubens. He also loved Rubens. He loved the grandeur and sweep of his landscapes and historical pieces. But it was his women that he said were luscious, even succulent, but they were definitely too fat for his taste. But it sounded like he'd like to eat them," she laughed.

"He really loved looking at the nudes. He especially liked Andromeda and the Three Graces. The Rape of the Daughters of Leucippus also appealed to him. It's funny that he would discuss that painting with me, only a kid, but the subject didn't matter. To him they were all just paintings."

"So not only did you look at the paintings with him but you picked up his intense feelings about the nudes," I commented. "Did he also introduce you to Gaston Lachaise?"

Again a pause. "Only briefly. He was kind of angry that Lachaise's females were not only fat -- they were grotesque. Their huge breasts repulsed him. In some of the sculptures he said the whole woman seems like two huge breasts."

"Well, we now know that your relationship with Wallace was deeply steeped in art," I said. "The artists that have so affected you were particularly involved in your memories.

What was Wallace's reaction to Botero?"

"I don't recall any," Angela said. "Wallace mainly discussed classical art and some modern, but rarely contemporary art. Maybe there weren't any art books about Botero when I was a child."

"He may not have been known to Wallace," I concurred. "Let's try to find out. Now relax and clear your mind. I want you to go to the place where you first heard of Botero?"

A fleeting look of panic passed over her before she spoke. "I remember it very clearly," she said. "When Jason finally gave up trying to rape me he said angrily 'when people see my painting of you they'll see you for what you are, just like I painted you.' Then he said, 'Someday you'll be fat and ugly like Botero's women. So fat you'd be better off dead.' Then he ordered me out of his studio. I can hardly remember how I got home but I took to my bed and was afraid to leave my room for several days."

For a moment she stopped talking and then she screamed out. "When I was able to return to work I had become a fat, ugly woman like Botero's pictures. I remember now on that day I weighed 124 pounds and for the next few weeks I hardly ate as I slowly lost weight. Only when I reached 118 pounds did I stop and look at myself without fear. I had become Botticelli's Venus."

Angela began to cry as the memory of that frightening and vicious scene returned. So most of the pieces of the puzzle had now fallen into place. Would they be enough to begin the arduous work of freeing Angela from the unrelenting grip of those memories starting with her childhood and ending with the attempted rape?

I had dealt with patients before who had adopted the identities of other people. Freeing them of this possession was often complicated by their intense need to hold on to these internalized figures.

Angela's condition was different from any I had ever encountered and was tied to a number of past traumas. One major bit of information was still missing. What happened between her and Wallace that had apparently ended their interaction? Angela had forgotten how large a role Wallace played in her life. Something had occurred that caused her to block those memories.

The next hour, using guided imagery, Angela returned to a time when she was alone with Wallace. She was eight. She regaled me with stories of how she and Wallace laughed together and how she made secret drawings for him. How he would wink at her at dinner when her mother wasn't looking. They were enjoying a warm and even loving relationship. She became imbued with his specific feelings about many artists. He was an outspoken lover and critic of art. She absorbed every word and was blossoming under his tutelage. The intensity of her relationship had now become evident. For a brief time in her life she had felt love.

Finally, I asked Angela to go to the very last time that she and Wallace spent time together laughing and discussing art. One moment Angela was happy. The next moment her face became ashen and her body crumpled.

"What is it, Angela?" I asked.

"One day, I guess I was almost nine years old, I was in my bedroom looking at another art book with Wallace and we were laughing and just having fun when Mama walked in. She almost never came into my bedroom. I thought she was taking her usual nap. Wallace hardly paused except to say, 'Hello, Lydia, come on in and see some of the wonderful drawings Angela made for me.'"

"What are you doing here with her?" she demanded.

Wallace appeared astonished. "What are you implying?" he asked. "I'm enjoying myself with your very talented daughter."

"Why didn't you tell me you were seeing her like this?"

"I saw no need of that. You ignore her and seem to have no interest in anything she does."

"What I do with my daughter is my business," she retorted. "You have no right to be with her, especially in her bedroom."

Wallace moved closer to Angela's mother. "I don't like the tone of your voice. This is the only place Angela feels comfortable and if you're suggesting that anything going on here is inappropriate, I'd wish you say it right now."

Turning to her daughter, her mother shouted, "You'll be sorry you had anything to do with this man. I know it's your fault that he's here and you'll pay for this."

Wallace hesitated before moving between Lydia and Angela. "Look, Lydia, this is getting out of hand. What's the big fuss about my spending some time with your daughter? It has never interfered with our relationship. And Angela certainly appreciates my interest in her art."

"So it's all about her art, is it?" she said. "Well, we'll see how much more art she does in this house."

"Lydia, stop this. You can't keep Angela from enjoying drawing and painting. It's just about the only thing she has that means anything to her."

"Wallace, I'm telling you to keep out of this."

Angela spoke in two very distinct voices: The loving voice of Wallace and the angry, hate-filled voice of her mother. She seemed to be on automatic and I felt her rising agitation as the dialogue suddenly stopped.

"Angela," I intervened. "This is a very sad and disturbing moment. What finally happened?"

Angela opened her eyes and looked at me. For a moment she seemed not to know who I was. Grimacing and shaking her head she replied, "Wallace never again spent time with me alone. I only saw him at dinner and then he avoided looking at me." Tears filled Angela's eyes and her body shook with a deep grief that only now was being expressed.

"What happened to your art?" I asked gently.

Angela thought for a moment as she wiped away her tears. "I remember I continued to do drawings at home."

"Perhaps that was a compromise that Wallace made with

your mother. He agreed not to spend time with you alone and she agreed to let you continue to draw in the house."

"I don't know. I don't know," she cried. "How could my mother do that to me. I loved Wallace."

"Yes, I can understand your loving him. He took you into his life as you did with him."

During the remainder of that session we spoke of her new realization that one person in her childhood had shown her love. With the abrupt ending of the relationship with Wallace his love became buried but remained tied to the artists and paintings he so admired. As a teenager, when she slept with Wallace, he again played a pivotal part in unwittingly solidifying her eventual identification as Venus. Later, it was only as Venus that she could fully feel love for herself.

Unfortunately, by disliking the obesity of the women in the art works of other artists that he loved, Wallace had created the matrix of Angela's identity confusion. Later, when Jason, the art teacher, painted Angela as huge and grotesque and then attempted to rape her, Angela was vulnerable to his verbal assault. By viciously shouting that he painted her as she really is and that someday she would be fat and ugly like Botero's women, he triggered her fixation with the artists' models.

The profound emptiness stemming from her mother's rejection and the two very different experiences with the two men who influenced her self-concept had set the stage for a bizarre case of body image distortion. Now I needed to apply this insight into changing her behavior and helping her recover.

During the next few sessions Angela developed a new series of imagery exercises to overcome the "seven models fixation" as she called it. Though she struggled with the desire to retain her belief in being Venus she understood that it would keep her from gaining control over her weight. Maintaining her weight at 118 pounds was reasonable. But feeling fat and ugly if she gained a few pounds was destructive to her self-esteem. She needed to overcome her identification with the various artists' models in order to become herself.

I suggested that we try to develop imagery to combat each of her seven body image identities.

> Angela visualized herself as Botticelli's Venus, weighing that perfect 118 pounds. As she looked at her body it began to change. She watched her weight swing to 119, and back to 118 and then to 117. Instead of seeing herself in a new body form she remained her beautiful self. She concluded the imagery by asserting that she will be just as beautiful no matter what she actually weighs. In the coming months she was able to swing her weight from 110 to over 130 pounds without feeling less beautiful. The original imagery of weighing between 118 and 120 was now replaced.

> She visualized herself as a Fragonard nymph playfully running about. As she was gamboling in the forest she changed her appearance to look like her real self. In her playful mood she ran over to a young man and wrapped her arms around him and gave him a kiss. When she told me this imagery she indicated it was really due to her growing feelings toward her new friend Sheldon. She ended by saying that everyone will love her for herself.

> She visualized herself as a physically powerful Venus de Milo admiring the athletic appearance of her body. Then with a huge smile she converted her athletic body into a soft and feminine one and converted the bodily strength of the statue into mental strength. She used her newfound belief in her real beauty to walk into gatherings of people and introduce herself to strangers. She was not only convert-

ing her body to a realistic one but was working to overcome her social fears, especially her fear of men and responding to them. She was learning to trust again.

Imagining herself as a Renoir nude took an entirely new approach. Instead of becoming thin and acceptable she decided to just look as big and fat as a Renoir nude and love herself in her fat body. I felt this was a major step forward in loving herself independent of her body size.

Visualizing herself as a Ruben's woman also took a totally different turn. She imagined being a Ruben's model then returning to her Venus body and repeating that she is the same person in either body. "I love myself no matter what body I have." Later she modified this imagery by going from Ruben's body to her own. Eventually the change was from a fat to a slim body. Her love was now encompassing all body shapes and sizes.

When she was constructing the imagery to rid herself of the Gaston Lachaise body I asked her to think of what made these bodies unacceptable besides just being huge and gross. She understood and created an imagery exercise to free herself of self-consciousness about her feminine shapeliness. She visualized herself as a huge Lachaise sculpture with enormous breasts, hips, and thighs and slowly watched this body become her own shapely body. When she became herself and remained nude she ran her hands over her entire body and marveled in her beauty. She did not have to pretend to enjoy the beauty of her body and femininity. The feeling was real.

Finally, we came to Botero's huge, obese women. Her visualization here was simple and direct. She saw herself as a Botero woman and then waved her hand at it and watched it blow up into a million pieces. In its place she appeared in her normal and beautiful body. She imagined leaping for joy knowing that she would never again be seen as such a grotesque woman.

On my suggestion she added an end-state imagery exercise where she saw herself in a variety of poses and situations in different clothes, including a bikini and an evening gown. In all of them, men and women admired her. She felt the pleasure of approval from all who saw her and enjoyed her newfound ideal self. She made it clear that her ideal self was not the same as her ideal weight of 118 pounds, but rather included her body at an indeterminate weight. Her new identity would be fulfilled by her growing sense of self and her burgeoning self-love.

I continued to see Angela for over a year and watched her grow into a self-assured and outgoing young woman. She began to date Sheldon and had her first enjoyable sexual relationship with him. Later by agreement with Sheldon she decided to date other men but continued to see him at times. Her increasing comfort with men developed slowly. Trust did not come easily.

She continued to use the original imagery exercises but gradually modified or changed most of them. They became an important part of her growing self-esteem and also played a part in her rekindled interest in art. She attended social events, sometimes alone. She resumed painting and took up sculpture. The day came when she told me that the seven artists' models who had invaded her mind had left for good. She had achieved her own identity.

When her therapy ended and she said goodbye I knew with certainty that Angela had grown from being a frightened, lonely child into a beautiful and self-confident young woman.

Four years later I was invited to attend her first one-woman art show. When she greeted me she took my hand and held it for a brief moment, then introduced me to her new husband. When we parted she kissed my cheek and whispered, "I will always love you."

Later, as I watched her greet friends and strangers and comfortably mingle in the crowd my eyes misted. I recalled the courage of this remarkable young woman who had finally found inner freedom. From the needed allegiance to seven artists she had cast all away and become just one. She had become the artist that she most loved.

CHAPTER FOUR

CARL: The Yo-Yo Man

My first contact with Carl was a brief telephone call. "I need to see you immediately," he insisted. "If I don't stop eating, I'll be a dead man." The laughter accompanying his comment alerted me that all was not what it seemed. Not detecting any evidence of depression in his voice I suggested we meet the next day. "Be on the lookout for me," was his cryptic response "I'll be there with bells on."

At his scheduled time I entered my waiting room. Even though I had heard the outer door open, Carl was nowhere to be seen. He had obviously let the door close without actually entering. Perhaps he was anxious about our first meeting. I returned to my office and left the door that separates it from the waiting room partially open. Almost as soon as I sat down I heard the outer door open and again went to greet him. As I entered the waiting room the outer door was closing. Carl was nowhere in sight. I waited a few moments and again returned to my office.

On the third attempt I quickly rushed to the waiting room, only to again be greeted by the slowly closing outer door. I began to suspect the worse. My new patient was either ambivalent about seeing me or too frightened to show himself. I sat down in the waiting room to greet him when he again entered. Within moments the door opened and Carl entered grinning from ear to ear. "I knew you'd be here," he exulted. "It always works the third time."

"Please come in," was my only response. His actions required some explanation, but first I needed to know something about him.

Without prompting, he told his story. Carl was forty-six years old, about 5' 8" and currently weighed 175 pounds. After eighteen years of marriage his wife had reached the end of "her rope" and was "discarding" him as "was her right."

"Since the beginning of our marriage I have been a classic yo-yo overeater," he said. "Up thirty, forty pounds. Down thirty, forty pounds. Always between 190 and 150. I swing up and down so fast even I can hardly keep track of which part of the cycle I am on. I make the full circle in two or three months. I am always going up or down."

"So that means four to six diets a year," I said.

"Righto," he agreed. "And can you imagine what that did to my wife. Half the time she couldn't feed me enough. The other half I didn't want any food. Nothing."

Carl's diets were simple. He would fast with only water and two glasses of orange juice a day until he lost everything he had gained in the prior up cycle. His discipline was extraordinary. He would sit at the dinner table watching his wife and two teenage kids eat. He would say nothing during the fasting. He just sat and watched.

The overeating part was equally devastating to his family. He would sit and gorge himself with all the food on the table. So quickly did he eat that his kids found that they would have to rush to get enough. He talked incessantly while swallowing his food. At times food dribbled from his mouth causing groans from his kids and hateful stares from his wife. She was never able to provide enough food. Eventually his kids refused to eat dinner with him. His nightly binging was "grotesque." He ate other meals normally.

"I was the dinner-time yo-yo man," he quipped.

Until now he had never considered seeking help from a mental health professional. He felt the problem was a dietary one and continued to hope that he would one day find a diet that would work. However, when his wife filed for divorce he realized that his yo-yo dieting had finally gotten out of hand. He sought help from a "diet doctor" who was also a psychiatrist.

"I haven't moved out of my home, although I'm looking for a place to live," he said. "My wife isn't putting pressure on me yet. As a matter of fact, she's being rather decent about it," he added sadly. "She likes the idea I'm seeing you because I want to do something about my crazy eating habits."

He revealed no significant facts from his background and no history of family obesity. At the homes of friends he managed to eat relatively normally. In recent years his eating compulsion and fasting extended to restaurants. His social life began to diminish as few friends wanted to go out with him and his wife. His wife slowly developed her own circle of friends. His repeated refusal to see a psychiatrist during their marriage prompted her to finally sue for divorce.

Near the end of our first session, I brought up his odd way of introducing himself. He laughed and said, "That's just me. A practical jokester. Don't worry I won't do that again to you."

As he was about to leave he asked if he could take the restroom key that was hanging on the wall in the waiting room. He said he would return it in a couple of minutes.

After seven or eight minutes with my next patient due to arrive shortly, Carl still hadn't returned the key. On a hunch, I decided to go the restroom to see what had happened. I opened the door with my own key. Carl was not there. However, resting on the sink in a pile of crumpled toilet paper was the key and one of his cards. On the reverse side was printed, "The Yo-Yo man was here."

This was not to be the last of the pranks that Carl would pull on me during the period that I saw him.

On his next visit Carl entered my office carrying a medium-sized suitcase, which he placed next to his chair. He offered no explanations and I asked for none. The tactic of patience paid off. He just sat and watched me for awhile, then he blurted out. "You know you're dying to know what's in that suitcase, so why don't you ask? By the way, you can call me Carl. I'll call you Marv."

So in a brief minute he changed our roles. He took the initiative and declared we could both use first names and directed his first comment to my supposed curiosity. Any direct answer would be seen as a victory. It seemed obvious that he needed to have control and reverse the patient-therapist relationship.

Sometimes the best response is no response. So I waited. Five, ten minutes went by. I noted controlled restlessness, but still Carl said nothing. Finally, he opened his suitcase and extracted a tablecloth, which he placed on the floor and took out two plates, utensils, and food—lots of food. "We're having dinner together," he announced grandly. "I'm in a feeding mood and I thought it would help my therapy if you had dinner with me. You would see me in my true binging element and be able to wave your magic wand and cure me once and for all," he laughed. "As you can see I'm in an up phase of my yo-yo dieting on the way to my usual 190."

"Carl, I appreciate your offer of dining with you," I said, while gazing at the growing stack of food. "But since I believe that what you're doing is trying to help me know you better, it would be more advantageous if I merely observe your eating. Also, if you are more comfortable using my first name that is agreeable to me."

His smile acknowledged that I was once again the therapist. I then witnessed an astounding demonstration of rapid-fire gorging. In less than fifteen minutes, Carl consumed all the food before him. This included a full loaf of bread, a quart of milk, several packages of cheese, many slices of ham, tomatoes, a quart of chopped salad, three or four bananas, a pint of pasta, a pint of coleslaw, and a full-sized pie. I estimated that he had eaten over 8,000 calories of food. He had just added over two pounds of fat to his body.

As he was taking his last bite I spoke, "Carl, I think your purpose in bringing all this food here was to demonstrate something I don't think I otherwise would have understood. Do you need to have someone watching when you binge like this?"

My question startled him. He frowned before replying. "Why yes, I guess I do. Why do you ask? Is that unusual?"

"Yes, Carl, it's highly unusual for someone to binge in this manner with anyone watching. Most bingers tend to be embarrassed by their compulsive eating. You apparently need to be watched. But it shouldn't surprise you that I asked. You gave me the clue when you described your binging at the dinner table. And for a long time you only binged at home and always at dinner."

At that precise moment the first breakthrough in his therapy came. Carl sat quietly on the floor, slowly gathering up the dishes, cartons, utensils, and putting them into the suitcase. He started to cry, uncontrolled and unashamed.

"What is troubling you so deeply?" I asked.

"I don't know," he blurted out. "I feel overwhelmed by some terrible sadness that I've never felt before." His crying intensified and he could no longer talk.

As I looked at him I thought. He is crying out everything he just put into himself. He must feel starved and tries desperately to fill himself with food in place of something else. No matter what he eats the emptiness remains. At that moment I wanted to sit by him on the floor and hold him. And then I knew what he was feeling. Without knowing anything about his past I knew that Carl was a man who was starved for love. He needed to be acknowledged. To be laughed at. To make certain I really experienced him so that he could somehow experience me. But why would the need for love require such an explosive and impulsive way of being expressed?

"Carl," I said. "I understand why you wanted me to sit and eat with you. All others are offended by your uncontrolled eating. But you hoped that I would share your food and not turn away from you. You wanted to know that I cared for you."

Carl looked up into my eyes. Seldom have I seen such longing. The voice of a small child spoke to me, a voice reaching out to me. "Do you care for me?"

"Yes, Carl, I do care for you and I want to help you."

He continued to look at me and I knew he felt gratitude for my words. In that short hour Carl and I had bonded almost like a mother and a child. Somehow I would find a way to give Carl the love he needed. My path had been laid out for me.

I saw a very different Carl one week later. "I don't know what happened last time," he began, "but when you asked if I always needed to have someone watching me eat that way, something broke inside me. I had the strange feeling that by watching me you were somehow feeding me."

"In what way did you imagine that I was feeding you?" I asked.

"I don't know," he replied cautiously. "But it was like you were the one stuffing the food into my mouth."

"Do you recall anything like that happening to you in your past?"

A subdued man faced me as he struggled to find memories from his childhood to explain his behavior. Nothing came to him. His mother, a schoolteacher, and his father, a dentist, were both devoted to him. As far back as he could recall the relationship with his only sibling, an older sister, was warm and friendly. There was no indication of any eating problem until after high school.

The first sign of a binging disorder occurred in Europe during a summer vacation between his second and third year of college. "I can easily recall the incident since it was the highlight of my vacation," Carl said. "I was having dinner with my traveling buddy in a great restaurant in Rome. The place was really busy and jumping. A group of kids about our age sat down at the table next to us. They were all Italian but spoke some English. We were soon gabbing away with them and I hit it off with one of the girls.

"We spent over three hours at the restaurant eating and dancing and I began to make out with that girl. Her name was Estella. Strange, I thought I had forgotten it. She appeared to be alone and no one seemed to mind that we gravitated together. It was after midnight when she asked me to come back to her place. After getting the nod from my buddy, I agreed. I remember telling him not to worry if I wasn't back until the morning. I was anticipating a wild night with her." Carl hesitated and in a quieter voice said, "And I had never made it with a woman till then."

Carl stared in my direction, eyes glazed, as the memory of that night flooded into his mind. "What I'm about to tell you doesn't seem so terrible now," he mumbled, "but back then it overwhelmed me."

He stopped speaking and gulped down deep breaths of air. "Somehow I think it's involved with my crazy eating." Again he paused.

"Go on," I said.

"I was surprised when the taxi she flagged down took us to a large estate somewhere outside the city. I didn't have time to think about where we were going or how long the ride took. In the taxi, she immediately opened my fly and took my penis in her mouth. Even though I had never had intercourse before, I enjoyed oral sex. But what Estella could do with her mouth and tongue was amazing. All the way to her place she continued and always seemed to know when to stop. So I never came.

"I could hardly walk out of the taxi when she sat up and told me to follow her. That's when I saw her place. She gave the driver some money, took me by the hand, and led me into her fantastic home. She took me upstairs and into an enormous bedroom. Adjoining it was a large kitchen, a sitting room, and a large bathroom."

Carl now paused and I could see sweat appearing on his face. "This is very difficult to talk about," he spoke at last. "I don't know why I feel embarrassed in front of you. Hell, we're both men and you probably would have done the same thing." Once more he stopped.

"Carl, sometimes an experience which appears in retrospect benign can be quite traumatic at first, especially if you're not in control."

"Yeah," he nodded. "Well, I want you to know that what happened was strictly what she wanted. I had no say or control at all. I was so turned on by my experience in the taxi that I was ready for anything. For God's sake, some men would probably say it was the luckiest night of my life.

"First she lit many candles that were placed around her room," he continued. "Then she took me into the kitchen and opened a bottle of wine and brought out some caviar and Brie, and three or four kinds of crackers.

"We sat very close to each other at an ornate table and just ate. We hardly spoke. I can still see the pictures of nymphs painted on the table. They were cute birdlike nude girls fluttering around but in very definite sexual poses. Strange how things stay in the mind," he muttered.

"Perhaps not so strange at all if those nude girls are connected to what happened between you and Estella." I said.

"Well, I suppose it's even less surprising because Estella and I would sit at that table at least another five or six times before the night was over. Can you imagine dozens of nudes painted on a dining table?"

Carl frowned. "I never realized it so clearly until now that her bedroom and the other rooms were filled with sexual objects. Sexy paintings on the wall, sculptures of couples having sex, even the bedspread was filled with sexy women and men with big erections. It was like going into a bordello."

Carl laughed. "I was a lamb being led to the slaughter by a really sexy and insatiable woman and until I was driven beyond my capacity I loved it all. Okay, you must be wondering what happened? Right?"

I waited.

"After we each had a glass of wine and caviar and some cheese she led me back into the bedroom and immediately began to dance. She did the most provocative striptease I've ever seen. By the time she was naked and came over to remove my clothes I was so turned on that I would have done anything she wanted." Carl paused and seemed deep in thought.

Something happened that night that became connected to his binge eating. So far, however, nothing I heard seemed related to it. Carl was a 21-year man on a vacation in Italy enjoying a sexual experience with a young woman. It sounded like the type of experience two young people who were turned on to each other would have.

"After she undressed me, she led me to the bed. We lay down together and kissed and touched and caressed each other. I became wild with desire.

"She guided my mouth to her breasts and I sucked them. Then she guided my head down and I kissed my way to her pubic area. I had never gone down on a woman. My only sex had been a few experiences of several women doing it to me. I don't know whether she thought I was inexperienced or not. When I got there I kissed her and nibbled at the area and she slowly guided me to do what she wanted. When she had her first orgasm I was astonished at how excited she had become. She let go with a loud cry of pleasure. She had me continue and she had several more orgasms.

"Then we stopped and for awhile we just held each other. Then she got out of bed and pulled me with her back into the kitchen. She poured another glass of wine for us and besides the caviar and Brie brought out other cheeses and different kinds of crackers and rolls. I think there must have been three or four different goat cheeses among others. She also brought out melon, strawberries, and blueberries. It was like a feast. And we ate. She would put cheese on a cracker and feed me. I did the same for her. It was a real turn-on. Feasting after sex. Then we went back to bed."

I watched Carl as he related the story of this astonishing sexual encounter. He appeared almost in a trance, enraptured by his own memories.

"And it happened again. The same thing. As soon as I was aroused she guided me down and after she had three or four more orgasms we went back to the kitchen to eat. She brought out additional foods and opened another bottle of wine. Then back to bed and again she had more orgasms. She never tired. My mouth and lips ached and at times I felt unable to go on. But she pressed me to continue and I did. She always knew when to stop and eat.

"By the third or fourth time I was already so stuffed with food that I just let her feed me, literally shoving food into my mouth. There was now a variety of chicken and fish dishes and all kinds of desserts on the table as well as cheeses, rolls, and jams. I wanted to stop eating but she would not let me. And when I felt I could eat no more she again led me back to bed. When I say this happened at least five or six times and maybe more I'm not exaggerating. We never slept. It was either oral sex for her or eating for both of us. I think she spent most of her time helping me gorge on food.

"By the time daybreak had come I think I had eaten more food than anytime in my life. I don't know how many orgasms she had. But I never came. Not once did she do to me what she did in the taxi. All my pleasure came from what I did to her and eating that incredible supply of marvelous foods. At least I really learned how to satisfy a woman orally," he said with a bitter laugh. "It was shortly after this experience that I began to get urges to binge."

The picture had radically changed. This was no ordinary brief sexual encounter. "What impelled you to binge after that experience?" I asked.

"I don't recall anything special happening. I just began to get impulses to eat and one day I think the urge just came.

When I sat down to dinner I binged. After that the urge just grew and grew. Within a year or two I had become the binging fool that I am today."

Something was missing from his story. It seemed unlikely that his excessive binging was just stimulated by sitting down to dinner. Frequently, binging is tied to feelings of rejection, childhood conflicts, traumatic experiences, or depression. Many bingers though remain unaware of the stimulus until they begin to examine their motives for binging. I needed to know more.

"Think back." I said. "Was there anything that seemed to act as a stimulus?"

"Like what?"

Before I could respond to his question, Carl suddenly exclaimed. "I remember something. Shortly after I was with Estella I wanted to masturbate. I began and thought of her and that's when I wanted to eat."

He laughed. "This all sounds to simple. I couldn't have developed such a crazy kind of binging strictly because I got turned on thinking of Estella, and it made me want to eat like I did with her that night."

"Wait a moment," he suddenly blurted out. "I remember that as I continued to give her oral sex I became less and less sexually excited. Near the end my mouth was so tired I could hardly do what she wanted. But the food she gave me was so delicious anyone would have had trouble stopping. Although I was stuffed, I just kind of kept my mouth open and she just kept putting more and more incredible things into my mouth. I think all that food turned me on. I also got pretty drunk by the time morning had come and she was finished with me."

"What do you mean finished with you?" I asked.

"Just what I said. You'd think with all the sex I gave her she would have wanted to see me again. But when the morning came, she got dressed and didn't even speak to me. After I got dressed, she called a cab, took me out to the street, gave the cabbie some money, and told him to take me wherever I wanted to go. She just said good-bye. No phone numbers, No saying she had a great time. No nothing."

A self-satisfied look came over Carl's face. "Now I remember when the eating began. I think I slept most of the next day. But the following night I became horny again thinking about her. That's when I started to masturbate. I thought of having sex with her. But all I could imagine was her going down on me and my doing it to her. I couldn't get the pictures of my head buried in her out of my mind. And I never came when I was jerking off. Instead I went out to a restaurant and gorged myself until I felt sick. That's what happened."

"What do those memories and feelings make you think of now?" I knew that Carl had made a breakthrough, but I didn't think his memories fully explained his binging.

"I know what you're driving at. I was her whore for the night. She wanted sex all night and kept me awake by feeding me between her sexual courses. I was in a sense forced to binge on that food to keep me interested in giving her sex. I was unable to stop. Or maybe I didn't want to stop.

"And there's something else I just realized. I haven't masturbated in years. I'm trying to remember when I stopped and I think it was shortly after I began to binge. Not long after sex with Estella. Before then I masturbated a lot."

"Do you believe that your binging is a substitute for masturbation?" I asked, wondering if that might actually be true.

"Well, it's certainly wild enough," he laughed, but immediately grew serious. "Are you implying that all these years I've been binging instead of jerking off?"

I was well aware that cases of binging tend not to be so simple, yet the evidence was there. What he had told me was certainly a primary stimulus for his binging. Other factors, if any, remained to be discovered. But his insight could be helpful in beginning to control his binging.

"From what you have told me and the connection you made to masturbation and your experience with Estella, it would appear that may be the case or at least, it's involved with the binging." The picture of Carl gorging on food in my office came into my mind. "Try to visualize how you appear when you binge."

"My God," Carl responded. "It's so obvious. Why didn't I see it before? After a few minutes of eating I'm in a kind of frenzy and need to almost uncontrollably stuff food into my mouth. I continue gorging myself faster and faster until finally all the food is gone and I give a sigh of relief and it's all over in a few seconds. Just like an orgasm."

My next question was obvious. "What has this done to your sex life?"

"What sex life," Carl said, with the first evidence of irritation in his voice. "I have sex maybe once a month with my wife and that's when she gives me a hand job. I do the same for her. And that's our sex life."

Although it appeared that the cause and rationale behind Carl's binging was tied to his rather auspicious first major sex experience with Estella, it was still not clear how it could have given rise to his intense eating compulsion.

When Carl entered my office for his fourth visit he appeared depressed. As soon as he sat down he blurted out. "I think I know what happened to me when I was a kid that makes me binge."

Without pausing for my reaction he continued. "During the past week each time I felt the urge to binge I tried not to do it. I was successful in controlling myself except on one occasion two days ago when I was having dinner with my wife. She is still willing to provide me with enormous amounts of food knowing that I get absolutely frantic if there isn't enough to eat.

"I was sitting there looking at all the food and trying to make myself not eat anything. I realized just how odd my pattern is. When I'm in my eating period I can't imagine stopping. Then I hit a certain weight and immediately start on my down spiral. The switch happens sometimes in minutes and always within a few hours. One moment I can't get enough food and the next moment the food repels me. My whole body goes against eating." Carl stopped, obviously perplexed.

"You're right," I agreed. "It is very unusual to suddenly feel repelled by the same food that minutes before you were swallowing with so much pleasure. In a way, and I know what I'm about to say seems peculiar, but it is also like having an orgasm. The binging period is the orgasm and the down period is post-orgasm when you have no further interest in sex."

Carl's look of doubt and even confusion caused me to overdo my explanation. "Most men immediately want to sleep after an orgasm," I said, already regretting what I had started. "There is a period when they can't have another erection. In this case, we're speaking about your entire binging period as one prolonged orgasm and your fasting period as the aftermath or refractory period when there is no interest in eating."

"Isn't that a bit far fetched, Marv," Carl said smiling. "That sounds too much like psychobabble."

"You're right," I agreed, laughing. "Ignore my comments since it's too ridiculous for even me to consider. Nevertheless, your entire eating disorder is not typical and we shouldn't rule out anything yet. Keep in mind that your experience with Estella can be seen as a form of binging. Having your mouth stuffed with food by Estella became your primary sexual pleasure for that entire night. And besides feeding you she watched you take every bite. And isn't it your wife who cooks and brings you those enormous quantities of food you eat. Much as Estella did."

"I never thought of that," Carl said, grasping the implication that his highly charged sexual experience with Estella somehow made binging become his form of sexual gratification. "So my binging the way I do, including being watched, all fits into that experience back in Rome."

"Let's call this our working hypothesis for it seems to fit," I said, putting an end to this subject. "You mentioned that something happened two days ago that also shed light on your binging."

Carl grew somber. "I was looking at all the food on the table in front of me. The kids weren't eating with us. My wife was watching me. I tried not to eat. I wanted to get up from the table and just run away but that has never worked. As I fought the impulse to eat, the deepest sadness overwhelmed me. I just sat there and cried. I felt tortured and devastated. I didn't know what was happening to me. My wife became alarmed and came over to hold me. I felt like I was falling apart. Then I remembered it."

Carl's body was shaking as tears rolled down his face. As I watched him I had the same urge to go over and hold him that I had several sessions earlier.

"I was around three and a half when my grandma died," he said in a barely audible voice. "I always knew the date, but until two days ago I had forgotten what had happened. She lived with us and everybody loved her. But I loved her the most of all. No one ever loved me as much as she did.

"I was sitting on my grandma's lap. She was feeding and kissing me." His crying intensified. "She would put a spoonful of food into my mouth and then she would take some. It was a game we played and we were both laughing." He stopped, then in a broken voice continued. "My God, I can't stand this. I see it so clearly, as though it's happening now."

I waited. Nothing I could say now would help him. Whatever he had remembered had deeply affected him. He needed to reexamine the experience and to overcome whatever effect it had on his life.

"One moment she was laughing and kissing and feeding me. The next moment her body began to shake horribly. She clung to me tightly. A terrible sound came from her." Carl put his hands over his ears as though trying to stifle the sounds he still heard in his mind.

"I screamed as something came from her mouth and covered me. I screamed and screamed. No one came. No one was home. Later, my mother came home and found me clutched to my grandma's body sound asleep. I awakened as she was trying to pry my grandma's arms from around my body. My mother was crying hysterically. I was terrified. My grandma was dead."

This time I did go over to him and put my arms around this sad and lonely man and sat with him until his crying gradually subsided. My own tears had come and gone as I waited for Carl to return from his terrifying memory. How does one undo such trauma to a small child? I have had other patients who suffered the death of loved ones in early childhood and it always leaves a deep scar. But few had suffered as he and none had to bury their feelings in a desperate sleep while being held in the unmoving arms of his deeply loved grandmother. When his mother found him, the memory had been thrust out of consciousness. However, Carl had provided me with the understanding of why his binging took the course it did.

The following session Carl and I reviewed our new understanding of his binging episodes as I tried to tie the memories of that intense trauma to his binging. He had known for years that his grandmother had died of a massive stroke when he was a child. But he had never been told of the circumstances of her death. That terrifying experience could explain, at least in part, the intensity of his binging. Now the connection would be made giving him an opportunity to undo its effect on him.

During that terrible incident a number of things happened to the small child. One moment he was laughing in the arms of his beloved grandmother. In the next, his joy of feeling her love and the warmth of her body was suddenly shattered. The shaking of her body and the horrifying sounds she made as she struggled for air and vomited all over him would eventually connect to his first sexual experience.

Carl's loss of his grandmother's love followed by his mother's depression left him bereft of love for a prolonged period in his childhood. His working mother had depended on grandma caring for Carl since his birth. In a way, Carl's grandmother had become his real mother. The loss of that love was devastating. The effect, however, would remain submerged until that time in Rome when he was 21.

What had happened with Estella would normally be a memorable though passing event in a young man's life. However, several aspects contributed to it becoming the stimulus for his compulsion to binge. He had been highly excited sexually and anticipated much gratification. Instead, he was never allowed to have his own orgasm during the total time of the sexual interaction. His primary gratification came from eating and what he did for her. She supplied unlimited and highly tempting foods to keep him in a state of heightened pleasure and sexuality. On that crucial night, Estella's shaking body and sounds of orgasm became tied to his eating. A night that began with joy and laughter had also ended with sudden rejection and dismissal.

The similarity to his experience with his grandmother was striking. Estella's body shook with each orgasm, She was highly vocal. She fed him food. Literally spoon-fed him. In a highly charged sexual experience his anticipated gratification had been tied to food. Once more the ending of this pleasurable eating experience was sudden and final.

Could a symptom such as binging develop out of this interaction of past events? The answer is yes. Most psychological symptoms are composites of multiple conflicts. Binge eating disorder affects over four million Americans and is the most common eating problem. Most binge eaters suffer from guilt, shame and depression. Rapid weight gain and obesity are common occurrences as are desperate attempts to lose weight with extreme diets. In that sense Carl fit the pattern.

However, most binge eaters try to hide their binging and usually eat alone. In this way he was atypical.

It was now time for Carl to begin his diet program. He saw the value of drinking water both before and during meals to reduce food intake. He decided to use far more water than most dieters since his capacity to eat enormous amounts of food was exceptionally high. Even Carl eventually felt full when he ingested enough food. To radically diminish his food intake he would add a quart or more of water during his binging episodes at dinner.

Although he was not in the habit of weighing himself daily he understood the advantage of doing so and especially in reacting to weight gain in a positive manner. During his binging period he fully expected to gain weight and knowing his exact weight mattered little. However, the special water diet interested him since his day-to-day weight fluctuated wildly. He agreed to start a journal and keep track of his water and food intake, as well as his daily weight.

He already was in an active exercise program, which did not require change at this time.

Carl recognized the value of the stabilization period but wondered if he could maintain it since his monthly weight swings could be in excess of twenty-five pounds. We agreed that he would start his actual diet program with a one-month stabilization period. Stabilization would also be the focal point of his first imagery exercises. Once established we would then create imagery to break the stranglehold his experience with Estella and the tragic death of his grandmother had on him.

He agreed to do the following imagery exercises a minimum of ten times a day.

Carl visualized sending searing flames of fire from his fingertips to consume the food placed before him for binging. He imagined laughing at and taunting the food and saying he was defeating its attempt to destroy him. "You," he said, pointing to the burning food, "will never enter my body again."

He visualized his wife carrying an enormous tray of food and trying with all her strength to break through an invisible but impenetrable wall that separated her from the dinner table where he sat. He shouted at her that she will never bring food for him to binge on again.

He also created imagery to control his binging in restaurants. He imagined one waiter after another attempting to put food on the table in front of him. But with a wave of his hand he would make the food fly into the air or would cause the waiter to tumble head over heels and spill the food on the floor. Only waiters who brought him a simple salad and a piece of fish were able to attend to his eating needs. He chuckled when he described this imagery to me saying that he's even imagining a healthy diet for a change.

He imagined his hands shackled behind his back so he was unable to reach out to pick up any food that filled the table in front of him. After struggling to get loose he sees a light bulb go off in his head and he now knows for certain that he has gained the power to stop his binging. He will never lift a hand to binge again.

Carl began using the four imagery exercises and the water component of the diet together. He imbued the imagery with near magical power and felt exalted by his visualizations. Within a few days he was drinking up to six glasses of water with each meal. His food intake diminished. He had told his wife about his imagery exercises but at his request she continued to bring food to the table. Only now, when he felt completely filled, there was still food left on the table. In that first week he only gained three pounds and was elated.

During his second week using imagery he added the following two imagery exercises.

He visualized sitting before a table laden with his typical wide variety of foods and deliberately selecting only vegetables to eat. For dessert he took several pieces of fruit. He was determined to change his dietary orientation to using fruits and vegetables instead of high fat and high protein foods that used to be a major part of his binging diet.

Using end-state imagery he visualized himself at his ideal weight of 150 pounds and knew he had conquered his binging compulsion. Wherever he went he was admired for his new body, and more importantly, he was admired and praised for having conquered his binging through the power of his mind. He was filled with love that he felt came from everyone because he had overcome his binging.

Carl knew that only by changing the negative beliefs that powered his compulsive eating could he hope to win his battle against binging. He was fully aware that all his images were reflections of his newfound hope and represented the profound changes he was undergoing. Visualizing himself, as he would be when he has reached his ideal weight, was a constructive antidote against his deeply engrained negative self-defeating mindset that he would never overcome his compulsive eating.

The week he added the two new imagery exercises he gained seven pounds. And he knew why. He had approached his wife for sex. However, she was still contemplating divorce. Based on his highly motivated attempt to finally control his binging she had put the legal process on hold. At this time sex was still out of the question as it had been for many months. His frustration and anger became translated into binging on the two subsequent nights. Then he regained control by adding even more water than usual. He upped his daily use of the six imagery exercises. His motivation to succeed had actually increased.

After five weeks of stabilization it was decided that Carl would start his actual diet. He had gained a total of five pounds, which was considered a success by Carl and me. He had made the first step to breaking the back of the binging compulsion.

Could he now, for the first time in his life, go on a rational diet to lose between one to two pounds a week? The time had also arrived to add imagery related to the sexual aspect of the binging. In the previous month Carl had probed into his feelings about sex and understood clearly how he had transferred his sexual gratification to food. By eating he not only satiated his appetite but also fulfilled his need for sexual satisfaction and even orgasm. He had made no further overtures toward his wife. They had established better communication and she was now following his directions to reduce the amount and type of food she placed before him at dinner.

Two new imagery exercises were added.

> He visualized beginning to binge on food and feeling the strong sexual feeling attached to it. As soon as he began to be aroused he imagined the food changing before his eyes into the body of his wife. She immediately welcomed his sexual overtures and together they engaged in mutually satisfying sex. His sexual feelings were now attached to his wife. He exclaimed in a loud and dominating voice. "Food will never take the place of sex again."

He again visualized binging on food and feeling sexual arousal. This time with a simple though powerful wave of his hand he made the food disappear and immediately felt the urge to masturbate. He had converted the sexual feelings that he once had for food to his own body and was overjoyed knowing he could see himself as his own sexual object.

In these two imagery exercises Carl was now attempting to regain power over his own sexuality and not give food the power to arouse him. Carl hoped that his wife would eventually accept his sexual feelings toward her and would be able to respond to him. At part of his healthy attitude toward sex he also needed to accept his own body for sexual fulfillment. Most important was breaking the sexual link to food.

Although during his first diet month Carl did not lose any weight, he only gained two pounds. For a person who fluctuated as much as twenty-five pounds up or down a month depending on which cycle he was on, such a small weight gain was evidence of the success of his efforts. The periodic relapses were now being handled by the special water diet and all urges to overeating were foiled. In a period of nine weeks Carl had gained a total of seven pounds. The first time in many years that he had held his weight to such a small change for so long. A new belief that he had finally found a way to break his binging compulsion was guiding his efforts.

During his next stabilization period I decided it was time to probe further into that terrible experience in his childhood. No imagery had been used in connection to that period although it had been explored in his therapy from time to time. Such a traumatic experience would leave a deep scar in the impressionable mind of a young child. It needed to be better understood. I introduced Carl to guided imagery as a method to help.

It was now time for Carl to reexperience his grandmother's death.

As soon as Carl was fully relaxed with his eyes closed, I said softly, "Carl, imagine you are back on your grandmother's lap in those minutes before her body began to shake and describe what you feel and what is happening."

Carl began to tremble slightly. "Granny is kissing me and telling me how much she loves me."

"Carl," I interrupted. "When you hear her talk, try to put her words into the dialogue. So you actually live out the experience. Also, try to speak in two different voices. It may be more painful but you will really understand the interaction as it's recorded in your own mind."

"Granny, I love you," Carl whispered. "I love you so much."

"And I love you with all my heart," Granny said. Carl's voice had changed to portray his grandmother.

"More apple sauce," Carl said brightly.

"Here you are and a kiss to go with it."

"More applesauce," Carl repeated.

"My, aren't you the hungry one," Granny said jokingly. "Here's some more and a kiss to go with it. And here's …"

"Granny, what's the matter?" Carl asked, alarmed. "Granny, don't shake. You're scaring me. Granny, you're hurting me. Granny, don't scream at me. Granny, Granny." Carl's voice shook with pain and fear as his body began to shake violently.

Carl stopped talking. Something must be happening, I thought. He couldn't have gone to sleep so quickly. I watched as his body quieted down and then saw a look of total panic on his face.

"Carl, try to describe what's happening," I said quietly.

"Granny, your arms are too tight. You're hurting me. Granny, say something. I can't hear you. Granny, talk to me. Granny, wake up. Granny, wake up. Granny, Granny," Carl screamed.

He had just become aware that his grandmother's heart

was no longer beating, nor was she breathing or making any sounds. Yet she held on to him in her unceasing death grip. In a state of terror Carl had become inextricably bound to his dead grandmother. Finally, he became still.

"Carl, don't go to sleep," I whispered. "Try to put into words whatever you are feeling."

Carl started to cry, "I know she's gone. She's left me. She's gone. I'm all alone."

Again he became silent.

"Carl, go on. Tell me what you're feeling."

"I can't tell you. It's something terrible inside me."

"Carl," I said, more firmly, "you can tell me whatever you're thinking."

"I'm afraid."

"I understand how frightened you are, Carl, but try to go on."

And he did.

"Granny, please get up. Granny, let me go. You're hurting me. Granny, you're hurting me. Please, Granny, get up. I love you Granny. Please don't hurt me."

With those words Carl dozed off and for a few minutes I let him sleep. It was the sleep that took away his pain, as he lay tightly held by his grandmother's stiffening arms.

"Carl, it is time to get up." I whispered. A frown crossed his face.

"Carl," I said louder. "You can hear me. It's the time that your mother has come home and is trying to remove your granny's arms from you. You are now awakening. Tell me exactly what comes into your mind."

A piercing scream came from his mouth.

"What is happening?" I asked, shaken by his intense fear.

"I don't know," Carl said, his childlike voice faltering and almost inaudible.

"Carl, you are now back at the very moment when your mother is pulling you from your granny's arms. Try to say everything that comes into your mind."

"It's a terrible smell. It's all over me. Momma is crying so hard it makes me afraid. Momma, Momma," Again, the scream of terror.

What Carl told me next appeared to be from the minutes and possibly hours or even days after his grandmother's death. Separate experiences in childhood frequently combine into one memory.

"Momma, where is Granny?"

"Granny has gone away, darling," his mother said, fighting back tears.

"No, Momma, Granny would never leave me."

"Yes, darling, Granny has gone away to Heaven to be with the angels."

"No, Momma, Granny would never leave me. Granny would never go away without me." I could barely listen to the cries of pain that came from Carl.

"Granny, Granny," Carl's voice was now the wailing of a lost and forsaken child.

"Granny, I want to go with you. Come back for me. I want to go with you. Granny, I love you. I love you."

"Darling, " his mother whispered. "Granny has gone to a place where you can't go."

"No, Momma. No. I want to be with Granny." The screams that tore from Carl's mouth seemed endless. "I want to be with Granny. I want to be with Granny."

"Carl, why do you want to be with Granny?" I asked softly.

"Then I won't be alone. Granny loved me. I need her."

"Carl, your granny is no longer living." I said, as I entered into the world of the three-year-old boy. "She has gone to another world. If you went with her you'd be gone from this world. You wouldn't be able to see your mommy and daddy."

"I don't care. I want to be with her. I love Granny."

"Carl, in grownup terms, you'd be dead." My voice was decisive.

A long anguished cry escaped from his lips. "I don't want to be dead. I know what dead is. I just want to be with Granny."

To a small child the real meaning of death is elusive and the need of reclaiming his grandmother's love and presence superseded his fear of his own death. Buried in his unconscious was the way to keep his grandmother alive. He needed to fill himself with the lost love of his grandmother through food, the food she was so lovingly and playfully feeding him at the moment of her death.

Without the powerful external stimulus provided by his night with Estella he might never have resurrected this long forgotten trauma. He might never have developed an eating disorder that symbolically satisfied regaining his grandmother's love. The act of binging was the act of reclaiming the love of his deeply loved grandmother. Granny had never really died. She had remained dormant in his unconscious, inexorably tied to food as she was remembered in those last few minutes of her life.

Following the reliving and discussion of his grandmother's death, Carl's life took a decidedly positive turn. He added two imagery exercises to help him work through the loss of his grandmother and its connection to his binging.

He visualized his grandmother at the moment prior to her death and imagined her kissing him goodbye and saying she is going on a long journey to another place but will always remain inside his heart. He will always know that she loves him. He saw his grandmother soar away and simultaneously felt her enter his body and heart. He knew that she remained alive in him and would always be with him. He no longer had to eat food to fill himself with her love. He ended the imagery by saying, "I love you Granny. I'll love you forever. I do not have to eat to keep you inside me."

He visualized himself sitting on her lap and feeling her shaking and hearing the terrible sounds coming from her as she died. At first he felt his fear and then saw himself grow up mentally and physically and come to understand that she had died suddenly and was unable to stop her death. In her dying moments as she was taking her last breaths he spoke to her saying, "Granny I now know that you didn't mean to frighten me. You could not help yourself. I am no longer afraid and I don't have to hide from my feelings. I love you now and for always. You are inside me. I do not have to eat food to gain your love. Granny, I love you."

In the months following the guided imagery Carl worked through his loss of love that occurred with the death of his grandmother and faced the anger and the resulting guilt that had subsequently developed. Being watched as he ate became the replacement for his grandmother's presence as she fed him those last mouthfuls of food. The striking incident with Estella tied binge eating to his grandmother and added the sexual gratification that came with his binging.

He was able to incorporate the full diet program into his life. He had overcome his binging compulsion and was in control of his food intake. His marriage improved and he and his wife resumed a normal sexual relationship. He managed to play a few more pranks on me during the latter period of his therapy. His practical joking was his way of saying that he hadn't given up the fun part of himself. One such incident happened about two months after the experience in guided imagery.

When I went into the waiting room to greet him I found him sitting there with the same suitcase he had brought to his second meeting. He seemed very distraught and kept dabbing at his eyes with his handkerchief. For a few moments I was puzzled and wondered if this was some massive relapse but my intuition suggested I look beyond the obvious.

He entered my office, opened the suitcase, pulled out a tablecloth and proceeded to empty his suitcase of a similar hoard of food as in the previous time. He had still not said a word except to invite me to have dinner with him. He felt we both needed a good meal. As before, I merely observed and did not join in the feast.

Throughout the session Carl sat on the floor, the huge pile of food untouched before him, while he chewed celery. He told me about his week's activities and the changes in his life. At the end of the hour he quietly gathered up all the un-eaten food and placed them back into his suitcase.

His parting words were, "Marv, when I first came here you saw the power of my compulsion to eat everything I had brought. Today you see the same food and I wanted you to see that now I feel no urge to eat it.

"I also want you to know that last night Janet and I had our first complete sexual experience since the first year of our marriage."

As he was leaving he opened the suitcase one more time, extracted a stalk of celery, and handed it to me. At the door he turned and smiled, "Don't forget to deduct that five calories from your dinner tonight."

In the year and a half that I worked with Carl I saw how the power of his imagination and the belief in his ability to change his life had radically altered his world. On his last visit he brought his wife and two children. They sat together and spoke of the many ways their family had changed. The same energy Carl had put into his binging he now put into bringing happiness and peace to his family. I watched and marveled at the degree of intimacy that now existed within the family. Their mutual affection was evident. Love had fully returned. Carl's grandmother had left her stamp on the entire family. There was no doubt that she truly resided in Carl's heart.

CHAPTER FIVE

JUDY: Taking Control

"Judy, either you tell the doctor exactly why I brought you here or I will. And I'll tell him everything. Do you hear me?" Mrs. G said, struggling to restrain her anger and frustration. Judy slumped in her chair, eyes downcast, and said nothing.

The previous week Mrs. G had called to make the appointment for her daughter after she had discovered her throwing up in the bathroom. The anger in her voice when she said, "I can't imagine my daughter doing such a thing," had stayed with me.

"All right, Judy, last chance," her mother said sharply.

Judy remained silent and slumped even deeper into the chair.

"Judy, would you prefer to speak with me alone?" I asked.

Silence.

"Doctor, forget her. I'll tell you everything," her mother said.

"One moment, Mrs. G," I responded. "Judy, if your mother leaves the office you should know that whatever you tell me would be in strict confidence. It will always remain just between the two of us."

Judy looked up. "You won't tell my mother anything?"

"Nothing, I won't even talk to her without your permission unless I thought you might do something to harm yourself. Even then, you would have the right to listen in to our conversation."

Judy shot her mother a look and smiled slightly.

"You do understand that, don't you, Mrs. G?" I said pointedly.

"Of course, doctor, I understand and accept what you say," Mrs. G said. "I only want to help my daughter." Without another word Mrs. G rose and left the office.

Trust comes slowly to a teenager and has to be established through interaction. Adolescents understand that I must protect them from harm. They're frightened by their loss of control or their strange symptoms and want help. Forming that essential connection to them is the crucial element in helping them. Later when trust and confidence has been established, they often want you to intervene with their parents knowing that you have their best interests at heart.

"I hate her," were the first words Judy spoke. "She always wants to tell me what to do. Do this, do that, that's all I hear."

"How long has this been going on?" I asked.

"Always."

"Even when you were a small child?"

"I guess it really started when I entered high school two years ago. I'm almost sixteen and I'll be getting my driver's license in another two months. I can take care of myself."

"Why are you here?" I asked. "I presume you know that I'm a psychiatrist."

"Yeah, I know. Mom thinks I'm mixed up and that I'm killing myself."

"What makes your mom think that?"

"Nothing special. I'm just like every other kid, but my mother thinks I'm completely screwed up."

"How come?"

There was fear or possibly guilt in her face as she again slumped in her chair and grew silent.

Finally she spoke. "Are you absolutely certain you won't tell my mother anything I tell you?"

"Yes," I said reassuringly. "You can depend on that. In

this office everything is 100 percent confidential."

Her struggle to believe that I could be trusted was evident.

"Judy, It's not easy to trust someone you've never met. Especially when you know your mother arranged our meeting and is paying the bill. By bringing you here your mother is showing a genuine interest in you and wants to help you. And she has accepted my way of doing it. Otherwise, I know that you would never feel free to tell me what it is that's bothering you."

A change came over Judy. She attempted to hide the tears that appeared in her eyes and she stiffened her body against the turmoil she felt.

"Judy, sometimes in life you have to take a chance. My only interest is helping you in any way that I can. Whatever is going on, I'm on your side and I'll always be absolutely straight with you."

No longer fighting to hold back her tears Judy cried without restraint.

Slowly the crying subsided. "Try to tell me what troubles you so much," I said gently.

Thrusting her face forward and shaking her fist in the air she cried out. "Look at me. Just look at me. I'm a blimp, a fucking blimp. I hate myself looking like this."

"Judy, it's no crime to be overweight," I said. "Certainly if you prefer to be thinner then we need to find a way to help you lose weight. But you seem so upset for just being overweight."

"I throw up all the time," she cried, "and I still gain weight. Nothing I do helps. I take laxatives. My mother doesn't know about that."

"Your mother mentioned that she caught you throwing up when she made the appointment."

"Did she tell you anything else?"

"No. Except that you were heavy and didn't like yourself because of it. Otherwise, I know nothing about you."

Judy looked at me warily. "And I can tell you anything and no one would ever know?"

"That is correct."

"I'm considered the class slut."

"What makes you think that?" I asked.

"Because I'll have sex with any guy who wants it. And even though I'm fat I know plenty of guys who want to get laid."

"Why does having frequent sex make you into a slut?" I asked, making it clear that I did not accept that idea.

"It just does. Would you want your daughter to have sex with anyone at all?"

"Judy, it's not a matter of how often you have sex. It's your feelings about it that disturb you."

"I have sex because it's the only way boys will like me."

"Does that feeling stem from your being heavy or do you overeat because you feel guilty about having sex?"

"I don't know," she said, crying. "When I entered high school I had a beautiful body and everyone made over me. Then I had sex with some guy I hardly knew. He was a friend of my brother and I thought he was nice. One afternoon he came to the house with my brother and came up to my room where I was doing homework. He said my brother had to go out for a while and he was waiting for him.

"He started kissing me. Then he offered me a few hits on a joint. I had tried pot before but had never really gotten stoned. This time I did, and before I knew it I was undressed and he was fucking me. I didn't know what to do. He told me not to tell anyone or I'd get into trouble. I never did. Later we smoked pot again and had more sex. I felt like I couldn't stop. I began to use pot all the time and would have sex with any guy who had some. I guess I wanted the sex too. But I felt it was terribly wrong. That's when I began to eat so much.

"When I entered high school I weighed 110 pounds. I now weigh 170 pounds. I'm gross. When I got to 140 or 150 pounds I began to make myself vomit. I ate more and more and didn't always throw up. I became this monster you see. And I sometimes vomited ten times a day. No one caught on until my mother saw me do it. I didn't even know she was home when she burst into the bathroom. That's the whole story. You now know everything about me."

"Judy, I appreciate your honesty. I know that these things are very painful to discuss. Maybe we can figure out why you reacted to sex and using pot by overeating and developing all this self-hate."

Judy stared at me for a few moments. "I won't lie to you," she whispered. "I'm desperate. I use other drugs too. Drinking, and some coke. I even had Ecstasy. I like the feeling I get but hate what I'm doing. My schoolwork has really suffered. It's a wonder my mother didn't tell you that when she called you. I need to believe in you because I'm terrified I'm going to kill myself."

Judy stopped talking. Fear was clearly written on her face.

"How strongly do you feel you might kill yourself?" I asked.

"You won't tell my mother, will you?" she asked, suddenly frightened.

"Judy, you have to trust my judgment in this situation. If I believed you would leave here and kill yourself I would have to alert your parents. The fact that you're so willing to talk about your feelings tells me you want to get well. That's a very positive first step to overcoming these feelings."

"I've thought of killing myself many times in the past few months but I don't think I would ever really do it. I want to get better. I've been afraid to ask my mother if I could see a shrink because she would want to know why."

"Maybe her catching you was no accident. It gave you a reason to see me."

For the first time Judy smiled. "I'm glad I'm here. And I like you."

"And I like you too, Judy," I responded warmly.

"Can you help me?" she whispered.

"I believe I can," I said. "Actually, I'm going to help you help yourself. The problems you have are serious and need attention but they can all be overcome."

During the remainder of the session she told me about school and her interest in science and music. She believed that her poor grades would hurt her chances of getting into a top college when she graduated in two years. Her only sibling, a brother, nineteen years old, was away at college. He knew about her drug use and the vomiting but tended to dismiss it. He kept her secret from her parents.

Her father who she described as "nice" was a high school teacher in a different school. From her brief description he seemed to be a rather shadowy figure in her life. She didn't feel he had any real impact on her development. What part he might have played in her present difficulties remained to be seen.

Her mother was an entirely different matter. She bore the brunt of Judy's anger. From early childhood her mother was preoccupied with Judy's education, moral behavior, and nutrition. Although her mother may have been a bit excessive, the advice she gave appeared to be reasonable. But for a sensitive child the advice felt like coercion. As Judy entered adolescence she began to rebel.

Her mother warned her about drugs, promiscuity, and the need to always eat a healthy and controlled diet. Her father and brother followed the dietary advice. Wanting to conform to her mother's wishes, she ate the right foods at home but outside, away from the scrutiny of her parents, she often indulged in junk food. However, it was never without pangs of guilt and remorse. Judy also felt that her mother was overly protective and was restricting her outside activities.

Before the session ended Judy promised that she would call me if she ever had the impulse to harm herself in any way. I felt our relationship had been established. For the first time in over a year she had hope.

During the next few sessions Judy described more fully her two primary disappointments: her inability to control her impulsive behavior and her poor grades in school. She did not mention the bulimia or her weight and I, likewise, focused on other areas of her life. By the end of the third session she began to figure out ways to improve her schoolwork and to stop using drugs. She had become determined to break the negative spiral that had carried her self-esteem to such a low ebb.

At the beginning of the fourth session she immediately began to cry. "I'm a terrible person," she burst out. "I couldn't help myself. I didn't want to do it."

"Judy, please tell me what happened?" I said concerned.

"Some guy gave me some coke and I had sex with him. Then as soon as we were finished he gave me some more and said a couple of his friends needed to get laid and he told them I would do it with them. I didn't even know these other guys and I did it, although I really didn't want to. I felt I owed it to them for the coke. When we were all finished and I was just lying there, maybe they thought I was sleeping, I heard one of the new guys say that maybe he'd bring some of his friends over to use the whore. I'm not a whore. I just couldn't help myself."

I felt the depth of her anguish and knew how degraded she felt. "Judy, those remarks were callous, but, nevertheless, it makes you aware of how much these sexual experiences are unacceptable to you. Sex is generally a beautiful experience but not when you feel used. Maybe this is the time to begin to find ways to overcome your need for drugs which lead to sex, and begin to take charge of your life."

"I want to change," she whispered, still sobbing. "I really do."

"Are you willing to use drastic measures to stop the use of drugs?"

"Yes, I'll do anything."

"We need to determine how strongly you're addicted. Do you use anything besides the three drugs you mentioned?"

"No, I never tried crack or heroin."

"Do you ever buy drugs for yourself?"

"No, I always get them from guys who fuck me. I guess everyone knows I'll put out for drugs."

"Do you seek out these guys?"

"No, but someone always wants to give me some. I do it almost every day."

"What happens if you don't use drugs for three days or a week?"

"I don't know since I've never tried going that long without them."

"Do you go on vacations?"

"Yes, and sometimes I go with my parents. I don't use drugs when I'm with them."

"Do you crave drugs then?"

"No, but I haven't been on any long vacations since last summer and that's over eight months ago."

"What I'm going to suggest is not easy to do but if you follow the plan it can lead to your overcoming the use of drugs. That would give you control over your sex life and above all make you begin to feel that you're in control of your life."

"I'll do anything," she whispered.

"Do you think you can refuse to accept any drugs that are offered you for a week?"

"I don't know."

"Do you crave drugs or just accept them when given to you?"

"I don't know. I think I want them when they're given to me."

"What if you were home with a bad cold for three or four days? What would you do?"

"I'd wait until I got better," she said and paused. "I think

I can do without drugs for a week."

"Good," I said. "Judy we're going to experiment. I don't want you to feel guilty if you have difficulty in doing what I'm suggesting. We need to determine whether you are physically addicted to drugs or are psychologically dependent on them. Perhaps you're using drugs to have sex in order to feel loved."

In a surprising burst of insight Judy said she thought that was the reason she gave sex to men. "When I use drugs I don't feel so guilty about all the sex. And it's gotten worse lately. I'm so fat and ugly no man would like me unless I fucked him. I hate myself when I do it. I don't want to do it anymore."

"Judy, you don't have to," I said. "I'm going to introduce you to the use of mental imagery, which can help you control your impulses. You can start using it today."

"What do I do?"

I proceeded to explain how imagery worked, the need to believe in its use, and the advantage of doing it while relaxed. It was clear that the imagery must address a number of areas simultaneously.

They included her need to improve her self-esteem and to feel self-love. Secondly, she had to stop using sex to provide the love she needed. Third, she needed to overcome her need for drugs. Fourth, she needed to stop overeating and overcome her bulimia.

The following imagery exercises were developed.

She would visualize knocking away the hand of anyone who offered her any drug. She would see the drug fly into the air and disappear. She would say I'll never use drugs again.

She would refuse sex with anyone she did not truly care for. She would visualize a series of men who wanted sex and tell each one that she doesn't need sex to feel loved. She would say to herself with great conviction, "I love myself very much. I love me." She would then physically hug herself as part of the exercise.

She would imagine a deep craving for drugs that burned in her like a fire. Then with a hose she would quench the fire and eliminate the craving. I felt this imagery would be useful since it was probable that Judy had some degree of physical addiction that would need to be addressed.

She would visualize approaching the refrigerator for food to binge only to find it sealed shut. A message on the door would state that the refrigerator would never again be used for binging. She would repeat several times, "I shall never binge again." Her eating compulsion was complex and it was important to introduce an imagery exercise to address it at this time. Later we would develop imagery for the bulimia.

Finally, an end state imagery exercise was added. She visualized herself at an ideal weight. In her case she believed that 125 pounds at her height of 5' 6" was perfect. At my suggestion she imagined herself in a variety of situations with her new weight. In a bikini on the beach being admired. In a form-fitting dress at a party. In a loose skirt and blouse, which hid her new figure but was as becoming as the others. She would be admired, but above all she would admire and like herself. With each change in dress or place she would say empathically that she loves her new self and will never overeat again.

These five imagery exercises were to start the program. Judy agreed to do them a minimum of ten times a day. I knew well the difficulties that lay ahead. We were simultaneously attempting to overcome a number of problems, each different but interrelated.

Many teenagers function impulsively and lack the persistence to markedly change behavior. As they fluctuate between attitudes that stem from childhood and those that are pulling them toward adulthood, persistent motivation and self-control may be in short supply. Judy would have to be steadfast and unrelenting in her use of the imagery. But even more important she needed to maintain the inner belief that she had the mental capacity to change her life. Today in her desperation she wanted to believe. Would she continue to believe it when she was once again offered a drug or had the impulse to raid the refrigerator?

As with most teenagers Judy needed to feel that her parents did not control her. What she was now trying to do would please her parents, and even though it was what she wanted to do, it might seem that she was conforming to their wishes. To her I, too, was an adult or parent figure who was guiding her. She needed something more to make these exercises work. She needed a reward that was real. Imagery by its very nature doesn't work quickly. It requires time, often months, especially when the needs are complex, as they were with Judy.

She needed to actually lose weight and soon. For the past two years her weight had steadily increased in spite of the bulimia. If she could lose six or seven pounds in the next month she would get an overall boost in self esteem and begin to believe in her new inner control.

At her next session I would introduce the Five Keys diet. I would also have an opportunity to see what kinds of resistances were erected to fight the imagery and determine what had to be modified. I might also introduce the use of a journal. I felt she would need as much input from me as possible. When I saw her one week later a transformation had taken place. She literally bounced into my office and plopped into the chair. "You'll never guess what happened," she announced grandly.

"I can't imagine," I said, smiling.

"I decided to change everything in my life at the same time, and I'm doing it."

"Well, that certainly sounds like a very heroic undertaking. I can see that you have already made some of those changes."

"Wait until you hear what I'm doing."

"I'm eagerly waiting," I said.

"Last week, after I left, one thing you said rang in my ears. Do you remember telling me that believing in yourself is one of the greatest gifts you can give yourself? You said that you can make anything happen that you wish for. You only need to find a technique to achieve it and imagery could provide that technique."

"Yes, I remember telling you that," I said.

"Well, the more I thought about it, the more I liked what you said and I told myself that I believe in myself." She smiled warmly and took a deep breath as she continued.

"When I was a little girl I found a tiny kitten lost in a field. It was crying. I took it home and washed and fed it. But after a few days it became obvious that it was sick and getting weaker. My father looked at it and said that he didn't think it would live and I had to adjust to that. I cried and he took the kitten to the vet who said the same thing. The vet was going to keep it and put it to sleep. But I cried so much that my father reluctantly brought it back home. Then I prayed all day for my kitten to get better.

"I saw in my mind the kitten starting to eat more and gaining weight and finally becoming well. I made my vision of the kitten so strong I knew in my heart that the kitten had to hear it. And a few days later it did begin to eat more. Very slowly it got stronger and one day it was perfectly well. My father said it was a miracle and that it was due to my love for it and the fact that I never gave up. He said I helped the kitten get well because I believed so strongly. He said the same thing then that you told me about myself. Doctor, I want to get better. I want to be well. I want it more than anything in the world."

She came over to me and put her arms around me and kissed me gently on the cheek. I felt her tears and I would imagine that she felt mine.

What she recounted the remainder of the hour was truly astonishing. In all my experience working with people using imagery I had never heard anything that approached what she was about to tell me. Judy had reached deep inside herself to find the resources to lift her from a life of desperation and self-hate. Her condition had not become fixed and her identity was still being formed. She had wrestled with her demons and overpowered them. She had risen in one brief week into a new world of being. This is her story.

"When I left you last week I kept thinking of what you said and that's when I remembered Gigi, as a kitten. Gigi has been with me almost eight years now. When I got home Gigi was lying on my bed. I picked her up and hugged her and I cried all over her telling her how much I loved her. I lay on the bed for hours crying and holding Gigi and slowly I begun to realize that I was about to become a different person. If I could bring a kitten back to life then I could bring myself back to life. I was going to do it all by myself.

"For the first time I really believed that I could do it. And I would use your imagery to help me. That's the same thing I did with Gigi. I knew she would get better because I saw her getting better in my mind. That's when I started to see myself getting better. And all week long I went through all the ways I was going to change. Each day that went by I knew in my heart that I was getting well."

I waited while she paused. I was amazed at what I saw and heard and didn't know what to say.

"During dinner my mom asked if something had happened to me and wondered if I was all right. I told her that something wonderful had happened and I was going to get better and she would never have to worry about me again. My father asked if it was due to anything that happened here with you."

Judy smiled sweetly at me. "All I said was that I loved you and you are helping me.

"After dinner I went upstairs and did my homework. That's when the visions began." She noticed my reaction and laughed. "No, not those kind of visions. These were visions from my own mind as I began to wonder what images I needed to practice to get well. I didn't even have to think them up. They just kind of came by themselves. I wrote them all down so I would not forget any of them. I must have over a hundred of them. Do you want to hear them all?"

Yes, by all means," I replied wholeheartedly. "All of them."

"I didn't get them all in one day," she giggled. "They came to me all week long and the last ones are from last night."

"Can you tell me everything in sequence, the way they came to you?"

"Yes, that's the way I want to do it. I finished my homework and was lying in bed thinking of what we had talked about. The very first image that I saw was my own body. I stared at myself like on a big movie screen. I examined every part of myself. I started getting upset and thought, am I really this ugly? The more I looked the more my body began to change. I told myself, I'm not ugly. I'm not ugly at all. I'm really very beautiful. Why have I always thought that I was ugly? Just like I was in a fairy tale I knew that I was turning into a beautiful girl. My body size didn't change. Only my thoughts changed. I began to cry and I hugged myself, saying over and over again, I'm beautiful, I love myself, I'm beautiful, I love myself. For the first time in over two years I didn't hate my body.

"Even as I began to see my body as beautiful, I realized

that I have to change all my thoughts about myself. Everything that I felt as negative has to be changed. For so long I have not been able to love myself. And I know I'm lovable. I know it. Don't you think I'm lovable?"

"Judy," I immediately responded. "You are lovely and lovable and beautiful. You have begun to know who you really are and to truly love yourself. Somehow you have made an important breakthrough in your thinking." Tears came to my eyes as I gazed at this extraordinary young woman who was opening her heart to me. "What happened then?" I asked softly.

"Then I thought that I've been sick for so long and I know it's because of how I think about myself. I want so much to get well and I know I can do it."

"Yes, Judy, I know you can, too. You are a very courageous young woman and nothing can stop you now."

"My very next vision came as I saw someone trying to give me pot and I screamed at him and said I'll never take drugs again. I know that drugs have nearly destroyed me and I'm through with them. I had more visions of using drugs. I began to imagine other people giving me drugs, kind of like the imagery you showed me about people giving me food. As soon as anyone came near me with any drugs, I screamed at them to get away from me. I did everything to make them leave me alone. I was convinced I would never touch drugs again. And, I know you'll be proud of me. I've touched nothing for the entire week."

"Judy, that's marvelous," I declared. "I am very proud of you. But best of all you did it by yourself and with your mind. Did your images tend to repeat?"

"Yes, some of the visions repeated every day but they were always different in some way. And every day I went over the previous ones many times. I wanted to burn them into my mind. I felt my mind changing."

"I have no doubt that your mind was actually changing," I said emphatically. "What were your next visions?"

"The very next one disgusted me. I saw lots of men invading my body. All they wanted to do was get inside me. And I knew that it was not my body they were invading but my mind. They were fucking with my mind. And I swore that no man would ever do that again. I would not have sex with any man unless I loved him and only when it did not involve drugs. It made me feel clean, like my body and mind were pure again.

"I began to believe in my ability to change who I was." Judy began to cry softly and I heard her murmur under her breath, "I want to be someone who is good. I want to be someone I can love."

"Judy, you already are someone who is good and who can be loved. But it has taken this wonderful change in your thinking that has brought that awareness to you."

She continued, "Next, I thought of how I eat. How I stuff food into my mouth. It has nothing to do with nutrition. My eating was all tied up with feeling empty and lonely and unloved. It's what we talked about last week. I was using food to make me feel loved and instead it was making me hate myself. I knew that I didn't want to use food in place of love anymore. I kept saying to myself that I love myself. Just like I love Gigi, I love myself. I realized also that my mother has always wanted me to eat good food. She always harped on it but now I know it was for my benefit and she was right.

"Also, I again saw my body big and fat and began to say that fat is beautiful. And thin is beautiful. I will love my body whatever shape or size it is. Can you understand how different this made me feel? Instead of saying I'll love myself because I'm thinner I'm saying that I'm going to get thinner because I love myself."

"I understand the difference," I said. "By loving yourself then you no longer have to prove that you are lovable by losing weight. Instead, losing weight comes as a reasonable choice you are making for your body. Just like you wouldn't love yourself because you played tennis well. Instead, it would be because you love yourself that you want to play tennis well. And by loving yourself you open up many doors to fulfilling yourself."

"Yes, that's it exactly," she said excitedly. "And then I thought of all the ways I binge. It's not only raiding the refrigerator. I'll eat food any place I can find it. In markets, on tables, anywhere. I knew that all I had to do was stop stuffing food into my mouth. Nothing gets by my mouth. It's closed by a enormous padlock." With that funny vision she broke out laughing. "I'm in style. Imagine carrying around an enormous lock on my lip, the world's biggest lip ring.

"Another thing I'm going to do is exercise more. I used to love to play tennis and stopped because I was so heavy and I thought people would laugh at me. I don't care. I'm going to play tennis and no one will laugh at me. I'll be the first to laugh if I look silly in a tennis outfit. I have lots of visions of my playing tennis and loving it. And I'm going to do other exercises.

"I wanted to ask you about the diet. I don't want to starve myself. I know you're a diet doctor and maybe you can help me with a diet."

"Before the session is over we'll discuss the first steps to take to lose weight and establish a healthy diet," I said. "But for now why don't you continue telling me about your new ideas and visions."

"I felt so excited about all these visions and the changes I was feeling that I wasn't prepared for the terrible dream I had the next day. I felt that I was being sucked down into a cesspool of mud and thought I was going to die. I struggled and fought to stay on the surface. Then someone threw me a rope and I grabbed it and was dragged out. I felt so relieved I just cried. When I looked around there was no one there."

"Let's take a few minutes and see what the dream might be telling you," I suggested.

"I already know what it means," Judy responded. "You are the one who threw me the rope, but I'm really saving myself."

I smiled and inwardly marveled at the progress Judy was making. I agreed with her interpretation and she went on.

"That afternoon and evening I had more visions. I would sit in my bedroom and close my eyes and wish to see things about myself and they would just come. I saw visions of growing old too fast, becoming wrinkled and hideous and even dying young if I didn't change my ways and take over my life. I mean really take it over. I would stare at the visions and keep saying that is my old self and I'll never look hideous or die young. I knew that I was now different and these old fears were groundless. They kept coming back a few more days but then just disappeared," she said triumphantly.

"Judy, it appears that in a very brief period you have already overcome some of your underlying fears. Because you have such a strong belief in your ability to change and you spend what appears to be hours going over and over the imagery, you are making major changes in your thinking. As you proceed always reexamine old imagery to see if there is any further need to work on residual negative beliefs."

"Oh, I will. I already do that. I try to bring some of the worse images back to see if I believe them anymore. If I do I just squash them with my mind."

"What a wonderful image," I said spontaneously.

"Did you really like that one?" Judy laughed.

"More than like it. You have an amazing imagination and remarkable mental power." I said, charmed by her enthusiasm.

She just giggled.

"Judy, we have to stop now in order for me to give you some ideas about your actual diet. But next week how about continuing to tell me about the visions that you've already had and the new ones that you may have next week?"

I then described the other four keys of the Five Keys diet program. She listened, made some notes, asked a few questions, and agreed with all aspects of the program. She loved the idea of the "friendly" scale as she called it and only frowned briefly when I said that diet drinks couldn't be used in place of water. She would begin to eat a healthy diet, including lots of vegetables and fruits and would let her mother help her. "You can't imagine how happy this will make my mother," she laughed.

We ended the session by my asking if she suffered any withdrawal symptoms from going cold turkey on all the drugs. She said that except for some queasiness in her stomach and feeling "jittery, like having pins and needles" for a couple of days she had no problem. "It was all in my believing I needed them, I think," she said.

At her next visit I knew things were different. She was no longer so bubbly and effervescent. "First, I want to tell you that I'm okay about eating and not using drugs and all that stuff but I've had upsetting visions about my brother and they scare me."

I immediately thought back on what I knew of her brother and wondered about her first sexual experience with her brother's friend. "Can you tell me about your visions?" I asked.

"I began to have visions of being alone with my brother and his tickling me until I was helpless with laughter, then he would lie on me saying he was just trying to calm me down. He really used to do that and I always felt funny when he did, but I loved him and we always had fun together."

"How old were you when this was happening?" I asked.

"Oh, I don't remember exactly but I think it began when I was eight or nine and continued till he went away to college, a year and a half ago. I was fourteen then. I…" She hesitated and I detected her struggle to avoid crying.

"So this continued almost a year after you had begun to have sex for drugs and love," I said.

"Yes, and he knew what was happening and never tried to stop me." Judy could no longer hold back her tears. "In the summer before Eddy went away to college he wanted to fool around with me. He would grab me and touch me and wanted us to be naked together. I didn't know what to do but I knew that was wrong. I never let him do anything, but sometimes he just wanted to rub against me and I didn't stop him. I feel so funny telling you this. I think I'm a bad person for letting him do that. Sometimes I even wanted him to do more."

Sexual feelings between siblings are common and at times acted on in varying degrees. Frequently, resulting guilt causes negative effects on the sexuality of both participants. It was important to determine what occurred between Judy and Eddy and whether there were residual effects.

"Do you feel up to telling me more about what happened?" I asked.

"I want to," Judy said. "Nothing really terrible happened with Eddy, but I've had awful visions all week about him and me."

"Can you describe the visions?"

"Do you remember I told you that I had my first sex with a friend of Eddy's?"

"Yes, I recall that," I answered.

"Well, Craig and I had sex quite a few times after that first time and it always seemed to happen when he was visiting Eddy. He would just come up to my bedroom and before I knew it we smoked a joint and were having sex. Then he'd just leave and spend the rest of the time with Eddy. Eddy never said anything but he must have wondered what we did when Craig came to my room. I used to think that Eddy had sent him up."

"That would imply that you connected your brother and Craig when you had sex with Craig," I said quietly.

"How did you know?" Judy uttered surprised. "That's exactly what happened all week. I had visions of many of the guys I had sex with and in the imagery I pushed them away and told them I would never have sex with them again and I would not use drugs with them. I did awful things to them in the imagery to keep them away and to make certain I would never again have sex with someone I don't like. A lot of the visions had occurred the previous week.

"But this week I imagined Craig and me having sex. Instead of pushing him away I decided that I really liked him and would have sex with him but without drugs. As we were doing it he turned into my brother. It was awful. I was having sex with Eddy. I had to force myself to change him back into Craig. Doesn't that mean I'm a terrible person having sex with my brother?"

"No, Judy," I replied. "First of all you weren't having sex with Eddy. You were visualizing sex with Eddy. That's a big difference. Secondly, your visions start with your having sex with Craig with whom you've had sex with a number of times. The fact that he's your brother's friend has complicated the situation. Also, Eddy has always been very sexual toward you and he might have wanted to do it with you."

"I think he did," she said, scowling. "But I wouldn't let him and that's when he would rub against me, well, you know what happened when he did that."

"Yes, I believe I know," I said, realizing that Judy had made the connection between her brother and Craig. "Because you wouldn't let Eddy go all the way with you perhaps he sent Craig up to do it in place of him."

"Oh, he wouldn't do that, would he?" she asked, shaking her head in disbelief.

"I don't know, but what is important is your feeling that Eddy knew Craig was having sex with you and apparently encouraged it. That could account for why you're having sex with Eddy in your imagery." I paused to see if she could accept that idea.

"But I wasn't having sex with Eddy, was I?" she asked.

"The answer is somewhat complicated, but you weren't really having sex with Eddy," I said, trying to find a way to present how she played out her sexual feelings for her brother.

"Imagery will often bring out hidden feelings and conflicts," I began. "Your imagery tapped into your sexual feelings for your brother. Since you had already recognized that Craig was a sexual substitute for Eddy you made the change in the imagery. You were strong enough to admit to yourself you did have sexual feelings for your brother and that is valuable in overcoming guilt about it.

"In a vicarious way you were having sex with Eddy. Being able to admit these feelings to yourself is an important step toward getting that feeling out of your mind. Remember this is what's in your mind. It's not what you actually did."

"Then I should feel good about knowing it."

"Absolutely. It's part of your courage in facing all your conflicts and that one was definitely connected to your use of drugs, which you're no longer doing."

"I feel better," Judy said more brightly, as a burden of guilt was lifted.

"So have you had other visions?" I asked.

"Lots more."

"Okay, I'm all ears," I laughed. "I've never had anyone think through so many problems so quickly using imagery as you have."

"Is this really a lot?"

"Yes," I said, "You are by far my champion imagery maker."

Judy clapped her hands. "And all I wanted to do was get better as quickly as possible."

I laughed. "Well, I think you're amazing for what you've done so far. Our job now is to make certain that you can stick by your new beliefs forever."

"Oh, I will, I will," she said with conviction.

"I think our time is about up so how about if you continue with the imagery at your next visit."

As soon as Judy bounced into the office I knew her week had been a good one. "I think I'm all better," was her first announcement. "And I'm going to become an artist," was her second.

"Great, on both counts," I exclaimed, laughing.

"I have loads more visions. Some are from the previous weeks I didn't tell you and lots from this week. But I don't think you have to hear them all unless you really want to," she said.

"We'll it's up to you," I said. "Do what you think is best."

"I guess I should tell you about the latest ones. I spend all day having these visions. I'm so good at seeing anything I want that I decided to become an artist. All I have to do is dream up a picture and paint it."

"Now that's a good idea. Many artists do just that," I said, wondering how realistic such a desire was. "Do you like to paint?" I asked.

"Oh, I love to, but I haven't done much drawing. But I started doing it," she giggled. "And the first drawing I did was showing you looking into someone's brain and seeing millions of pictures."

"Well that could certainly be an interesting drawing," I acknowledged. "After all, looking into your mind has provided me with more images than anyone I know."

"Am I really fun to work with?" she asked.

"More than fun," I said emphatically. "You make me realize that a truly high spirited and motivated young person can do almost anything she wants. Anyway, Judy, I have truly enjoyed my work with you. So now tell me why you think you're all better."

"Well, I changed my whole way of eating. My mom thinks you're a magician who made me want to eat healthy food. So I told her you were and that you hypnotized me to do what she wanted. She almost believed it, but then I laughed and said you didn't need to hypnotize me because you told me to use the visions in my head to do whatever I wanted."

"And believe me you're already an expert at using your imagery," I said.

"Do you know what else I did?"

"No. Tell me."

"I gave my bathroom scale a special name. I call it Marvy. Is that okay?" she asked, suddenly aware I might not like her using my name.

I laughed. "Why that's the best compliment I've had in a very long time. So what else makes you think you're better?

"I just am."

"Well, you certainly appear that way."

"I don't think about Eddy anymore. Drugs and alcohol are only words. I love my body and I'm determined to be 125 pounds. Don't you think that will be perfect?"

"Judy," I said smiling. "You already are perfect. You just have to bring your body to the size you prefer and if 125 pounds seems right it won't be long before you're there. Do you have any questions about the dieting? Or stabilizing your weight for the following month and alternating diet and non-diet periods until you reach 125?"

"No, I get it and I'm going to do it exactly the way you say."

"Good. The main thing is to do it because it makes sense and will actually help you control your weight easier and forever. Now how about any visions you have had that you would like to tell me."

"I still do imagery to stop stuffing my mouth but I do it in different ways."

"What are some of the different ways?"

Judy began to giggle and only with effort was she able to stop and describe her imagery. "Promise you won't laugh at me," she asked.

"What if I can't help it?" I chuckled.

"Well, in that case I guess it's okay."

"So how about telling me one of the funny ones."

"All right. I blew up a big balloon until it was bigger

than my head and it got stuck to my face and every time I tried to get food into my mouth some air came out of the balloon and sounded like a big—you know…"

"No, you've got to tell me."

"It sounded like a big fart." Unable to control her embarrassment Judy broke into gales of laughter. Finally getting control, she added. "And when I heard that I thought it's just too gross to stuff food into my mouth."

I laughed with her. "That is a funny picture and I can see how it works. Any more?"

"Every time I open my mouth to stuff food in it Gigi leaps up and grabs the food away. She then scolds me by shaking her head at me and makes me promise not to eat so much anymore."

"That's another good one," I said chuckling. "Any more?"

"Lots. I just keep making up new ones all the time. One of my favorites is seeing all my favorite foods on a table suddenly get up and start dancing as soon as I come close to picking up something to eat. When my hand reaches for it the food dances away. I try to chase it but can't catch it. Only when I promise never to stuff my mouth can I pick up a single piece of food to eat."

"I like that one too," I said.

"I have a really gross one," Judy said slightly frowning. "I reach for a hamburger and suddenly there's a million hamburgers crawling all over me and stuffing themselves down my throat. I become as big as a house and only when I promise not to stuff myself anymore do the hamburgers stop. Then all the food comes flying out of my mouth. Really gross. That's the only one like that. I don't even think of vomiting anymore. I know I'll never do that again but I guess I'm still afraid that I might get tempted to eat and that's why I'm doing all the imagery to stop stuffing myself."

I continued to marvel at her uncanny insight and how she knew precisely what imagery she needed and what would work.

"What is this about becoming an artist?"

"I have always loved art," she responded. "I don't know if I'm good enough to become a real artist but I'm going to try. And using the imagery is such a wonderful way to paint. I have the picture in my mind before painting it. And if I don't like it I can change it in my mind and then change the painting."

"I think you've hit on something really important for you. You will also find you can use imagery for making up stories or to practice acting or directing a play or improving your skills in almost anything."

"I know. I've already tried it to play chess and it worked."

I continued to work with Judy for over a year as she steadily lost weight and became in her body what she had already become in her mind. In the latter part of our work together I only saw her every two weeks but her determination to remain free of drugs and overeating never faltered. She became aware of impulses to relapse and at such times doubled and trebled her imagery. She had set a new course for her life and was determined to never go backward.

Judy represents some part of all of us. We all have great hopes. We dream of change and growth and self-control and creativity. Some of us gather our strength and move forward more slowly, but equally unrelenting, and reach goals set years before. Others move more rapidly. Most have frequent periods of gathering moss or even temporary backsliding. But we all have within us the capacity to achieve in our own time period what Judy did in hers.

Her ability to take complete control over her life and make such drastic changes in her mind and behavior in a few short months left me in awe. Adolescence is a time of fluctuation and change, and young people in that formative period are capable of powerful surges of inner power. I believe that Judy epitomized the potential capability of most young people.

After I stopped seeing Judy professionally I kept in touch with her throughout her high school years. She reached 125 pounds sixteen months after starting with me. When she left Los Angeles for an eastern college she called to say goodbye. Although that was my last contact with her I have a warm and lasting feeling for her. She was truly a young woman of great courage. Her parents knew I had formed a special relationship with her and occasionally contacted me with news of her continuing development. Judy maintained all her gains through undergraduate college. When I heard she had decided to pursue a career in science I was not surprised. Her unlimited and unbridled enthusiasm and imagination were the perfect ingredients for Judy to explore the highways of the universe.

CHAPTER SIX

SCOTT AND MARILYN:
The Stranger in My Bed

"Doc, how much do you think we weigh together," Scott chuckled, as he and his wife sat before me.

I silently observed them as I considered how to respond and watched rather fascinated as I noticed Scott's hand lazily kneading Marilyn's thigh and very slowly moving upwards. Marilyn pretended not to notice but her breathing became noticeably heavier.

In the first fifteen minutes, Scott and Marilyn took turns reciting their history of obesity. Marilyn, an elementary school teacher, age forty-four and 5' 4" tall, exuded a rather indefinable aliveness, almost pixie-like, certainly attractive. Her luxuriant dark hair, which surrounded her face, was a definite attention getter. It drew one's eye and to some degree minimized the largeness of her body. She smiled easily and warmly and I felt immediately drawn to her. She was obviously not put off by her obesity.

She came from an overweight family that included both parents and an older sister who had Type 2 diabetes. Her father had died of stomach cancer at the age of sixty-one. In her childhood she was pudgy but not excessively heavy. During puberty her body shot up and considerably widened, as she described it, and by early adolescence she had joined the ranks of her obese family. Ever since, she had fought the battle of her increasing waistline with one diet after another. She described herself as another of the millions of yo-yo dieters with her weight continuing higher and higher to its recent peak. "At my current weight of 247," she laughingly exclaimed, "I need a diet that works. My weight is finally interfering with our exercise." She smiled briefly as she stole a look at her husband. I had the distinct feeling she was being coquettish, including using the words "our exercise" for sex.

Scott kept his roaming hand almost continuously on his wife's thigh as he described his dietary problems. An occasional glance at his wife's face as his hand approached her groin was evidence that his hand's activity was no happenstance. Was he unaware that I would certainly be observing what he was doing? Or was he doing it as much for me as for himself?

Scott was forty-seven, 5' 9" tall and weighed 260 pounds. I also felt drawn to him. His lively and penetrating eyes seemed to probe and make contact. Not staring, but more like visiting me. He was a young-looking and quite handsome man.

Similar to Marilyn he also came from a family of obese people. His father, considerably overweight, died in his early fifties of a heart attack. His mother had been overweight since Scott's early childhood and suffered from serious Type 2 diabetes. She was constantly struggling with diets, insulin injections and elevated blood sugar. Three sisters filled out the family pedigree of obesity. He made it clear that his eating was strictly an out-of-control compulsion that truly dominated him, but it didn't bother him that he was fat. He was here strictly because of Marilyn. "If Marilyn goes on a diet I go on a diet," he laughed, rather raucously. "When Marilyn goes up, I go up. When Marilyn comes down I come down. We are the yo-yo couple."

When his laughter subsided he said, "Doc, Marilyn heard about you and wants to add you to her list of diet gurus. Believe me, she doesn't miss anyone." Again the laughter. His hand was now squeezing his wife's upper thigh. Marilyn appeared not to notice.

In the first twenty minutes of my initial interview several things stood out. Couples and entire families are often struggling with weight control. Enlisting the entire family in a diet program often facilitates the family maintaining the motivation and necessary discipline to continue any diet. However, it is unusual for couples to enter therapy with a shared weight problem. More likely, one person comes to therapy and shares the diet program with the family.

Also, a couple will rarely sit so close together and exhibit overt sexual interactions. Many couples will hold hands in mutual support and offer comfort to their partner if one is markedly upset. The meaning of Scott's action remained obscure. Was it a way of telling me that his mind was elsewhere? Did Scott come here under protest and not want to diet but felt obliged to follow his wife's diet programs?

"Perhaps you'd like to tell me of the problems you had with your other diets?" I asked, not directing my question to either one.

Scott turned and looked at his wife and nodded. Immediately Marilyn brightened. "I want you to know that I follow every program I've ever tried faithfully and I always lose weight and so does Scott. But I never seem to be able to keep my weight off and neither can Scott. Believe me, just as Scott said, we've tried everything. I like them all. But I can't figure out why after a few months or so we just start gorging ourselves again. Don't we Scott?" she said, looking at her husband.

"You bet, baby," he responded with gusto. "It's like that eating bug bites us and we just dig in and stuff ourselves. Remember the time when we had both lost over thirty pounds and we decided not to press our luck and swore that we'd never gain even an ounce back. We were convinced that we had finally reached nirvana and were so excited that we went out to celebrate." Scott literally exploded in laughter and seemingly spontaneously reached over to squeeze his wife's breast. She laughed and wiggled her body.

"Wasn't that a feast?" she bubbled. "I remember that we had a contest to see who could find the most pecans in our dessert."

"Right, and you won, but let me tell you I enjoyed giving you the prize as much as you enjoyed getting it." Scott chuckled as he recalled that celebratory dinner and the aftermath.

"I wouldn't mind a little of that prize right now," Marilyn said, in a very sexy voice.

I was clearly puzzled. For all intents I wasn't in the room as they regaled each other with memories of the failure of a particular diet and obviously enjoyed the feast and its "prize." Although I was tempted to intervene and make my observations known something told me to sit tight. Somewhere in this interaction were clues to help them.

And without any hesitation Marilyn put her arms around Scott and gave him a long and sexy kiss. When they parted she gazed at me and rather sheepishly said, "Don't think I'm so forward with everyone. It's just Scott. I'm just crazy about him. And we know it's okay to do anything in a psychiatrist's office. You do want us to be perfectly natural, don't you?" she murmured.

Both now looked at me.

"Why, of course," I said, in my straightest voice. "What you're doing happens all the time here."

We laughed together at my poor excuse for a joke.

"But, Doc, Marilyn really wants to try your diet. We hear it's a humdinger. Heck, if it works, we can all go out and celebrate, but no prizes," Scott added.

And once more they hugged and without hesitation Scott's hand gripped his wife's bottom. She squirmed comfortably in his grasp.

Anything may go here, I thought, but what is all this exhibitionistic sex? And what does it have to do with their weight problems? In a way their freedom to be sexual together was refreshing. So far they seemed to have a mutually supportive relationship and appeared to be in love and very responsive to each other. But I have long learned that what seems to be one thing in an initial interview frequently becomes quite different as I come to know each patient.

At Scott's urging I proceeded to describe the basic components of the diet program. They accepted at face value everything I said. No questions. No request for elaboration. Using water to fill their stomach and help curb their appetite resulted in "great idea, we'll do it immediately."

I asked about their current use of the bathroom scale. They looked at each other and after a brief, hardly detectable nod from Scott, Marilyn answered. "We both hate to get on the scale so we hid ours a long time ago."

I asked Scott if he felt the same way. "Absolutely, the exact way Marilyn said."

However, once I pointed out how to use the bathroom scale as a positive force to help their dieting, they immediately agreed to change their attitude and use the scale to help them. They were lavish in this praise when I told them how the special one-day water diet worked. By now I had become quite wary. For people who had failed on all their previous diets, they were accepting my suggestions too easily.

Exercise needed little encouragement since they were both on reasonable exercise programs. Identical ones, I might add. However, when I indicated the need to alternate diet with non-diet periods on a monthly schedule, I came to their first hesitation. The stabilization period seemed difficult for them to accept.

"We really like to totally accept a diet, to give it our full cooperation and make it work," Marilyn said. "Once we start, nothing stops us."

"Yes, but something must happen to you that causes you to gain all your weight back," I said.

"Yes, that's true," she agreed. "But that has nothing to do with the diet. We just love to know we can lose weight. No one does it better than we do. And the faster the better."

She winked at Scott.

"Although," she said rather sheepishly, "we're not blind to the problem that diets don't mean much if you quickly put your weight back on. And in the past couple of years we haven't even been able to lose that much before we give up."

"The stabilization period is designed to avert that specific problem," I said. "Increasing difficulty in losing weight is due to the decrease in your metabolic rate, which tends to happen with continual and frequent weight loss. I can understand your wish to continue to lose weight once you start a new diet. However, the real purpose of dieting is to lose weight and develop permanent weight control. Isn't that your objective too?"

"Of course it is," Marilyn stammered. "But won't that be difficult to do. Stopping in the middle of a diet."

I smiled and carefully explained the rationale behind the stabilization period. Marilyn was also openly upset when I told them that dieting tends to be more successful when monthly weight loss is held to between four to eight pounds, excluding the first month when water loss tends to be high.

For the first time I saw Scott and Marilyn's zeal and motivation falter. The ultimate objective for most dieters is to lose weight and keep it off. Their objective was apparently quite different despite their lip service to permanent weight control. Something in their combined attitude, perhaps solidified by an almost symbiotic relationship, had become a major barrier to losing weight permanently. They seemed to have a sense of joy in merely losing the weight, even knowing that in short order they would regain it. Unlike typical yo-yo dieters who grow guilty or angry at their inability to keep weight off, Scott and Marilyn seemed to thrive on such radical swings in their weight.

I was struck by the uncanny similarity of their responses and moods as our interaction continued. There was no mention of their lack of self-control and increasing ill health. With backgrounds of heart attacks and diabetes neither could afford to continue this yo-yo dieting much longer. My course of action had suddenly become clearer.

I began cautiously. "Have you always followed each other's change in weight with such exactness?" I asked.

"You have it wrong," Scott replied. "I find it easy to diet when I follow Marilyn. She always starts a diet and I just go along with it."

"Have you always followed her dieting?"

"Not exactly," Scott said hesitantly.

I waited a few moments as the first silence in the session began. For the first time Marilyn was looking toward the floor. A palpable shift in the levity and humorous interaction had occurred.

"Can you tell me what you mean?"

"I don't think that has anything to do with our wanting to try your diet program," Marilyn broke in, raising her eyes to look directly at me.

"Understanding how your compulsive eating and diet programs became connected to each other may be useful in helping you gain the control you seek. You have an unusual pattern of dieting and regaining weight. I readily admit that I've never worked with a couple who so intimately interconnect their diets as the two of you. I believe it will be helpful to examine all aspects of your eating patterns."

Something in their marriage had become an obstacle to their gaining control over their eating. How much it would contribute to understanding their mutual compulsive eating remained to be seen. But first I had to find a way to encourage them to reveal their past. And why the reluctance to tell me?

"Why don't you just tell us how to do the imagery exercises, which I know you teach everybody," Marilyn said.

"Although it is generally better to get a more complete understanding of your background, I'd be happy to work out some imagery exercises with you now," I replied. The resistance to examining their early dietary problems was too great to overcome for now. If they returned to see me I would have another opportunity to gain the understanding necessary to help them break their tenacious pattern of dieting.

I described how imagery works, the value of positive and negative imagery, and the need for choosing imagery targeted at their compulsions. After discussing the ways they tended to overeat, we developed the following imagery exercises.

They visualized seeing mounds of food piled high on their dining room table. As they reached out for it, the food turned into a wide-open mouth, almost like the mouth of a hungry baby bird, and tried to swallow their fingers and hand. They laughed so hard over this image that they finally gave up reaching for food. It was impossible to eat. They rejoiced saying, "We're not going to binge on table food again."

They visualized going into a restaurant and ordering an enormous feast. Just as they reached for the food the waiter would come over, shake his head, and say, "naughty, naughty." They broke up laughing and rolling on the floor in glee. They felt it was now impossible to gorge on food in a restaurant.

They visualized entering a cocktail party and being approached by the hostess or a waiter with hors d'oeurves. Each small morsel of food flew up and found a way of crawling down Scott's shirt and pants and Marilyn's blouse or dress. Again the ubiquitous laughter. "We'll never overeat at a party again," they roared.

They created a second restaurant imagery exercise. Here they entered a restaurant and ordered a feast. As each course was brought to them the food grew so large it was impossible to eat. Everyone in the restaurant watched them trying to take the food into their mouths to no avail. They finally gave up saying it's impossible to eat any food in a restaurant.

Finally, they visualized sitting at the beach having a grand picnic. As they brought the food out of their picnic basket the food ran away from them. As much as they tried to catch the food while it ran all over the beach the food always managed to escape. They were laughing so hard over this funny scene that they swore that picnics would no longer tempt them to gorge.

I was struck by the uniformity of their reactions to being enticed by food. Neither attempted to create any individual imagery. Each imagery exercise ended in laughter or joy, which stopped their eating. All the imagery appeared to have sexual overtones. A mouth swallowing a finger was clearly sexual. The words "naughty, naughty" alluded to sexual playfulness. Food that grows larger and larger could certainly refer to an erected penis or an enlarged breast. Even the final imagery suggested flirtation. All the imagery was highly pleasurable and positive.

They were embarking on a path to overcome compulsive eating with sexy and humorous imagery. Certainly atypical among dieters. But why not, I thought, such imagery may fit their needs perfectly.

Was sexualizing their eating at the root of their compulsion? The connection between sexual gratification and eating is well known. Sexual frustration will frequently lead to bouts of binging in many people, even those who are not overweight.

Scott and Marilyn thoroughly enjoyed collaborating in the creation of the positive imagery and seemed quite animated as they recounted them. Once they understood how the imagery was to be used they quickly created the five exercises. At the end of the session they agreed to practice the imagery six times a day, using the rag doll relaxation technique that I described to them. They agreed to return for another session in one week.

Marilyn and Scott walked in with broad grins, making a genuine attempt to control their laughter and handed me a large colorful box. "We really like you, Doc," Scott said with much enthusiasm. "We love the imagery and we made some new ones. Great stuff," he added, nudging Marilyn in the ribs. She could hardly suppress her laughter.

"Thanks for the box. But why would you bring me something?" I asked, setting the box on my desk.

"Oh, just our way of showing how much we learned from you already."

My inner alarm went off. Therapists are always wary of gifts and we tend to discourage them. But when a new patient offers something it is both difficult to refuse it or to analyze the meaning behind the gift.

"Do you mind if I open it later?" I asked.

"No, we really want you to open it now," Scott said, grinning.

Without further comment I picked up the box, untied it and took off the lid. Without warning a colorful "jack-in-the-box" sprang out with wide-open mouth and popping eyes. I was taken by surprise and stumbled backward. Marilyn and Scott howled with laughter. "That's us." both cried out in unison. "That's us."

"Well, that did surprise me," I laughed. "And it certainly does look like the two of you."

Both howled again.

As I was about to put the box down, Scott shouted, "That's not all. Check out what's under the doll."

Still wary I removed the jack-in-the-box. Underneath was another box, which I carefully picked up.

"Don't worry, Doc," Scott said reassuringly. "This one won't bite you. On the contrary you'll do the biting." The laughter erupted again.

Inside was a medium-sized fruitcake, glistening and very tempting. "Go on, have a piece," Marilyn chimed in. "We're going to celebrate the beginning of your fabulous diet with an absolutely guaranteed to help you lose weight piece of fruit cake. It's made without fat or salt and it's all fruit, honey, and whole grains. We didn't want you to think we didn't know anything about eating low calorie food."

The cake easily weighing one pound had already been divided into three parts. "We thought you would enjoy eating a little snack while we talked," Marilyn said. "I can vouch for all the ingredients since I baked it myself."

I quickly reflected on my options. Were they pulling my leg? Each piece of the fruitcake, even without fat, was at the minimum 600 or more calories. That could be almost half the daily calorie input of someone on a careful diet. Did they really expect me to eat it during the hour? What would my eating it or declining to eat it mean? Were they telling me that no matter what I tell them they would control what they eat without regard for calorie reduction? Or were they naïve about calorie content? Using the uncertainty principle that allows therapists to avoid falling into therapeutic traps I said, "Well, it certainly looks delicious and I look forward to eating it, but first we'll use it to learn more about you. Would that be agreeable?" I asked.

Marilyn and Scott looked at each other. "Why, of course," Marilyn said. "But what could our bringing you an afternoon snack possibly tell about us other than we like you and brought you some fruitcake?"

"How about playing a game with the food," I said, avoiding their question. "Kind of like show and tell?" I had conceived a plan to help them talk more easily.

Scott glanced at Marilyn then looked at me and said loudly, "Great idea. How do you want to do it?"

"First we take a small bite of cake. Then each of you tells me something about yourselves that might help me understand your dieting problem."

Without hesitation Marilyn chimed it. "Sounds good. First we eat."

I immediately broke off a small piece of fruitcake with my fingers, put it in my mouth and licked my fingers clean. Scott and Marilyn watching me carefully did likewise and clapped their hands as they enjoyed the cake and made a big show over licking their fingers. It seemed I had scored a point with them.

"OK," I said, looking at Marilyn. "Let's start with you. I'd like to hear anything you want to tell me about why you might be overweight and having trouble dieting."

"Is that what you mean by show and tell?"

"Yes. We each show how much we enjoy your fruitcake and you tell me something about your eating problems so that I get to know you better."

For a brief moment her face darkened, the humor had fled, but just as quickly she regained control. I now felt that something upsetting lived not far below the surface.

"All right, I guess that's fair," she responded. "Right after my father died, I met Scott. It was love at first sight and although I already weighed about 170 pounds Scott didn't care. We were all over each other from the time we met. It was so wonderful even now I can recall how I would shiver inside whenever he touched me. And I still do."

She stopped. I waited. She looked at Scott. He smiled briefly.

"From the beginning we celebrated all our love making by eating afterwards. If we had sex five times a day we'd eat five times a day. We did crazy wonderful things like eating food off our bodies and our sex life was absolutely the best. Scott, should I tell him how you liked me to, you know what...."

Scott did not look at her, but he whispered, "It makes no difference. Tell him what you want."

"It's all right, Scott?"

"I said it's okay."

"The thing that Scott likes best is for me to smear all kinds of things on his penis and then I lick and suck it clean. I love doing it and it became part of our feast whenever we had sex. I would smear all kinds of jams, or honey or chocolate cake or chocolate syrup, even ice cream on it. We tried everything. He was in Heaven when I did it. I couldn't get enough of doing it to him because I enjoyed it so much too. After awhile Scott began doing the same thing to me. In the beginning we spent hours every day doing it. We hardly had any other kind of sex.

"After a year or so when we had both gained over twenty pounds we knew we had to diet or we'd be so fat we couldn't even enjoy sex. That's when we began our dieting and made it part of our sexual fun. We'd diet rapidly and then celebrate with more sex and gorging ourselves on food. We'd quickly gain all the weight back plus a few extra pounds. Then we'd diet again." She stopped.

I knew that what she told me was not easy. I also felt there was more behind this way of enjoying sex than what had thus far been revealed. Countless people enjoy oral sex and certainly smearing food on sex organs, as part of oral sex, is not unusual. But rarely is it used to the degree that Marilyn had described.

I turned to Scott who was looking at the floor. "Scott, what would you like to tell me about your eating problems?" I asked.

"Let's have another piece of cake, first," he suggested.

"Fine," I said, and immediately broke off another small piece and ate it. This time I did not lick my fingers. However, after eating their piece of cake, they again licked their fingers. Neither seemed to notice that I had pulled a handkerchief from my pocket to wipe my fingers. The mood had definitely become more somber.

Scott began, "When I first met Marilyn she was having a fit over her father's death. He had died only a month earlier.

She needed to be held all the time and she cried at the drop of a pin. If I was more than a minute late on coming to pick her up or calling her, she would be upset and it didn't take much to make her cry. I did everything I could to try to cheer her up. I already loved her deeply.

"At first we didn't have much sex. Not until Marilyn told me she wanted to eat me." Scott paused and appeared deep in thought. "I remember thinking that was an odd thing for a woman to say, eating a man, even though men say it all the time about oral sex with women. Anyway, what she wanted is what she already told you. Sure I loved it, who wouldn't, but she was the one who started it. It was the only way that I could get her to laugh and begin to enjoy life."

Again Scott paused. "I don't think I ever told her that sometimes when she went down on me I felt that I was like a mother feeding her. She needed to be filled up and I was only too happy to oblige. Only much later did I do the same for her. By then oral sex had become our primary way of having sex. By the time we began dieting, sex and food were inter-changeable. Frankly, Doc, I can't separate the two. As far as I'm concerned we could go on doing it forever. The real reason we're here is because our family doctor has said that unless Marilyn and I lose and keep our weight off we're both candidates for an early death. My cholesterol is so high it's off the charts."

The picture had certainly changed. For the first time I had a sense of what might underlie their symbiotic and compulsive eating. I could now direct my questions to areas of their past that remained obscure.

"Let's have another bite of fruitcake," I said. "I appreciate your being open and frank with me, knowing this isn't easy for you."

Marilyn and Scott looked warily at each other but said nothing as we all reached for another piece of cake.

"Marilyn," I began, "it sounds like you took your father's death very hard and meeting Scott helped you get over your grief. Could you tell me more about your relationship with your father?"

Marilyn hesitated. "There's nothing much to tell. I guess you would say I was very close to him, especially when I was a child and teenager. We did everything together."

"Did those activities include your sister?"

"Not most of the time. She was four years older than me and seemed to prefer her friends or doing things with our mother. She generally ignored me. My father loved both of us but he clearly favored me."

She stopped speaking. A dark cloud swept over her face. I waited for a minute or two.

"Marilyn, I realize that the death of your father was a major loss and how fortunate it was to have met Scott who helped you during your grieving. Are you able to tell me more about your relationship with your father?"

Marilyn gazed longingly at Scott who did not look at her or touch her. A definite change had occurred in their interaction since the previous hour. "I loved my father more than anyone in my life."

She moved closer to Scott and tentatively put her hand on his thigh. "You understand, don't you, dearest, that my love for my father was different than what I feel for you?" Her need to reassure Scott was so evident I wondered if her love for her father had caused difficulties in the past.

"Of course I understand," Scott said with a slight irritation in his voice. "I told you years ago that I didn't ever expect you to love me as much as you loved your father."

"I know," she stammered, "but I never really believed you."

"Your love for your father is your business and anyway he's dead, so why don't you just tell him what he wants to know." Gruffness had entered his voice.

"I'm afraid you'll be angry at me."

"Look, Marilyn, we've gone over this and I won't be angry. Let's just stop the joking around and tell the man what he wants to know."

I sat quietly, baffled by this abrupt change of behavior in both of them. I merely looked at Marilyn and nodded.

"As long as I remember, my father doted on me," she continued. "Even when I was little, maybe only three or four I used to go everywhere with my father. I don't remember my sister or mother ever being with us. It always seemed that my father and I were a pair and my sister and mother were a pair. My mother and father hardly ever did anything together and ignored each other most of the time. Sometimes I felt that my mother disapproved of all the time I spent with my father and all the affection he showed me. It made me feel there was something wrong with my father kissing and touching me all the time. No, not sexually," she said, as though anticipating that I would ask, "but it was all the time, especially when we were alone. I loved him so much and I craved all the affection and wanted him to never stop."

She hesitated. "Do you think any of this is important?"

"Yes." I replied softly. "It may be difficult to talk about, but your relationship with your father has affected your life somehow."

"He loved me so much that he would often say that without me he would not want to be alive."

Her breathing became deeper, almost like she was sighing. Her pain was apparent. Whatever had happened between her father and her had never been resolved.

"When I was about eleven and beginning to grow into womanhood his kissing and touching me grew more intense. He would never kiss me on the mouth but would nibble my ears or put his tongue into my belly button. He loved to do that until I would beg him to stop. It tickled me so much.

"Scott," she said, turning again to look at her husband, "I know you don't like me to talk about this but I have to tell him. What we did was wrong. After all these years, I still can't get the thoughts out of my head.

"Doctor, you have to understand that my father would

never hurt me and what he did was because he loved me so much. And I loved him," she added.

Obviously embarrassed, Marilyn looked away from me as she continued. "My father and I would often go swimming and into the Jacuzzi when we were naked. When I turned eleven I was aware that my body was changing. I was getting taller and my breasts were developing. I had some pubic hair. I never thought it was wrong to swim or be with my father without clothes. Nudity between us was natural. And I liked to feel his body when he hugged me and kissed me. One day we were in the Jacuzzi and, as I said, I was beginning to develop breasts. We were splashing each other and having fun when he again began to kiss me. For the first time I felt funny as though he shouldn't be doing it. When he started to kiss my breasts I had a terrible feeling that he would bite them off, but all he did was kiss them."

"You mean suck on them, don't you?" Scott broke in.

"I guess that's what he did," she said reluctantly.

"Tell him what else happened," Scott said.

Marilyn sat very still as she continued, "I know this was wrong but when my father was...was sucking on my breasts I felt funny down there, I mean in my crotch. I felt what he was doing was wrong and I wanted him to stop. Yet I didn't want him to stop. Can you understand that?"

"Yes, I understand that," I said gently. "Such an event would be both exciting and yet seem wrong. You were deeply involved with your father at that time and kissing you had been going on for years. Thus the change in how he kissed and what you felt must have taken you by surprise. Can you go on?"

"Yes, I can tell you what happened then, though there's not much more. And Scott has heard all of this before."

How often have I heard stories like this one? How the intimacy of a loving parent and loved child turns into a painful and often traumatic episode when sexual feelings suddenly erupt. Her father did not appear to be a predator of young children but rather a lonely man bereft of his wife's affection. Needing love he had turned to his young daughter for affection and companionship. But the apparently innocent playfulness and caring had an underlying sexuality that turned decidedly unpleasant. In a single incident the love and trust that bound Marilyn and her father were undermined and possibly shattered.

"I didn't know what to do at first. My father so loved to kiss me and he appeared deeply absorbed by kissing my breast. I wanted to tell him what I was feeling down there but couldn't get the words out. It was only when he moved his body closer to me and I felt his penis hardening and touching my leg that I became scared. I guess I lost control and jumped out of the Jacuzzi and ran into the house naked. I didn't know what to do. I felt something terrible had happened to me.

"I was old enough to know about sex and I had some sex education in school, but none of that seemed to matter. I suddenly felt dirty and bad. I sat down on the hallway floor and cried. In a few minutes my father came over to me. He had dressed and sat down beside me. He covered me with a big towel and just held me saying over and over again how sorry he was for what happened. He said he just lost control and felt sexually aroused by me. He said it was not my fault at all. He had turned our innocent and playful closeness into something frightening and terribly wrong.

"I continued crying and he kept on talking about how beautiful sex is, but it should never happen between a father and daughter. Maybe he said that he had let his loving caresses and kissing get out of hand or go on too long. He just talked and talked and what I mainly remember was his repeating that what happened was not my fault and it would never happen again. And it never did."

I watched as Marilyn dabbed at her eyes trying to stem the tears rolling down her face. Sexual abuse comes in many forms. Although there can be some repair, such incidents frequently continue to affect the victims into adulthood. How this colored Marilyn's life and marriage must now be determined. Also, what part did it play in her eating compulsion?

"I realize that recounting that experience with your father was painful but it does help me understand you better," I said. "Perhaps this is a good time to hear more from Scott?"

"No," Marilyn immediately said. "I need to tell you what else happened between my father and me."

"Of course. Please continue."

"From that time onwards my father never touched me again and slowly we developed a different kind of relationship. We never talked about what had happened. We became close again but more as friends. I grew to love him in a different way. He and my mother got divorced when I was fifteen. To be near me he found a place to live not far from our home. He would often tell me how lonely he was. I tried to convince him to meet other women, but he didn't feel comfortable doing it. He needed me more than ever, and I guess I was his only friend and companion.

"I often cried when I saw how unhappy he was when I wasn't with him. He shared his deepest feelings with me. I spent much of my spare time with him. I even went to college in the city near where he lived so I would be able to see him. After I became a schoolteacher I would visit him in the evenings and weekends. I hardly dated while he was alive. His stomach cancer was inoperable by the time it was diagnosed. I watched him slowly waste away and die."

As though a cover had been lifted on her feelings, Marilyn broke down and cried uncontrollably, her body shaking with her deep sorrow. Scott moved to her side and just held her. Minutes passed. Gradually her crying ceased. In the seventeen years since her father had died her pain had lived on.

What part did her father's death play in the type of relationship she established with Scott? The unusual symbiosis between Marilyn and Scott must certainly be connected to the very close relationship she had with her father. Could her pleasure in oral sex be connected to her father? And what part did Scott play in their eating patterns and ritual. His duplicating her diets and following her weight up and down, year after year, must serve some need of his. It was time to hear more about Scott's background.

Scott needed no encouragement to describe his past. "My background is rather tame compared to Marilyn's," he began. "The event that most troubled me was my father's sudden death when I was seventeen. One day he was alive. The next day he was dead. Until then my life was a typical one. I have one older sister and two younger ones. We're all close in age and all fat just like both of my parents. I'm getting close to the age when my father had his heart attack. He was fifty-one and, as I told you, I'm forty-seven. It's one of the reasons our family doctor is concerned about my weight."

Scott paused and gave Marilyn another hug. She had composed herself but the sadness still lingered on her face. "Is there anything in your past that might be related to the way you duplicate Marilyn's eating pattern?" I asked.

"I don't think so," he replied. "It's just that I love her so much it's easy to follow what she does."

"Perhaps you could elaborate a bit on the relationships you had with your parents and siblings," I suggested.

"We were close to each other. Except for the usual scrapes that kids get into, nothing special happened. My father was quite heavy, drank a lot of beer and was a jokester. He worked in the sales department of an automotive accessory shop and did quite well. My mother was the heaviest of all of us and ate continuously even though she had diabetes and needed to take insulin. I remember days when she would sit in the kitchen and just gorge herself until I thought she would explode. She made the best cookies and cakes, and sometimes I would sit with her and we'd gorge together, just the two of us.

"I remember a time when I was about eight or nine that

she and I had a contest to see who could eat the most pea-
nuts, one at a time. These were peanuts in the shell not loose
ones in a jar. It turned out that the contest tested our skill in
opening peanut shells. I was faster and thus ate more pea-
nuts. When I was ahead of her and was getting filled up and
wanted to stop she said, 'no, it's not fair to end yet. You have
to give me a chance to catch up.'

"And we continued to eat more peanuts. I think it must
have been hundreds of peanuts. At least, I recall it was some
enormous number. After that we had other contests always to
see who could eat faster. We used cookies, watermelon slices,
raisins, cherry tomatoes, grapes, all kinds of nuts, peas, string
beans and even flakes of Wheaties or corn flakes, one at a
time. When it came to eating cereal flakes I became so fast at
doing it my mom called me the fastest-eating boy alive. I
really loved those times with my mom. We stopped doing
that when I went to high school. By then I was pretty fat but
I didn't care.

"We were a pretty happy family. Everything seemed to
revolve around food. My mom was a great cook. She made
all sorts of delicious things. It seemed that dinnertime was
always a feast. I remember that all the food would upset my
sisters since they were getting fat. And we all really lost it af-
ter my father died."

Scott had already provided me with information that
could tie into his duplicating Marilyn's eating habits. The
eating contests with his mother could have set the stage for
the pattern established with Marilyn. What part did his fa-
ther's death play in his eating compulsion?

"What do you mean that you all lost it after your father
died?"

"Well, my mother drowned her sorrows in food. She ate
everything in sight and craved company when she went on
her binges. My sisters and I became sitting ducks. Whoever
was around she'd coerce into eating with her. She told us she
needed company. If we refused, she'd cry until we sat and ate

with her. Naturally, because of the games she and I played when I was younger, she always tried to get me into these eating marathons with her. And frankly I didn't mind doing it. She never stinted on providing delicious food, whether she cooked it or bought it. This continued for about a year and then I went away to college."

The session was drawing to a close and all of us realized that a change had taken place. The levity and sexual interaction had given way to a much more serious tone. Their next appointment was scheduled for a week later. I needed to find a way to help them break their pattern of yo-yo dieting. I had no doubt that using the Five Keys diet would work with them temporarily, but unless their circular eating pattern of losing weight and then regaining it through a ritual celebratory feast was broken, my program would be no more successful than others.

Imagery exercises would help but unless they were willing to give the imagery time to work and go through at least several stabilization periods, it appeared doubtful the Five Keys diet would work permanently. Were they candidates for guided imagery and what would I expect to accomplish using that technique? Guided imagery would require having separate sessions with them. Would they agree to that? Or was it possible, considering the nature of their symbiotic eating compulsion that entering guided imagery sessions together might prove effective. The determination would be made at their next meeting.

As soon as they sat down to begin their third session Scott spoke. "We've given your program some thought and we don't think you can help us. We came here to learn how to lose weight and to try to break our pattern of always gaining the weight back. All that stuff about our childhoods was too painful to endure and we don't see what it has to do with losing weight."

Marilyn remained silent.

"I can understand your feelings," I said. "It is not always

easy to see how childhood experiences can play a part in overeating. It does appear that there is reason to believe the experiences you described to me have influenced your eating patterns. If so, certain psychological changes need to take place. Mental imagery has been a basic tool of my program for years and has proven very useful to help dieters make those mental changes.

"However, I'd like to suggest another approach. I sometimes use guided imagery with my diet patients."

I stopped and waited for any show of interest. There was none. It appeared they had decided to end their sessions. What was frightening them? Did they need to hold on to their compulsive eating? With their background of diabetes, heart disease and cancer it was important for them to lose weight permanently.

"Do you know what guided imagery is?" I asked, trying to generate interest.

"I was once in a course given to teachers to help us understand how children react to adults." Marilyn responded. "The instructor used guided imagery. It was quite interesting. The instructor told us to imagine going into a classroom and see ourselves as a young student in our own class. She had us interact in a variety of ways with the children and to see the effect on our child-self in the class. I was surprised that I would become angrier at myself as a child than to the other children. Then to make up to my child-self I would hug her and finally hug all the children. There were a lot of other things she had us do. I enjoyed it."

"Sounds like you had a meaningful experience," I said. "I have found it a very powerful tool to overcome various conflicts. Would you be interested in trying now to get at some of the underlying elements in your compulsive eating?"

"I guess that would be okay," Marilyn responded cautiously, glancing at Scott.

"How about you, Scott?" I asked

"I still don't see how getting at hidden problems will

help us?" Scott said grudgingly.

"Since you're already here and we have most of the session remaining how about trying it out and then you can decide if you want to continue."

"Scott, we're already here. Let's do it," Marilyn said.

"Okay."

"Unlike your classroom experience when there were a number of teachers following the guided imagery and thus it precluded anyone speaking out loud, my approach is to have the participant verbalize everything that is being visualized and to speak all the words that take place in the imagery. And I sometimes interact with one or more of the characters in the imagery."

"That sounds exciting," Marilyn said. "I'd like to try it."

"All right," I responded. "Are you comfortable having Scott here when you go through it, realizing that things could be revealed that could be quite upsetting?"

"Yes, I have nothing to hide from Scott. I want him to know everything about me."

"Scott, would you like to remain in the office while your wife is going through this? Keep in mind that you must not say anything, no matter what Marilyn says."

Scott glanced at Marilyn who smiled at him. He agreed to stay. His interest had definitely been awakened.

At my suggestion Marilyn quickly went into a relaxed state using the rag doll technique she had learned. "Marilyn, I want you to go back to your childhood to a time before the experience you had with your father in the Jacuzzi at the age of eleven."

Marilyn sat quietly with her eyes closed but her lips tightened and a grimace appeared on her face. Two minutes passed.

"Marilyn, it is important that you describe everything you are experiencing. Don't worry about what it means. Sometimes the meaning isn't clear at first and it only becomes apparent as the imagery unfolds."

Marilyn took a deep breath, her face grim but determined. "I'm sitting in the kitchen with my mother. She's making dinner. I'm holding a schoolbook. She's ignoring me."

"How old are you?"

"I'm about eight or nine."

She became silent.

"Please try to describe what's happening," I said.

"I can't," Marilyn whispered. "I can't tell you. I feel so alone." She began to cry.

How quickly she had entered a place of pain. "I know what you're experiencing is painful, but try to tell me what it is."

"My mother is just ignoring me," Marilyn said, directing her words to me. "I want help with some homework. My daddy isn't home. He always helped me. She never does. I don't know why I even try to get help from her."

"Marilyn, try to say all the words that you and your mother speak. Be as natural as you can."

"Mommy, I can't understand my arithmetic. Daddy's not home. My teacher will be angry if I don't finish my homework."

"Don't bother me." Marilyn now spoke with the angry voice of her mother.

"She doesn't want to help me," Marilyn again addressed me. How difficult it was for her to face this painful part of herself in the imagery. But I felt that Marilyn was very capable of going deeper into herself.

"Ask her again," I suggested. "More strongly."

"She'll get angry with me."

"She's already angry with you," I said. "Ask her again."

"Mommy, I need you to help me with my homework," Marilyn shouted.

"I told you not to bother me." The anger in her mother's voice was increasingly evident.

"Demand that she helps you," I directed. "Make it clear

you must do your homework."

"Mommy, you must help me," Marilyn was now scream-
ing. "You must help me. If daddy were here he'd help me.
He always does. You never help me."

"Get out of here," her mother shouted. "You can just
wait for your father to come home, that crazy man."

"She won't help me," she said. "I can't do this anymore."

"Yes, you can," I said strongly. "You're doing fine. You
need to know how much your mother rejects you."

With a newfound determination, Marilyn confronted
her mother. "Mommy, you're a bad mommy. I need you and
you never do anything for me. You hate me. You never
wanted me. You only love Julie. You always help her. I hate
you. I hate you."

A torrent of tears flooded her eyes. The picture had be-
come clearer. A deep hatred toward her rejecting mother was
imbedded in Marilyn. The tie to her father became more un-
derstandable. She had no one else. Without her father she
would have died inside. And her father also suffered the same
rejection by his wife. They needed each other. In a scant fif-
teen minutes the underlying bond to her father had become
known. She and her father were bound by a common need to
be loved.

Could Marilyn take another step and see that the rejec-
tion by her mother had left her with an insatiable need to be
fed? I now believed that this need was tied to her compulsive
use of oral sex for feeding.

"Marilyn," I said, "it's time to let out all your feelings
about your mother."

No further encouragement was needed. Marilyn's tor-
ment and anguish filled the office. Scott sat and cried as he
heard the pain coming from his wife. "Mommy, didn't you
ever realize that you were killing me. I would have given any-
thing to be loved by you. For years I thought I was a bad per-
son and you didn't want me in your life. I felt like I would
disappear and you wouldn't even care. No matter how much

daddy loved me I felt there was something terribly wrong with me. Why couldn't you just love me a little? I would have loved you back and loved you more than anyone. Mommy, I was only a little child when you told me you never wanted me. How could you not want me? Was I so bad when I was born? And the times you slapped me for holding on to you. Sometimes I couldn't let you go. I felt I would die. Mommy, why didn't you love me?"

No words can convey what Scott and I felt during the remainder of that session as Marilyn came to understand the extent of her deep emptiness and deprivation caused by her mother. As the session was coming to an end, I intervened.

"Marilyn," I said, "You suffered much pain in your childhood but now try to face your mother with the intent of becoming free of her hate and rejection."

My words acted like a catalyst as she quickly composed herself and made the transition from hate, to resignation, and finally to separating from her mother. All her life she had desperately needed her mother's love and has never been free of her inner belief of worthlessness.

In a clear vibrant voice, no longer the helpless child, the words poured from her. "Mother, all my life I felt that something I did made you hate me. But starting right now I will never believe that again. You neglected me when I most needed you, but I no longer need you. I'll live my life as fully as possible because I love myself and I live with someone who deeply loves me. Mother, I'm sorry that we never had a chance to share the wonderful love that mothers and daughters often have. Once I wanted that desperately. Today, I no longer want it. I never want to feel that I'm waiting for love that will never come from you. I'm saying good-bye to you, mother."

I knew that in intense periods such as what Marilyn had just experienced, a person feels momentarily different, more alive, and even free of past deficiencies. To some it is perceived as an epiphany but in the real world it is only the first step to cleansing oneself of such anguish. However, the groundwork had been laid for meaningful change.

As the session was ending Scott agreed that next time he would enter his own inner world.

As soon as Scott and Marlin sat down Scott said, "I'm ready to begin." Marilyn looked at me, a slight smile came to her lips and I saw the words "thank you" form on them.

Scott closed his eyes and began to relax. "Scott, I want you to go back to some period of your life before your father died. Your father is with you."

Almost a minute passed before Scott spoke. "I'm sitting at dinner with my mom and dad. My sisters aren't there. My mom is nibbling at some cake she had baked. My dad is looking at her funny-like."

He stopped.

"Anything else happening?"

"No."

"Scott, ask your dad why he is looking at your mother funny-like."

"Dad, why are you looking at mom in that strange way?" Scott asked.

"I'm not looking at her in any special way," he responded irritated. Scott had spontaneously used a lower gruffer tone for his father's voice.

"Yes you are. I saw you. Don't you like her eating all that cake?"

"Look, Scott, your mother is a sick woman, she has diabetes and if she continues to gorge herself you'll soon be without a mother."

"Scott, how old are you in the imagery?" I asked.

"I guess I'm about fifteen or sixteen."

"Okay. Continue, perhaps responding to your father's remark about your mother dying."

"This is strange, since I know that my dad is going to die soon and my mother is still alive."

"I know, but imagery taps into the unconscious and reveals many things if you describe everything without holding back. Go back to the imagery."

"Howard, I don't like you scaring Scott about my diabetes and dying," Scott said, speaking for his mother.

"Then why don't you stop gorging all the time," his father snapped back.

"If you'd spend more time home with your family and did more things with us I wouldn't have to eat so much," his mother retorted.

"Don't blame your sickness on me," his father said. "If you weren't so fat I'd want to spend more time with you."

"You've never wanted to spend time with me," his mother countered. "None of your children really know you, you're away so much. Out with the boys, you say. I bet it's with the boys."

"Look, Charlotte, don't get snippy with me. Just look at yourself. You're disgusting. Your mouth is going all the time. And look at what you've done to the kids. The whole damn family's a bunch of pigs."

"You're the biggest pig of all. You just don't eat here most of the time."

"At least I'm not a slob, and don't have food dribbling down my chin like you." Scott's voice had turned ugly.

Scott was now speaking more rapidly and was sweating. He was immersed in his imagery, his eyes shifting back and forth, watching the interplay between his parents.

"You did this to me," his mother said. "You always had other women; don't think I didn't know it. You never enjoyed us and only came home for an occasional meal and to get laid. And you never even want that anymore."

"Getting into bed with you would be like rolling in a pigsty," his father said with disgust.

"You can't get it up anyway. Don't think I don't know what bothers you. You're not even a man anymore."

"You bitch. I wouldn't get it up for you even if I could."

His mother laughed and appeared to have spat at her husband. Scott had seemed to lose contact with me and was mesmerized by the events in his head. I suspected that he was playing out things he had heard between his parents over a period of time. As in night dreams, imagery often combines events from different time periods.

"Don't spit at me, you goddamn whore," his father screamed. "Don't think I don't know what goes on with you. Any tramp who wants a piece can come here and get it from you."

"You lying bastard," his mother screamed back. "Why don't you just stay away? I'd be better off if you were dead and buried."

"Scott," I broke in. "Ask your father why he called your mother a whore."

For a moment Scott just stopped talking. My voice had broken his focus on the argument between his parents. Then he yelled at his father. "Why did you call mom a whore?"

Silence ensued briefly. Then his father erupted. "You keep out of this. It's none of your goddamn business what I call your mother."

"It is my business. I love mom and you make her cry. You're making her sick."

"I'm telling you to keep out of this. You don't know everything that goes on here and what kind of woman your mother is."

"How dare you tell Scott lies about me. I'm a good woman and a good mother. And you're a piece of shit as a husband and father."

"Watch out, Charlotte, before I knock some sense into your head."

"Yes, that would be like you to hit me, wouldn't it? You heard him, Scott, threatening to hit me."

"Don't fill your son with a lot of lies. For two cents I'd smash you, you damn whore. I..."

Suddenly Scott clutched at his chest, his breathing came

in tortuous gasps and for a moment I thought he was having a heart attack.

"Scott," I ordered, "leave that scene with your parents and just breathe normally."

"No, leave me alone," Scott cried out. "It's my father. He's having a heart attack. I need to help him. What did I do?"

"Scott, you did nothing wrong." I assured him. "What's happening to your father?"

"He can't breath. He's dying. It's all that anger and he's dying from it. My father hated us and he's dying from it." Scott began to cry, gasping for breath. Marilyn, alarmed, rushed to his side and held him. I quickly walked over and took his pulse. Elevated but not extremely. He did not show pallor or any signs of faintness. Though concerned, I trusted that he was experiencing a frightening emotional reaction caused by reliving the period of his father's heart attack. Scott had witnessed a composite of years of torment from the unremitting battle between his parents. Its effect on his own state of mind was devastating.

"Oh, my God, my father's fallen," Scott screamed. "Dad, Dad, don't die, please don't die."

I was deeply shaken by the quick display of events that Scott had visualized leading to the death of his father. I had not known that he had been present when his father had died. I had no doubt that the enactment in his imagery was a real event.

Scott cried quietly and for many minutes I waited. I knew that he had left that frightening period of his life. Finally, he opened his eyes and looked at Marilyn and then at me.

"My father was so tortured and unhappy. I hardly saw him in those last few years and I'd almost forgotten that he had died during one of his terrible arguments with my mother. I watched, unable to stop it. Maybe I could have done something. I felt how much he hated my mother. I didn't know he would die. He had never had heart trouble that I knew about. But I just sat there and watched him die."

His crying gradually subsided.

"Scott," I said. "There was nothing you could have done. You were not responsible for your father's death. But you can better understand now why you became so close to your mother. Your father was disgusted with her and was hardly around. He gave little to you or the family."

"Darling," Marilyn said, a deep sadness in her voice. "I love you so much and I never knew about how difficult it was for you growing up. I didn't know that you were there when your father died."

As Scott slowly recovered from his pain he and Marilyn held each other. No longer did I sense their touching as sexual. They had come to know each other's torment and shared tears and frightening memories. Holding each other came from deep caring and love. They had taken that first step to fill their lives with love without making it a feast of food.

During the following month, I had two additional guided imagery sessions with each of them. Although deeply loved by her father, Marilyn had grown up knowing she was an unwanted child by her mother. At my urging Marilyn contacted her mother by telephone and confronted her with her memories and feelings.

Her mother flatly stated that she had never wanted Marilyn. It was especially painful for Marilyn to learn that her mother would have left her father if it weren't for her birth. On more than one occasion she threatened to give her away for adoption. Only her father's insistence that they keep her prevented that. From the resulting compromise, her mother and father moved into separate bedrooms and lived separate lives until they divorced.

As Marilyn searched her past she could find no evidence that her father had a single friend. She became increasingly agitated realizing how her father's tie to her had been partly orchestrated by his desperate loneliness. His possessiveness dominated her life. She recognized how much she needed his love but had never understood that her early attempts during adolescence to become a separate person was forestalled by intense guilt over hurting her father if she left him. In a strange quirk of fate his unwitting sexual arousal when she was eleven became the leverage she needed in her efforts to extricate herself from his grasp. But it had not been enough. Guilt over leaving him, even as an adult, prevented her from living her own life.

Sadly, she felt that if her father had not died she would never have been able to leave him. Her guilt over this wish to be a separate person had been deeply hidden and her marriage to Scott had helped keep her guilt at bay. For in Scott she had found another man who desperately needed her and worshipped the ground she walked on. Her relationship with her father was being repeated with Scott.

By offering her nourishment and love, Scott also fulfilled the desperately needed role of a good mother. Scott had become as essential to her well being as she had been for her father's. She had assumed the same neediness to be loved by Scott that her father had of her. She had identified with her father's desperate loneliness. Self-esteem based on self-love was foreign to her.

At times people meet and fulfill each other's unconscious needs. This is sometimes called the unconscious contract that couples bring into a marriage. Scott's relationship with Marilyn was also tied to the past. As a young child his father, a salesman, was away much of the time, often for a week or more. Almost refusing to believe the memories that stormed into his conscious mind Scott admitted seeing many different men enter his home when his father was away. At times the men would give him a toy or even money. The understanding was clear. Do not interrupt his mother and the man. Scott's anguish on realizing that his mother had "loved" many men was overwhelming. His father was right. His mother was a whore. His father's absence may have contributed to his mother's prostitution, but certainly did not cause it.

On examining his past, he was unable to find any period when he felt his parents were close or loving. He grew up in an estranged and empty home. His only solace were the eating episodes with his mother. He painfully recognized that little else existed between him and his mother. If he didn't eat with her, he would have had no other evidence of being loved by her. His love was tied to food. The connection between his eating indulgences with his mother and those involving his wife had been made. By duplicating Marilyn's eating pattern, including the short lived binges, he was continuing his eating relationship with his mother. His need for his mother's love had influenced much of his relationship with his wife.

Toward the end of their second month of therapy we decided to add additional imagery exercises to their diet program. Their motivation to overcome the emotional links to their compulsive eating had been established. They abided by the Five Keys diet program and even found that the stabilization period was acceptable and useful.

I suggested that each develops individual imagery. They agreed.

Marilyn's imagery:

> She visualized her father holding her tightly. She was about 12. Despite feeling guilty she slowly extricated herself from her father's arms. No matter how he tried to hold her she gradually tore herself lose. Her father cried and ranted but she broke free. Without any remaining guilt she told her father, "I love you, but I must be free to be my own person. You can no longer use me to fill yourself with love. I will never again eat food to hide my feeling that I must be free of you."

She visualized seeing her father dressed as a woman and representing her mother. He kept repeating that he loved her. Then she watched, as her father became wholly himself. She pushed him far away knowing she would never use him to replace her mother again. She said loudly, "I will never overeat again because I was not loved by my mother. I love myself."

She visualized putting a wall between her father and herself and seeing her father wither and fall to the ground. She was in her early twenties. She shouted at her fallen father that he can't stop her becoming a separate person even if he believes he'll die without her. "You must live your life as I must live mine. You can't make me guilty by making me believe you will die." With those words her father rose from the ground and turned his back and walked away. She exulted in a new sense of freedom as she felt the burden of guilt lift, her father no longer part of her life.

At my suggestion she created several other imagery exercises where her parents were seen as food that replaced love.

Her father, who also represented her mother, became covered with wonderful delicious foods. He held out his arms and invited her to eat the food off his body saying that then she'd know that he loves her. She loudly refused and said to him, "I will never use you for food to replace real love. I will not eat food for love. I'll never again eat food when I feel empty and need to be filled with love."

She visualized covering Scott's penis with food and as she was about to eat the food she stopped and said, "I don't need to do this anymore to feel you are feeding me with love. You are not my father. Your penis is just a penis and is not food or love."

Finally she added the following end-state imagery.

> She imagined having a beautiful thin body, the result of her dieting and self-control. She admired her naked body in a mirror and paraded before Scott who likewise admired her. She felt love for her body not because she was thin but because it represented herself. She knew her love was real. She hugged herself repeating, "I love myself and I am lovable to others."

Scott's imagery:

> He visualized that he was a teenager sitting at the dining table and eating with his mother. As he ate he became aware that each bite filled him with love. He had made the food serve as love. Then in one sweep of his arm he shoved all the food from the table to the floor. Instead of eating he reached over to hug his mother saying, "The only love I want from you is from your heart, not from the food you make. I will never eat food again in place of being loved."

> He visualized his father and mother having a terrible fight and his father accusing his mother of being a whore and not loving anyone but herself. He turned to his father and said, "You were away and mother was unhappy and needed love, which you never provided. You also never loved me. But I understand your anger for what she did. Now you and mother can fight your own battles but I'm no longer taking sides. I will no longer be angry with either of you or

be guilty for what happened. I will no longer need to eat food with mother to make her feel I love her in place of you loving her."

He visualized seeing Marilyn gain weight and instead of immediately eating to keep up with her he did the opposite and became thinner and stopped overeating. He would no longer see Marilyn as his mother or follow her eating patterns.

He visualized making love with Marilyn through intercourse with full satisfaction. There was no oral sex despite Marilyn's entreaties for it. Instead he told her that he loves her and will always love her and she doesn't have to feed from his penis to feel loved. He is not her mother but her lover. Eating will no longer be connected to food or sex.

He visualized being with Marilyn night after night without sex though feeling intense hunger. Despite feeling sexually aroused and knowing she also wanted sex, he stated that he is going to separate sex from eating. "Neither of us will starve to death nor feel unloved. Sex and food will no longer be tied together. I will not have sex until it comes from sexual desire and not from hunger."

He also included an end-state imagery exercise.

He imagined himself having lost 90 pounds, which would put him at his ideal weight. He admired his thin and attractive body and felt a new and deep love for himself. Wherever he went, everyone complimented him on his new body. Marilyn was enthusiastic about his new look and told him how sexy and handsome he was and how much she wanted to touch his body. He marveled at his new self and ex-claimed how much he loved himself.

They agreed to add these new imagery exercises that incorpo-rated their new insights into their daily imagery schedule. In order to change their eating patterns, they understood that they needed to stop repeating the past conflicts that remained from their childhoods.

After this session their therapy took on a new direction. They wanted to break the connection between sex and eat-ing. They wanted to remove connections to their parents. They were willing to experiment. At times they would go for a week or more without sex. Or they would have oral sex without covering their genitals with food. They even repeated their old pattern but this time making it just a part of fore-play and always ending with intercourse.

They set aside special time during weekends to help each other create new imagery exercises and tried guiding each other using guided imagery to further explore their past. For over six months they lost weight and fully believed that in a couple of years they would be completely different people physically and mentally.

Then their first major relapse occurred. Scott's first words as they entered my office that fateful day were like a pronouncement of doom.

"I made her do it. If I hadn't insisted it never would have happened." He had obviously been crying before entering my office. Marilyn sat still, her face grim and unmoving. Her clenched fists betrayed her tension.

Scott broke down and cried. Marilyn was silent. I was completely in the dark. I quickly mentally reviewed the pre-vious hour. Nothing unusual had occurred.

"Please tell me what happened," I said, looking at each of them in turn.

Without glancing at his wife, Scott whispered hoarsely. "I don't know what got into me. I awakened three days ago feeling strange and depressed and had the impulse to cover Marilyn with food and just engorge myself. I went to work and could hardly concentrate on the stock market. When it closed, I went to buy food. I tell you it felt like something was making me do it. I brought all the food home hoping Marilyn was there, and yet hoping she wasn't. She was. When she saw what I had done she was angry, but I pleaded with her that I needed to do this one more time. We argued for over an hour until I got angry and ....I'm so sorry about this Marilyn," he turned to her, "I still don't know why it happened. I tell you something made me do it."

"Don't give me that shit," Marilyn finally spoke, angrily.

Scott hesitated and then picked up his story. "I begged her to let me eat her and eat all the food from her body. I was frantic and almost tore the clothes from her body. She agreed, I guess because she found no way out." Again he turned to his wife, his desperation apparent. "Darling, I need you to forgive me."

I was stunned at this turn of events. We had talked about relapse and how to handle it if it were to occur. And indeed they had gone through several episodes of binging and once eating from their bodies without interfering with their diets. They had learned that relapses are common and will generally not affect a diet program if one evaluates the cause and resumes the diet. They had done just that before. So what happened this time?

Scott continued, "I think Marilyn was frightened and I know I was. I felt I was out of control. In the past, whenever one of us slipped, we helped each other and immediately went back on the diet. But now I felt compelled to drown her in food. Not like anything we had ever done. But literally to cover her and eat from her body till I was stuffed. At first she didn't know how extensive it would be, but when I brought all the food into the bedroom and she saw the quantity she resisted. So I did it little by little, putting food on her and eating it and putting more food on her until finally I literally poured food all over her. I could no longer control my-self, I poured a bottle of honey on her and smeared layer cake, ice cream, applesauce, even coleslaw and pasta over her. It was a mess and I didn't care. I had no thought but to eat everything. When I was finished, Marilyn just lay there. She wouldn't talk to me and has hardly talked to me since that afternoon. I have been miserable and I can't stop crying. I don't understand what happened. You've got to help me."

"Scott," I said, racking my brain for clues, "you said that you awakened feeling strange and depressed."

"Yes, I remember that very well," he said.

"Did anything happen the previous day or night that seemed unusual to you?"

"I don't think so," he replied hesitantly.

"Take your time and think carefully about what you were involved with at work or home or even in your thoughts."

For a few minutes he did not speak. Marilyn turned to him. "Scott, you told me you felt weird as we were going to bed. Don't you remember?"

"I do remember that," he said. "Oh God, I know what happened and I didn't tell you, even though there was noth-ing to hide. When I was returning home after meeting with a client in Hollywood a young woman came up to my car when I was stopped for a red light and asked to get in my car. She said she would make me happy. She held on to the door handle and I was afraid of driving on when the light turned green. I didn't want to hurt her. I told her to let go and she replied that she needed the money and could I give her a few dollars. I was afraid of even opening the window. The door was locked. She looked at me with such pleading eyes I felt torn. And she was beautiful. For just a second I felt the temp-tation to let her in and felt an overwhelming sense of guilt that such a thought would enter my mind. Marilyn, you do understand, don't you?" he said, once more turning to her.

Marilyn did not respond.

"I finally opened my window just a little bit and slipped her ten dollars. I saw tears in her eyes as she thanked me and left. I couldn't get her out of my mind all evening. Then I went to bed and had those weird feelings when I awakened, which led to my need to do what I did."

"Do you recall any dreams on awakening?" I asked.

Scott was silent for a minute then his face became ashen. "I did have a dream," he murmured. "It's all coming back to me."

I waited.

"I saw the same streetwalker. She asked me for money. As I gave her ten bucks she turned into my mother. Then she changed back to the hooker and I felt the impulse to have sex with her. I invited her into my car. Then my car became a bedroom. We both undressed and as I was about to enter her she turned into my mother again. I was disgusted and re-pelled, but my impulse for sex was too great. I prayed she would turn back into the hooker. I think she had turned back when I plunged into her and came. I didn't remember the dream until now."

For the first time I saw Marilyn's face soften. Scott sat there and cried. Long buried sexual feelings for his mother had surfaced temporarily, but long enough to have set in mo-tion the episode that had occurred three days ago. In the years that he sat and enjoyed the eating episodes with his mother, inwardly knowing that she indeed had given sexual favors to other men, he remained unaware that these eating games covered a strong sexual desire for his mother.

Meeting the hooker, who represented his mother, had become the catalyst to bring his sexual feelings for his mother into a dream. The need to repress his forbidden sexual feel-ings stimulated the need to turn Marilyn back into his mother, but only for food, not for sex. The compulsive bing-ing act resulted.

"Scott," I said quietly, "although what happened has caused much pain for both of you, we need to put it into context and understand what it means. This is important for both of you since Marilyn had come to represent your mother. The picture is now clearer."

"All right," he murmured.

"I need both of you to help me ferret out the remaining obstacles to your weight control program. First, Marilyn, can you try to tell us what you make of Scott's overwhelming need to eat off your body again, now that you know the precipitating factors?"

"Why should I start this thing? Isn't this Scott's problem?" she responded glumly.

"Yes and no," I replied. "If Scott wasn't in this very special relationship with you, there is the likelihood that his fantasies of sex with his mother would never have become conscious."

"Okay, what do you want me to do?" she asked more cooperatively.

"Now that the sexual fantasy is known, we need to break the link to both your pasts. Scott, you have to overcome seeing Marilyn as your mother. Marilyn, you have to stop seeing Scott as your father, who is really a composite of your father and mother. I believe you will benefit by going together into a guided imagery experience where we may be able to find a way to more substantially end these connections."

Marilyn looked at Scott who had stopped crying and then looked back to me. "I don't know exactly what you intend to do but I'm willing to try anything that will prevent that happening again."

I looked at Scott.

"I'll try anything too," Scott gasped. "I'm so sorry for what happened."

"Okay, we'll begin. It is important that you listen to each other's imagery and make spontaneous choices whether to follow your own or your partner's imagery. Most of the time it will just happen. I'll be here to guide you as well. Ready to start?"

Both nodded and we entered a strange world that none of us could have predicted.

"Please close your eyes and relax," I said. "I want you to both go back in time to a period before you actually met. Each of you tell me where you are and then we'll decide which scenario to follow."

Marilyn spoke first. "I'm about fourteen, a freshman in high school, all grown up, but I'm afraid of boys since I still haven't gotten over what happened with my father. I'm in the high school cafeteria and Scott is sitting across the room and looking at me. I had never seen him before."

As soon as she finished Scott began, "My scene is quite different. We're both in our twenties but had never met. Marilyn's father has just died and we're meeting for the first time. And it's love at first sight."

I quickly evaluated the two imagery settings before I responded. "I believe it would be more advantageous to follow Scott's setting except for a few changes I'd like you to make. You have known each other for several weeks and are in love. Marilyn sees that Scott is also her father. He looks like her father, although it is still Scott. Scott, you see your mother in Marilyn and realize that your strong sexual feelings are for both Marilyn and your mother. Despite your mutual awareness you remain deeply attracted to each other. Try to see if you can visualize each other in the manner I described."

"I feel kind of weird," Scott said, "imagining Marilyn as my mother. But I definitely can see her that way."

Marilyn began to cry. "Seeing Scott as my father is very hard. He seems to go in and out of being Scott or my father and I'm having trouble feeling this deep attraction to him. It's easier when I feel it's affection rather than sexual."

"Since this is very close to the time you actually lost your father," I said, "it will be painful but try to keep your feelings sexual rather than just affection."

"What do we do now?" Scott asked somewhat timidly.

I knew that what lay ahead would not be easy. It's one

thing to have the insight that you had lived out an uncon-
scious incestuous relationship in your marriage. It's quite an-
other thing to allow yourselves to act out those fantasies in
guided imagery. "I have no scenario at this time," I re-
sponded. "However, your objective is to break the connec-
tion that exists in your own sexual relationship to the remain-
ing sexual feelings toward your parents. Also, you need to
eliminate, or at least reduce, the effect this connection has on
your compulsive eating. So one of you just start describing
what is happening in your imagery. The other will follow it."

"Father, what are you doing in my bedroom?" Marilyn
asked.

"Did you call him father or something else?" I asked. I
wanted this to be as realistic as possible.

"I called him dad or daddy," she replied softly.

"Start again," I suggested.

"Daddy, what are you doing in my bedroom?"

"Oh, I'm here because I love you," Scott responded hesi-
tantly.

"I love you too, Daddy. Do you want something?"

"Yeah, I think I'll just lie down here and rest and maybe
give you a hug."

"Do you think that's all right?" Marilyn sounded con-
cerned.

"Remember, you two are deeply in love in real life, but
you now recognize that there are also parental aspects of your
love that need to be eliminated," I said.

"But I can't get the picture that she looks like my mother
out of my head," Scott said.

"Scott, lie down beside Marilyn who is under the covers,
but you feel her body beneath your hands," I said.

"Darling, why don't you undress and join me. I want to
feel your body too," Marilyn was obviously visualizing Scott
as himself.

"I'd like that, honey," he replied, "I'm undressing and I
can't wait to feel your body."

"Oh, Scott you feel so good. Press closer to me."

"Marilyn," I broke in, "now visualize Scott as your father pressing closer to you."

"Scott, Daddy, what are you doing to me." Anxiety had come into Marilyn's voice.

"I'm just showing how much I love you, darling."

"Scott, visualize Marilyn as your mother," I said. "Both of you continue to retain the parent's roles."

"I can't do this," Marilyn cried. "It's too much like what happened to me."

"You can do it," I said decisively. "Remember, this man in your bed is really Scott. Your memories have made him your father. But now I want you to see him as your father."

Marilyn started to sob.

Scott said, "Darling, I love you. You're the only one I have in the entire world. I need you to love me. What would I do without you? It's all right whatever we do. We do it out of our love for each other."

I smiled. Scott had introduced Marilyn's words from the recounting of what her father had done to her.

Marilyn remained silent. Scott stopped talking.

"Go on, Scott, what are you imagining?" I said.

"Shouldn't Marilyn say something?"

"Not until she's ready. Remember, she's following your imagery."

"Hmm, that tastes delicious," Scott continued in a husky tone.

"What are you doing?" Marilyn almost screamed.

"Why, darling, I'm only sucking on your breasts," Scott said, innocently.

"No, you mustn't do that."

"But you love me to do it. It's like I'm feeding myself on you. I want to feed myself." And almost instantaneously Scott's voice changed. "No, I didn't mean that."

"But you did, Scott," I added. "Continue. Don't falter now."

"Yes, you wanted to do that, you nasty boy," Marilyn now retorted. "You like taking your father's place with me, don't you? You can admit it. You know I love you as my son, but you're also my big man."

How clearly Marilyn's defensive side took over. She had quickly converted her anxiety about Scott being her father to suddenly becoming his mother and seeing him as a little boy. What was to follow was an astonishing display of their fluid and rapid exchanging of roles as the non-touching interaction continued. From parent to child to self they pursued their personal agendas, now intricately connected.

"Yeah and you want to suck my cock, don't you, Mom, don't you?" Scott said, with rising excitement in his voice.

"Don't you dare to say that, you bad boy."

"But you love it, admit it. You love it."

"Stop sucking on me. Get away. Don't press that thing against me." Marilyn's voice was shrill. Scott had again become her father.

"No, I like doing it to you. I really want to put it inside you."

"You can't do that. Stop it."

"No, you want me to do it. You want it. You love me the way I love you. Tell me you want it inside you."

"No, I don't. Get away from me."

"No. Open up to me, my little bird. You want me. You love me," Scott gloated.

"Use parental names," I again broke in.

Marilyn took a deep breath. "Oh, Scotty baby, Mommy really wants you inside her. Come to Momma. Come into me."

"Ok, my little cookie, Daddy has always wanted to do that. You're old enough to take me. You really want me."

"Daddy, what are you doing to me?"

"I'm just loving you, baby."

"No, daddy. This isn't right."

"Yes it is. We're doing it out of love and you can always

feel filled up with me inside you. Whenever you want to feel filled up you can just take me right into you."

"Daddy, I'm so hungry for you, I do want you. I want you to fill me up, can I suck on your breasts like you did me."

"No, but my cock is like a breast and you can suck on it as long as you want and just fill yourself up."

"I'll feed you forever, Scotty baby, Momma loves you and you can take my breast too. Do it. That feels so good. You like to feed from my breast."

"Momma, I want to do whatever you want me to do. I like sucking on your breasts."

"Whenever you come inside me you're part of me. And you can do that whenever you want."

"Now," I said. "I want both of you to imagine you're having oral sex, then intercourse and continue to holler out the names of your parents. Remember, in this imagery you're having sex with your parent. And when you individually feel you're about to climax scream out as loud as you can that you know you are making love with your real life partners and not your mother or father. Call out your real names. Say them over and over at the very moment you are climaxing."

What happened next went beyond my wildest expectation of what this conjoint venture into imagery might produce. For about five or six minutes Marilyn and Scott writhed in their seats, even as they shouted the names of their parents. They had become deeply immersed in the incestuous pattern they had learned about. It appeared that they truly felt the rhythm and excitement of the sexual imagery.

The climax started when Marilyn began to shriek and thrust her body against the sofa. Scott very quickly responded to her climax with his own guttural and explosive outpouring of words. They began to scream out their real names. Their climaxes went on longer than could have occurred in reality. I watched with true astonishment and came to that inner realization that these two people had really joined feelings, perhaps their souls, in their sexual blending within the guided imagery. Their symbiosis was so complete that when the incestuous meaning was known and then undone, the ecstasy was shattering. I hardly dared to imagine what they would say when their imagery ended.

I waited.

As the screaming and moaning finally stopped I said very quietly. "Keep your eyes closed and just see yourselves in bed with your adult selves. Feel as deeply as possible what you have just experienced. You have taken an enormous step today. Now with your eyes closed go back to that moment when the climax is over and you are resting comfortably together. Then each tell what you felt and what this has meant to you."

"You start, sweetheart," Scott said softly.

"I'm completely overwhelmed by what I was feeling at the end," Marilyn began. "It felt so real that I forgot it was only happening in my imagination. At first though, I couldn't get into it. I had to fight not to stop what we were doing. It seemed so strange seeing Scott as my father. He seemed like a stranger in my bed. I couldn't tolerate the idea. It took some time for me to get involved. The memories of what happened with my father up until the time he died were very painful. I realize how much of a captive I was to have taken care of him out of guilt and because I thought he truly loved me.

"I can understand now more clearly what it meant to be fed by Scott and in that sense he was like my mother. When Scott got into bed with me at the beginning of this exercise and pressed against me I was shocked to actually feel real disgust just like what happened when my father did it in the Jacuzzi. I hope it's all over now and that Scott and I can truly enjoy a genuinely close relationship. I don't ever want my father to be part of our loving each other. And I certainly don't want it to be tied to my eating."

And Marilyn stopped. She cried, but I suspected they

were not tears of sorrow but tears of relief and hope.

A few moments passed and then Scott started.

"When I got into bed with Marilyn and felt I was her father I felt some anger that I didn't express. I guess realizing how her father's possessiveness had hurt her really angered me. When she began to play out the role of my mother I found I was excited and repelled at the same time, but I was surprised to see how intense my sexual feelings were toward her. I think Marilyn really caught my mother's sexual needs and when I finally abandoned all restraint I was caught up with having sex with my mother. It sounds so repulsive now that the feelings have disappeared. I can see how these feelings made any true sexual relationship with Marilyn impossible. To think this was going on all those years when we were playing eating games. And like Marilyn, I never want any of this to ever intrude into our relationship again. I love you, darling. I know that our lives will be different from now on."

I looked at these two remarkable people who faced and overcame enormous obstacles in their love for each other. They sat quietly, waiting. "Continue to rest with your eyes closed," I said. "There is little that I can add to what you have experienced. You both took very important steps toward eradicating deeply embedded conflicts that have seriously affected your lives.

"What is most important is to know that because of your own efforts to change your lives, you are now conscious of your personal conflicts. They won't continue to operate underground. You actually experienced during this one hour the intense emotions that governed those conflicts. The real love that exists between the two of you will continue to benefit. The link of your mutual eating compulsions to your past has been clearly recognized and I believe has been broken. Now you must do everything possible through continual use of imagery and your unceasing efforts to change your behavior to once and for all put these conflicts to rest."

During the following eighteen months that we met they steadily lost weight. I never commented on the fact that week by week, month by month they lost almost identical amounts of weight. In the two years that I saw them, each lost about 80 pounds. They had continuously modified their imagery exercises, used journals, maintained the steadiness of their weight during stabilization periods, handled brief relapses without guilt or anger, and developed a loving and satisfying sexual relationship. Although we continued to explore residual feelings about their past the major breakthrough that happened in that one extraordinary session was the turning point in their therapy.

I heard from them from time to time for another three years. Scott said he had stabilized his weight at 170 pounds and Marilyn at 135 pounds. The only mention of their sex life was that it never quite approached the intensity of their orgasms during that momentous breakthrough session. I really do think they were pulling my leg, but on the other hand they both did experience very prolonged and vocally resplendent climaxes.

CHAPTER SEVEN

NANCY:
Twelve More Pounds and I'm Perfect

"I hope you can help me lose weight," were the first words spoken by an attractive young woman I was seeing for the first time. "I've tried a million diets but I just can't seem to lose the last twelve pounds that I want too. I'm getting close to that point again in my latest diet and I'm afraid that I'll start stuffing myself again."

Nancy was a thirty-six-year-old divorced sales manager in a large department store. She was trim and carefully dressed with just a sense of casualness in her physical appearance. Her clothes were formfitting and it was clear that she could not be considered overweight. Possibly a body image problem, I thought, as I waited for more information.

"My problem is a simple one," she went on. "During my marriage, which only lasted four years, I began to gain weight. It's no mystery why I overate. I was very unhappy and felt neglected by my husband after only a half year of marriage. When I suspected he was stepping out on me I became depressed and began to eat too much. For a few months he didn't seem to notice but when our sex life just seemed to stop I asked him if he was getting sex somewhere else. He shouted that I'd become a fat slob and that's why he wasn't interested in me. I knew he was lying. At that time I was only about seven or eight pounds overweight."

"Do you recall what your actual weight was then?" I asked, wondering what her criteria for being overweight was.

"I'm 5' 3" and I weighed 115 pounds when I got married. I was twenty-five at the time. He thought I had the perfect body back then. When he called me a fat slob I weighed maybe 122 or 123. I admit I was heavier than I wanted to be, but certainly not fat." A note of anger crept into her voice.

"For the next three years my life was a living hell. Not only did my husband neglect me, but he also hollered at everything I did. On two occasions he even hit me." For a few moments I thought Nancy was going to cry, instead she went on. "He frequently stayed out all night and never even bothered to call and let me know. I got divorced when I was twenty-nine. By that time I weighed about 150 pounds and I looked like a pig."

She paused and smiled briefly. "But I discovered that men still found me attractive and sexy. Still, I hated myself and decided to finally go on a real diet to lose all the extra weight and just start a new life. Up till then I would dabble in losing weight, but frankly I was just too unhappy to stick to any diet more than a few days.

"I had a job that I loved selling cosmetics in a department store and I wanted to make something of my life. I went on my own diet, determined to return to my old weight of 115 pounds. I just ate less, a lot less, and in three months I'd lost over twenty pounds. I was ecstatic. But I should have known that something wasn't right because I had to really struggle to lose additional weight once I got under 130 pounds, even though I ate less food than before. Somehow I got stalled at about 128 pounds the first time I dieted. Then I just lost all control and indulged in my love of chocolate and ice cream and undid everything I had done in the previous few months. That became my diet pattern. Back up to about 150 where I would start to diet again. I do this two or three times a year. My absolute lowest weight in the last seven years was 127, which I managed to reach twice."

"What impelled you to eat when you reached the low point of your weight cycle?" I asked

"Whenever I reached 127 or so I got this crazy need to eat and I just couldn't stop it. And all the time men wanted me. I had more sex in the last seven years than you can imagine. Although I loved the sex and had some great lovers I still felt fat and ugly. Men would gaze at my body and touch me and hold my breasts and tell me how beautiful I was. I thought they were just caught up in the sex and didn't see me as I really was. But I loved it. I think I craved sex as much as food."

As I listened to Nancy I began to formulate possible reasons for her barrier to losing weight. She was extremely intelligent and articulate and appeared to have some insight into her inability to lose and maintain her weight loss. At her age and body frame her goal of 115 pounds seemed realistic.

"Please tell me more about your previous diets," I asked. "How you used them, how they ended, and the types of diets you tried."

"I tried every diet that I read about. And some of my own. Low carbs and high carbs. Low fat and high fat. Low protein and high protein. I've been on the cabbage soup, grapefruit, peanuts, starvation, and carbonated water diets. You name it, I tried it. The only thing I haven't tried is drugs. I'm afraid of them. Everything I've heard about them indicates that as soon as I would stop taking them I'd gain my weight back faster than ever. Anyway, I know the problem is in my head somewhere. It just doesn't make sense that I can't lose those last twelve pounds."

"No, it doesn't make logical sense but it may make psychological sense," I said. "There's no physiological reason for you to always stop at a certain place like you do and resume overeating. The body weight control mechanisms don't exert that kind of control. Something else is going on with you."

"I agree, and that's why I'm here. I know you're a psychiatrist who deals with overweight people. A new friend told me she had gone to you and you helped her in ways she hadn't known about. When I start gaining weight after losing it for three or four months I hate myself. I detest what I'm doing. l cry and hide away until I need some loving. Then I call one of my boyfriends for some sex and it helps a while."

"Does having sex help you control gaining your weight back?"

"I think it does since I crave more sex as my weight climbs. I know this sounds crazy but I can't seem to start my diet until I reach about 150. I always start out thinking I'm going lose all I want. But I don't. Lately, it seems that I hardly eat anything in order to lose those first twenty pounds."

"What do you weight now?" I asked.

"I weigh 133 on the way to my usual 127 or 128. I'm really having trouble getting down past 133, although I touched 132 two days ago. I just hope you can help me find a way to keep going past 127. I really need to do that. You have no idea how I feel when I'm at that weight and then lose control and start eating again."

For the first time I detected the beginning of tears. I could sense her underlying despair and how this feeling must intensify as she again approached that seemingly impenetrable barrier of 127 pounds. That it was a psychological barrier I had no doubt. That was the mystery waiting to be solved. But first she needed to stop trying to lose weight before reaching her resistance at 127. Her first visit was almost up and I needed to introduce her to the stabilization period before she left. She needed to leave with hope and not despair.

"Nancy, have you ever heard of using a stabilization period in any of your diets?"

"No," she replied. "What is it?"

"It's a period in your diet program when you attempt to keep your weight constant instead of trying to lose more weight. One month you diet. The next month you stabilize your weight. You continue this alternation as long as you need to diet."

"Doesn't that make dieting much longer?"

"No," I responded. "It actually is one of the most useful tools to lose weight that I offer. Because you're not dieting more than a month at a time your metabolic rate doesn't change, which is one of the reasons your overall dieting doesn't take longer. For now you need to have a different way of controlling your weight. You're having trouble losing weight now because your metabolic rate has diminished from previous diets. The same calorie reduction you used some years ago no longer works for you. We need to break that cycle so one day you can eat a more normal diet."

"I don't know what a normal diet is. I haven't been on one for years. I'm either eating too much or eating almost nothing to try to lose weight. It's been awful." Now the tears began to flow. Her underlying sense of hopelessness had surfaced.

"Nancy, I can understand how you feel being out of control for so long. You need to finally find a way to establish permanent weight control and the first thing to do is stop losing weight."

"No, I can't do that," she protested. "I feel ugly. I can't stand my body."

"I know, but such feelings are undermining your ability to control your weight. Although there are a number of elements in my diet program you will soon learn about, the very first is your need to stabilize your weight. Rather than make a decision now, why don't you think over the prospect of not losing any more weight for a period of a month. I would like to see you again tomorrow if you're agreeable."

"All right," she said. "I'd like to come back tomorrow and I won't do anything foolish before then."

I noted the use of the word foolish but said nothing.
People attempting to lose weight face many obstacles in their search for permanent weight control. Knowing your ideal weight is not as simple as it sounds. Nancy is a case in point. Many would consider her body weight ideal. Every dieter has to know the difference between an idealized body image and

an ideal one. The idealized one is fraught with dangers to the dieter since they tend to be unrealistic and are based on cultural or social norms that may be unattainable. Ideal weight, on the other hand, takes into account body frame size, distribution of body fat, and one's level of activity. It requires one to accept a reasonable goal on the weight-height spectrum.

The problem of being stymied before reaching their ideal weight and finally giving up dieting is common among dieters. Over the years I have discovered that the most effective method of overcoming this barrier is through changing belief systems about dieting and understanding the value of the stabilization period. It's a matter of thinking differently about eating and approaching the weight problem using a new paradigm.

The following day Nancy arrived very upbeat and immediately said. "I thought over your idea of a stabilization period and I realize that it could be helpful, so I'll do it. I weighed 133 this morning and that's what I'll keep it at."

"That will definitely help you," I said. "Now to make it easier let's go over how to use your bathroom scale."

"I already weigh myself every morning," she responded.

"That's fine. What do you feel when you see you've gained weight?"

"Why terrible, of course, wouldn't anyone?"

I smiled and then proceeded to explain about using the scale as a psychological assistant and how it's used with water to control food intake. She smiled as she thought of the scale as a friend but agreed to change her attitude about it.

Her exercise routine seemed adequate and was not changed. I emphasized using the techniques of the Five Keys diet during the stabilization period as well as during subsequent periods of dieting. Although she had already heard of my use of mental imagery from her friend I postponed discussing it. Now I needed more information about her eating patterns.

"Since yesterday," Nancy said, "I've tried to imagine

what could be stopping me at the same place every time I diet, but nothing seemed to make it any clearer to me."

"What other things did you consider in your reflections?" I asked.

"Well, I didn't really think about anything else. It's all so frustrating."

"Try to reflect on what it means to lose that last twelve pounds."

Nancy blushed. "I hope you don't take this wrong, but I often think that if I lost that last twelve pounds I would be perfect."

"Nancy, why would I take that wrong?"

"Oh, you know what I mean," she said flustered. "I know I'm not perfect but weighing 115 would seem to be so wonderful it's kind of like being perfect. You do understand, don't you?"

"Is being perfect that important to you?" I asked.

"Wouldn't it be to anyone?"

"Perfection is often seen as an unreachable state," I said. "Have you felt perfect in other ways?"

Tears glistened briefly and her lips compressed before she answered. "I've never been able to be perfect in anything I've ever done no matter how many times my parents told me how wonderful and perfect I was."

"When did your parents tell you that you were perfect and to what were they referring?"

"They said I was perfect in everything. No matter how terrible I did something, I was always their perfect little girl. I always knew they lied but I also needed to hear it."

"What made you think they lied?"

"Because Josie, my sister, was really the perfect one." I saw anger in Nancy's face though quickly controlled. "Everything she did was just too good for words. I mean everything. And my parents never said that Josie was perfect when I guess she really deserved to hear it. So I knew they were lying to me to cover up that I was a big disappointment to them."

"What makes you so certain that your sister was perfect?"

"She just was. She was three years older and my only sibling and she constantly picked on me and told me I was horrible and dumb and not to bother her when I needed help with my homework." Nancy was no longer hiding the anger that suffused her words.

"What did your parents do about her criticizing you?"

"Nothing, absolutely nothing. They never believed me when I told them," Nancy said grimacing. "Josie never did it when my parents were around. She always pretended she was my sweet adoring sister whenever my parents could hear us. Josie always got the highest grades in school and my grades were always average. I didn't think I could ever be as good as she was. I hated her then."

So the theme of perfection had been established early in her childhood. We needed to understand how it became attached to her weight.

"If you only did average work in school what made your parents say you were perfect?"

"My parents thought I needed to be constantly flattered to feel good about myself. But it didn't work. I thought they were trying to cover up that I was just an average kid, a nobody."

"Does being average really mean you're a nobody?" I asked.

"Being average in my family means just that. My father is a famous writer and my mother is a history professor. My sister went to medical school and is now writing a book on Obstetrics. I'm just a nobody, do you understand me? A nobody."

Nothing stopped the tears that flowed down her face. Nancy had tapped into a long and highly disturbing feeling that had festered in her for years. Could reaching the perfect weight be her way of proving that she is worthwhile, not a nobody? Could having a perfect body help her overcome this terrible feeling she carried with her?

"Then you believed that because your parents constantly said you were perfect that they lied to cover up the fact that you were a nobody?"

"Yes, that's right," Nancy said bitterly. "I knew it when I was just a kid. I knew that I was a fake."

"Nancy, it appears that something has prevented you from doing the one thing that might make you feel good about yourself. Somehow those last twelve pounds exist to defeat you and maintain your belief that you're a nobody. Something in you has done this. Do you have any idea what it might be?"

Nancy stopped crying and stared at me. Her eyes seemed wild and unfocused. She shook her head as though to negate some unacceptable thought. I waited.

"I hate myself," she said softly. I could hardly hear the words. But they were unmistakable.

She became silent.

"Why do you hate yourself?"

Breathing deeply, anguish etched on her face, she whispered, "Because I have wanted to kill them, all of them, for years." Nancy broke down and cried uncontrollably.

I felt her deep pain but knew this was not the time to assure her that she was not a hateful person. More needed to be known about her past. "Nancy, you have suffered enormously much of your life carrying those painful thoughts. It may explain why you have been unable to reach the level of achievement you desire in anything you've tried, especially in losing weight."

For a few minutes Nancy was silent, as she struggled to regain control. Then she said, "And I love my parents. I even love Josie. How could such thoughts be in my mind?"

"Nancy" I said, "many children have periods of hating their parents while growing up. At times though the hate continues in the form of obsessive thoughts. It's the way we often punish ourselves for hating those we also love. Your feelings of guilt have made it nearly impossible for you to believe in your own values and goodness. Being perfect to you is a myth that you have carried since your parents emphasized it falsely. They wanted to reassure you and, in so doing, actually did the opposite."

"I know they meant well," Nancy sobbed.

"Yes, I believe that's true," I said thoughtfully. "But your anger and guilt made you do the opposite of what you wanted. You hurt yourself by remaining mediocre and unable to achieve any goal you felt would be a worthy one. At the same time your lack of accomplishments effectively punished your parents. It would appear that this became tied to your inability to lose all the weight you wanted. Your eating habit alone would always make you feel inferior to your sister. Whatever your true capacity is remains buried. You have been on a self-defeating path since childhood."

"Yes, that's what happened," Nancy said, brightening. "I always wanted to believe that I could do anything my sister did. I would pretend that I was as smart as she was. I used to write poems and short stories, which I quickly tore up so no one would find them. I would deliberately leave things out of term papers saying they were unimportant and invariably the teacher would tell me that I overlooked certain things. I did that over and over. And my grades remained just average. It seems I was determined to remain a nobody. I was doing it to myself."

Nancy cried, but no longer tears of suffering; they were tears of a new understanding. Tears that gave evidence of the enormous breakthrough in her insight during this one hour. I marveled at the quickness of her mind and felt that she was destined for greater things ahead.

During the next few sessions Nancy solidified her new understanding. She was determined to overcome the negative beliefs that had governed her life and prove she could accomplish anything she set out to do. Instead of seeking perfection, her goals became more reasonable.

Following her fifth session she visited her parents in New York to attempt reconciliation. They had never understood why she had withdrawn from them and believed that living 3000 miles away had changed her. She told me that her mother and father cried with her as she described the terrible feelings she carried. They both understood and begged forgiveness for what they had inadvertently done. Her father had held and kissed her when he said, "If only I could undo all those times my words made you suffer I would do it. I would do anything to make you happy."

She learned that her parents truly believed she was a brilliant child but had reacted to her lack of accomplishments by falsely praising her. Unknowingly, they had caused her intellectual development to suffer. She also discovered that her parents had saved some of her early poems, written at the age of 11 that she thought she had thrown away. She brought them with her the next session and left them for me to read. They were beautiful and showed a precocious understanding of relationships and a deep sensitivity for the sufferings of humankind.

Finally, Nancy told me that she was no longer seeking bodily perfection by weighing 115 pounds. She still wanted to lose the same amount of weight since she saw it as her ideal weight. The concept of becoming perfect had been laid to rest.

The time had come to open up the avenue of mental imagery and the rest of the components of her diet. She had now been in therapy for six weeks and had reached the end of a prolonged stabilization period. She had begun to use a journal for focusing on resistances and feelings while dieting. She understood how to use water and the special one-day extra-water diet. On her own she had stepped up her exercising.

She was already eating a relatively low calorie diet just to maintain her weight. Even with exercising an hour a day five times a week she estimated she burned between 1,600 and 1,700 calories a day. We decided to limit her weight loss for her first diet month to a half-pound a week. She would need to reduce her calories by 250 calories a day. It was important not to reach her previous barrier of 127 pounds until she had induced certain mental changes through her imagery exercises.

On her eating binges Nancy ate whatever food was available. It could be from a few peanuts to gorging on an entire box of chocolate candy. Even though she hated it when she lost control and binged she realized that it made her feel better. She understood that binging served as a form of punishment necessitated by her guilt over the hate she felt. By binging, she suffered; and the suffering relieved her guilt.

On grasping this mental process she exclaimed, "No wonder I could never fully lose all the weight I wanted to. I didn't deserve to be perfect with so much hate and guilt. And my need for punishment almost guaranteed that I would binge again as I approached my perfect weight."

Each bit of insight added to her self-esteem. Her determination to break this eating pattern was now powering her drive to overcome the conflicts that stemmed from her childhood. She understood that she had transferred those conflicts into her compulsive eating.

Nancy was ready to develop her imagery exercises. She decided on the following ones.

She visualized seeing herself about to gorge on piles of food on her dining room table. As she reached out for her first bite, the foods sprang up assuming strange quasi-human form. In unison they screamed at her that she could no longer use food to make herself suffer. All together they spewed fire from their grotesquely human faces and burned her if she came too close. Even when she backed away they pursued her screaming, "Say you won't use food for punishment or we'll burn you to a crisp." She swore that she would no longer binge on food to relieve her guilt and need to suffer. She ended the imagery by shaking her fist at the food and saying she's finished with all of it. And she felt a powerful feeling of newfound strength course through her body.

She imagined approaching a dining table filled with food and feeling the urge to binge. Immediately an impenetrable mask covered her entire face so she could not see, eat, or smell anything. A voice from outside her shouted, "You will never binge again. It is forbidden to you. Say you accept this pronouncement." She immediately said with enthusiasm, "I accept that I shall never binge again." And the mask fell from her face.

She visualized running a race against her mother, father and sister. At the beginning of the race she fell behind but as the race continued she gradually caught up and as the finish line appeared she spurted ahead to win the race. She exulted, saying I shall be able to finish anything I try. I shall always win my race.

She visualized the number 127 and imagined her body at that weight. Then with a flourish of her arms she crossed out the 127 and wrote 126 and watched the slight change in her body. She continued to do the same for all numbers down to 115 pounds and saw her body at its ideal weight and size. She felt she had overcome the major barrier to her completing her life and now knew she would always be able to do whatever she wanted.

She visualized herself walking down the street and beautiful in her ideal body at 115 pounds. No one watched her but she knew that her body was right for her. She said to herself, I know in my heart that I am now the way I want to be. I am beautiful and fulfilled and in full control of my weight and myself. I love myself and will never again feel the need to suffer because of my past.

Finally, at my suggestion she added another end-state imagery to include external reactions to having reached her goal.

She visualized herself at her ideal weight and feeling beautiful. She again walked along a busy street, this time attired only in a bikini. All eyes turned to gaze upon her with obvious approval. Her parents and sister were among those who admired her. They realized that she had become a fulfilled and accomplished person in her mind as well as her body.

These six imagery exercises were the first ones she used. Over the succeeding months she would change some, eliminate some, and add others. Sometimes she used as many as twelve at each imagery session. She jokingly said that twelve was her magic number because it was the number of pounds she needed to lose.

During her first diet month she lost close to three pounds. She remained at 130 pounds during her second stabilization without any relapses. She only used the special water diet twice in those two months. On her second diet month we decided she would again lose a half-pound a week and try to reach 128 at the end of the month. Again she did exactly that. She was now at the upper end of her major weight barrier.

At the beginning of her third diet month Nancy became anxious knowing that for the first time, if she continued her same weekly weight loss, she would be on the verge of penetrating the barrier. She had never been able to reach 126 pounds.

I anticipated a struggle. Although she had engaged in her imagery exercises for four months and had changed her life enormously in other areas breaking that barrier could be daunting. Was her need for punishment still too great to achieve real success? Breaking this barrier could arouse inner conflict despite her conscious belief in her new self. Once more I cautioned patience and again advised losing a half-pound a week.

"No," Nancy asserted, "I'm not starting this diet month with hesitation or doubts. I'm not going to lose just a half-pound a week. I don't want to be cautious." She was deter-mined to make a clean and decisive break below 127 pounds.

I smiled, acknowledging her decision. "By throwing cau-tion to the wind you have decided that you have the power to break the back of this barrier," I said.

But now hesitation appeared. "I can't understand why I feel frightened," Nancy admitted. "I feel confident in so many ways that I never did before but I have a strange fore-boding that something in me is going to stop me from doing this."

"Do you have any idea what it is?"

"No, but I feel like it's alive."

"Nancy, there is another technique we haven't used but I'd like to try it today. It's a variant of mental imagery we call guided imagery."

"I've read about it," she broke in. "You guide me through different visualizations and I follow your ideas."

"Yes, that's it. As soon as I stop talking you immediately pick up and describe as fully as possible whatever images come into your mind. I'm not going to do any preliminary exercise since I know you have a vivid imagination and visu-alize easily. Would you like to try it?"

No hesitation here. "Yes, I want to do it."

"To become more suggestible it is good to go into a state of deep relaxation. Close your eyes and imagine you are a rag doll. Take a slow deep breath and as you exhale slowly imagine that you are pouring your mental self into your rag doll self. Again take a deep breath and as you exhale pour your mental self into your rag doll self. You are now in a state of deep relaxation."

I thought how quickly she accepted the rag doll technique. I watched her slow breathing and knew she had entered a deeply relaxed state.

"Nancy, earlier you said you had a strange foreboding that there was something frightening inside you. Something that was going to stop you from breaking this mental barrier to losing any more weight. You need to face that frightening part of yourself. Are you willing to go inside yourself and face it no matter how frightening it is?"

"Yes, I want to do it. Please don't stop no matter how frightened I become. I mustn't fail."

"No, and you won't fail," I said, reassuringly.

"Imagine being on a narrow mountain path going up to an unknown place. As soon as you see yourself, describe your surroundings."

Without any time lapse she picked it up. "I'm all alone. The mountain is barren. There are no sounds. Nothing seems alive."

"Continue to walk," I said, "and as you round a curve you come to a plateau, a dead-end, except that you notice an opening to a cave."

"Yes, I see the opening."

"Enter the cave."

"I'm afraid to enter it," she exclaimed.

How quickly we've come to the feared object, I thought. Not even being able to enter the cave usually indicated severe anxiety about what would be confronted. Entering caves in guided imagery represent entering the unconscious, the repository of our past memories and fears.

"What seems to frighten you?"

"It's dark and there is something inside that can hurt

me."

"Look closely and you will discover near the entrance to the cave a flashlight that you can use to light your way into the cave. Do you see it?"

"Yes. I have it. I'm entering the cave. The walls are filled with pictures."

"Can you describe them?"

"Yes they're very clear. But I don't understand what they could mean."

"Describe them."

"Well, there seems to be all sorts of things a little child would play with or eat. There's a wagon, a ball, a furry animal, lots of furry animals. There's a baby bottle, a cup with a straw, a high chair, a..." Nancy let out a scream. "That's terrible."

"Go on," I encouraged.

"There's a large doll with her head cut off." She stopped and I saw her body stiffen. "The head of the baby, I mean doll, seems to be crying."

"Nancy, do you feel you want to continue?"

"Yes," she answered, hesitantly. "I don't know what all this means but, after all, it's only like a dream."

"Nancy, I'd like you to go forward, which may mean something very disturbing will appear. What this means we don't know yet, but it's definitely tied to whatever is frightening you."

"I want to go on," she stated.

"At the far end of the cave is a tunnel. Follow it."

"It's getting darker, even though I have the flashlight on. It's almost like the battery of the flashlight is dying."

"Continue to go forward and describe whatever you see."

"Everything is just dark. No more pictures. I'm feeling scared. It's getting harder to walk. I need to stop. The walls are almost touching my body. I'm trying to..." Nancy suddenly flung her arms forward and let out a terrible scream.

"Nancy, what's happening?" I asked, alarmed. Her reactions to the imagery were already exceptionally intense and I was concerned about what we would find.

"I'm falling. I can't stop myself. I'm going to be killed." She now wailed.

"No, wait. I'm landing in a room. I know the room. It's the kitchen of my home when I was a little child."

She became silent. "Try to continue," I encouraged.

"I'm sitting on my sister's lap. She's looking at me and all I see is hate in her face. I'm afraid of her. She's going to hurt me."

Silence. I waited.

"Nancy, how old are you?"

"I'm about two years old. Mommy's not around. Only Josie and me. Josie hates me. She wants to hurt me." Nancy began to shiver and her face tensed.

"Can you go on?"

"Yes. Josie is squeezing me. Stop it, Josie. You're hurting me," Nancy screamed.

"Why does she hate you so much?" I asked.

"I don't know."

"Ask her."

"Josie, why do you hate me so much?"

"Because you're a terrible baby. You're a bad girl and always cry and scream when I come near you. Nobody likes you. You don't belong here. I hate you."

"Mommy, Josie is hurting me," Nancy cried out.

"Is your mommy now in the room?"

"Yes. She just came in."

"Josie, I told you that you must love your little sister." Nancy's voice had totally changed. Her adaptation to the use of guided imagery had occurred so quickly that even I was surprised.

"She doesn't love me. She says I'm bad. I'm a bad girl." Nancy struggled not to cry.

"Josie, you must never say that to Nancy. She's not a bad girl. She's a very good little girl. She is a wonderful sister and you must love her, just as daddy and I do."

"No, she's a bad, bad girl. I hate her. You never should have brought her home."

Another scream rent the air.

"Nancy, darling, are you all right? Josie didn't mean to push you off her lap. It was an accident." Her mother's obvious concern was clearly evident in Nancy's voice.

"No, it wasn't. I hate her. I don't want her on my lap. She's bad, bad, bad." Josie's voice was venomous.

"Josie, you could have hurt your sister. If you ever do that again I'll never let you hold her."

"Nancy, it is now time to confront your sister and mother in what you have experienced. You have been able to witness feelings and memories of your early childhood. Such images are a composite of much of your early relationship with Josie and your mother. Are you game to confront them with their abusive behavior?"

"Yes. I don't want to carry these feelings any longer."

"Stand up and tell Josie that you will no longer let her holler at you or hurt you."

Nancy sat straighter in her chair. "Josie, I'm a good girl. You are the bad one for hating me. I'm little, but you can never tell me that you hate me again. I won't listen to you. If you ever say it, I'll hit you. I'll hit you hard."

Again silence. Fear was evident on her face.

"Go on, Nancy," I said.

"You have always thought I didn't belong here. But I do. I belong here as much as you. I'll always be your sister and if you don't want to love me then I won't love you." Tears came to Nancy's eyes.

How difficult that must have been to say, I thought.

"Nancy, your mother seems to feel that she has to encourage Josie to love you, even threatening not to let her hold you if she pushes you to the floor again. Is there anything you want to say to her?"

For several minutes Nancy remained silent gathering her

thoughts, bringing into focus the many feelings and thoughts that were flooding her mind. When she finally spoke a new decisiveness had appeared in her voice.

"Mommy, you have been a bad mommy to me. You made Josie do things she didn't want to. You made me feel that I have to let Josie hurt me because you wouldn't stop her. You never really took my part or you never would have let me be alone with her. She always did something bad to me. And you let it happen over and over again." She stopped.

"Go on," I said. "There's more you can say to her."

In a stronger voice Nancy continued. "Mommy, you have made me feel like you don't really love me. You made me feel like I wasn't as good as Josie. You always needed to reassure me that I was good. You said I was perfect. No one is perfect. Why did you keep saying that to me? It made me feel like there was something wrong with me and you wanted to hide it from me. You were the one who stopped me from getting stronger and feeling that I was as smart as Josie. Mommy, you have stood in the way of my becoming something I could be proud of. I will never listen to you again. You didn't speak the truth. I'm a good and smart person."

"Nancy, you can't leave it that way with your mommy," I said. "Is there anything you want to say to show that you realized she thought she was helping you?"

"Yes, yes," she immediately replied. "I don't want to end this with anger toward either Josie or my mother." Her words indicated that Nancy had now grown up and would face her sister and mother as an adult.

"Mother, I may at times have given you much trouble and you had to bear with me during those times. I know you thought you were helping me and never wanted to hurt me. By my not accomplishing more I added to your suffering. You felt responsible for my failures when it was my own lack of direction and belief in myself. Mother, I love you. I love you, knowing deep inside myself that you love me."

Nancy sat and cried. Without my saying anything further Nancy continued.

"Josie, I now understand how difficult it was for you to accept a sister. For three years you were all alone and I know you must have been a wonderful and perfect child and were dearly loved. Then I appeared and it was obvious that mother and dad loved someone else. You were only a little child yourself and I understand your jealousy. I forgive you for hating me. I didn't make it easy for you because I hated you in return. I want us to love each other and make up for how distant we've been over so many years. Josie, I love you."

Now Nancy's tears flowed without restraint. I was greatly touched. It is unusual for someone to reach so deep inside in such a brief period of time and to come full circle in important relationships. Within an hour Nancy had felt intense hate, experienced reconciliation and forgiveness, and finally found the love that could now become the force that would bind her to her family. In the coming weeks and months I would help her solidify what she learned today.

Nancy broke through her psychological barrier convincingly during her third diet month. At the end of the month she weighed 123 pounds. Her enthusiasm and joy were boundless. Not only because she finally conquered what had appeared to be an insurmountable obstacle, but because of how different she felt. Several weeks after her pivotal psychological breakthrough she called her mother and confirmed much of what she had discovered.

Shortly after, with a sense of apprehension, but with great anticipation, Nancy contacted her sister and they arranged for just the two of them to meet in San Francisco. Josie readily admitted the extent of her jealousy and begged forgiveness. She said she had always felt that Nancy was the smarter of the two and couldn't tolerate knowing her younger sister was better than she. Josie had cried as she spoke of the intense jealousy she had felt and how it had made her suffer all these years.

Nancy told Josie how much she hated her and at times how she wanted to kill her. They hugged and continued to cry together as Josie kept saying that she understood how terrible it must have been for Nancy living with such feelings. At the end of that weekend the two sisters had found a new beginning in their lives together. They agreed to share at least one full weekend a year alone together to renew their bonds and love.

Nancy cried as she told me how sad their parting was. As soon as Nancy boarded her plane to return to Los Angeles she wrote a letter to Josie to cement their love for each other. From this beginning a truly loving and close relationship developed between the two sisters. They both came to understand that there are forces that can control us and steer us into tainted grounds. Only with awareness and the willingness to forgive and love again do such past episodes resolve and pass into the psychic history of each of us.

Nancy felt that the power of her guided imagery experience was so great that she did not need it to be reinforced. Instead, she developed new imagery to foster her inner growth and creativity. A newly awakened dream of becoming a writer had surfaced and she created the following new imagery exercises to promote her dream.

> Nancy imagined herself as a spirit capable of moving into any part of her body or mind that she wished. As a spirit she floated into her heart and experienced deep love, knowing that she could now write about the greatest love that existed. She floated into her stomach and intestines and felt the turmoil and pain of her existence and knew that she could now write about such anguish. She then floated into her brain and mind and created pictures of one idea after another. With subsequent use of this imagery the ideas constantly changed. Sometimes she imagined faraway galaxies and strange civilizations. Other times

she would hear the words of love or hate or envy and pictures would appear of those ideas. She knew she was tapping into her unconscious where the dreams of writers are born. And each time she used the imagery she felt she was giving birth to another idea or feeling. She told herself I am preparing my mind to write.

The other significant imagery involved visualizing herself sitting at her computer and allowing all the feelings and ideas from the previous imagery to penetrate her fingers and she would watch the images translate into words before her eyes. She said I will be able to create by merely tapping into my inner self. What I see in my images I can write.

Nancy reached her ideal weight of 115 pounds during her sixth diet month. She acknowledged this milestone briefly by noting that though it was the perfect weight for her it was only one part of her new self-esteem. Far more important was the knowledge that she was capable of changing any negative beliefs that hindered her development.

She had continued to create further imagery to develop her newly revived interest in writing. Her imagination was boundless.

Although we did not meet again after she stopped therapy she wrote several letters telling me how much at peace she was. She no longer thought of food as having any claim on her life. She found love in a new relationship and when her first book appeared she was heralded as a major new writer. It was a novel about the discovery of love.

CHAPTER EIGHT

JEFFREY: The 375-Pound Man

Jeffrey was a child in the body of a huge man. Twenty-seven years old, yet he reacted with the spontaneity of a youngster let loose in an amusement park. His initial greeting was to slap me playfully on the shoulder and then pat his belly and laugh loudly.

"Well, Doc, I'm your captive for good or bad. Do with me what you want. The odds around the lab are ten to one that you'll spin your wheels and end up scratching your head about your impossible patient. But I promise to do everything you ask even if I have to cut down on my junk food."

Jeffrey's laugh was infectious. I was quickly caught up in his humor and warmth. Yet there was something very odd about his unusual greeting.

Jeffrey was a brilliant young physicist. His physician father, who referred him to me, spoke glowingly of Jeffrey's many accomplishments during his brief academic life. He had already written over twenty highly regarded scientific papers, contributed two chapters for two text books, and had received a grant that gave him almost unlimited freedom to conduct his research. At the age of twenty-six Jeffrey had been promoted to assistant professor and had become the "darling" of the Physics Department.

But Jeffrey was on a path to an early death if he didn't find a way to lose 200 pounds. His medical records indicated early enlargement of his heart, frequent arrhythmias, high blood pressure that proved difficult to lower with medication, the beginning of Type 2 diabetes, and a loud wheezing that I easily heard as he sat in my office across from me.

"Jeffrey," I asked, "do you always have such difficulty breathing?"

"Always," he replied, "but this is nothing. You should hear me when I walk a hundred yards. I'm thinking of hiring myself out as a fog horn or a bird caller on weekends," he laughed.

"Jeffrey," I began.

"Call me Jeff," he interrupted.

"Okay, Jeff. Do you always treat your overweight condition with such humor?"

"Look, Doc," Jeff said, suddenly becoming serious. "I think being here is a waste of time. If I didn't want to placate my father who went to the trouble of finding you and arranging for me to come, I wouldn't be here. I've tried many other diets and nothing works. I've got a genetic defect and diets are useless with me."

"What makes you think that you have a genetic defect?" I asked.

"Both of my parents, an uncle, an aunt, and two cousins are grossly fat, although nothing like me. And most of all I've tried not eating and nothing makes any difference. If I manage to lose any weight at all, I gain it right back. My body just wants to be this way and that's how it is. So why don't we call it a day. I'll pay you for the visit and you can go out and play a round of golf." Again that boisterous laughter.

I believed that Jeff was frightened and unable to face the possibility of another diet failure. My experience with overweight patients having a family history of obesity indicated that losing weight following a proper diet program would be successful, though it might take longer to achieve the desired results. Looking at the huge man in front of me I could easily conceive that a genetic defect was partially responsible. But this was by no means certain.

"Jeff, since you're here, why not tell me about your over-

overweight condition and what diets you have tried in the past?"

Jeff said nothing for a long minute, and then blurted out. "Look, I told you this is a waste of time. I'm leaving. Just tell my dad I was uncooperative."

As he attempted to rise he was defeated by his weight and fell back into the chair. Before he could try to rise again I spoke out. "Jeff, I can understand that you might be afraid of trying another diet and failing. It's sometimes easier to just give up and accept your condition rather than face your fear."

He looked at me. Were those tears glistening in his eyes? He lowered his head.

"It's okay to be afraid and failing again might make you feel totally helpless," I said softly.

Jeff began to breathe heavier.

"I'd also understand if you cried," I added.

"I think I'm dying." He said in a barely audible voice. He still did not look up. "And I'm scared."

This is the real Jeff, I thought. The rest is a cover-up. "Please tell me why you believe you are dying."

"In the past four or five months I've been unable to walk without feeling I'm about to have a heart attack. My chest hurts and I can hardly breathe. What scares me the most is I can't stop eating. I've gained another thirty pounds in the past three or four months. My parents noticed it, which is why they insisted I see you. I feel helpless to control myself.

"I weigh 375 pounds. I'm not even six feet tall. Do you understand what that means? I eat all the time. I just can't stop."

"What happened three or four months ago just before this current eating binge began?" I asked.

Jeff frowned as he thought back. "Nothing happened then, I just began to eat everything in sight. I've had previous binges but none that lasted this long."

"Continue to think back. Anything happened in your career or in a relationship or to you physically?"

"No, no, I tell you nothing happened then," he said hurriedly.

He's hiding something, I thought.

Both of Jeff's parents were very overweight as was the father's only brother and one of his mother's two sisters. However, his only sibling, David, three years his junior, was of normal weight. Many other family members of this and previous generations were also extremely overweight. It had long been considered a family trait. The family obesity almost always started in childhood. No member of the family had been successful in overcoming their obesity through dieting.

Jeff was chubby as a preschooler but really began to balloon out after entering the first grade. By the age of ten he was considered obese and was the butt of jokes and hazing from other children. He took most of it good-naturedly and found he could win kids over with humor. His parents dismissed his obesity by saying it ran in the family and he should just accept it.

As a child he showed precocious skills in reading, writing, and science. His prodigious mental gifts were evident in many areas. He played the piano and clarinet, had formidable artistic ability and was able to perform amazing mental feats in mathematics. In high school he quickly became the leader of a small group of students known collectively as the "brain trust." He became editor of the school newspaper and contributed original jokes each month. He participated in a weekly TV show for teens. By his junior year he was one of the most popular kids in school.

As we proceeded I sensed Jeff had developed a tentative interest in working with me. I knew he was terrified and hoped that this would provide the impetus to give another diet a chance. I had no clue why he went on a four month eating spree. Perhaps it was tied to his fear of dying.

His family doctor had informed Jeff that he had definite physical changes in his heart. Could that have been the trigger? His obesity had produced heart symptoms and fear of dying. Such fear could have increased his overeating. The added weight would have intensified his heart symptoms, frightening him more, and fostering further eating. I decided to address what appeared to be a life-threatening cycle.

"Jeff," I began. "I'm aware how frightening your situation must appear. Your heart is burdened by your overweight condition and you're understandably afraid. You need to lose weight quickly and rapidly. But diets in the past have failed you. You have a belief that having a genetic predisposition to obesity means that losing weight is impossible for you."

"Doc," he interrupted. "It's not a genetic predisposition. It's who I am. I'm genetically wired to be heavy and there's nothing I can do about it."

"If you believe that, then why did you come to see me?"

"Because my father insisted and said your program is different. You're a psychiatrist and you look at heavy people differently. But I don't believe you or anyone else can help me."

The challenge was obvious—how to change Jeff's beliefs that his obesity was permanent. Other patients with a strong family history of obesity rarely took such a strong negative stand against dieting. Many were motivated to begin a new diet through changing attitudes.

A feeling that something else was determining his very negative attitude bothered me.

"Jeff, I'm aware that you might leave this office and not return. You have told me something of your fears. You believe that your obesity is fixed and that you're on a path to an early death, but I feel that other unspoken things are part of that fear. My diet program is different from others and is quite simple to follow provided you have sufficient motivation to use it.

"The primary barrier is not believing in your ability to help yourself. Believing that your genetic background prevents you from losing weight is a powerful negative belief that has defeated your other attempts to lose weight. Losing weight is still a factor of calorie intake and utilization. However, starting and staying on a diet is a matter of attitude and beliefs."

"I understand that," he responded glumly. "After all, doing research based on vague theories and yet having the willingness to spend unlimited hours in experiments requires a strong belief in what I'm doing. I always do what I believe in and I don't believe I can lose weight."

"And you'll hold on to that belief, despite my telling you that proper dieting can overcome any genetic element that may be contributing to your obesity."

"Yes, that's what I believe."

"Can I be frank with you without you getting up and leaving?"

Jeff looked at me curiously. "All right. Say what you want. I won't leave."

I felt his tension rise as I paused before speaking. "Jeff, I believe that something else, something you haven't told me, is behind this strong belief you have about not being able to lose weight. I'm not even certain you have connected your obesity to anything else, but I sense that you're hiding something from me that may be crucial to my understanding your condition."

Jeff stared at me. His face was expressionless. But his breathing became louder. I had touched a raw nerve.

"You may be right, but it has nothing to do with my being overweight. I've been fat since childhood and what I do now is unrelated."

"We often have difficulty in seeing connections between thinking, behavior, and symptoms," I responded. "But your extreme negative attitude about not being able to lose weight indicates to me a mental obstacle beyond the knowledge of your family history."

Jeff became extremely still. He seemed lost in thought.

I waited.

"I'm an evil person," Jeff said, speaking through clenched teeth.

"No woman would want to have anything to do with me. I'm so fat I even disgust myself. When I was about twelve or thirteen I discovered porn. I've never told anyone about this until now. First Playboy and Penthouse. Then Hustler and videos. Finally, I began to write my own stories about sex. I wrote everything imaginable. I thought of things that no one else would ever imagine. I spent half my time masturbating to the stories I wrote."

"But why does writing stories about sex and masturbating make you an evil person?" I asked.

"You would have to read my stories to understand what I think about. It's an abomination to think the way I do. I feel compelled to masturbate everyday and my stories are more and more bizarre. And I can't stop it."

"Does your sex involve anyone besides yourself?"

"No, of course not."

"Then I have difficulty in understanding why you think of yourself as evil. Whatever your thoughts they remain limited to you."

"I didn't think you'd understand. No one would." Jeff grew silent and I felt him withdrawing.

"Jeff, I believe that a person's thoughts belong to him. Acting on thoughts that are destructive or harmful to others is a different matter. If someone has obsessions and frightening thoughts or unusual sexual fantasies and they remain with the person, then they remain his business. It would appear that your thoughts remain your own and you are reacting with extreme guilt over them and thus condemn yourself as evil."

"You psychiatrists are all the same. You can always find a way out of anything. When I say I'm evil I know what I'm speaking of. Don't try to placate me. If I didn't feel guilty about these thoughts, I would be beyond redemption."

"Jeff, I respect your feelings," I said, realizing that he needed to feel guilty and consequently evil to avoid believing his sexual fantasies came from someone inhuman.

"How do these sexual fantasies contribute to your being overweight?

"Being fat keeps women away from me."

"So you're saying that if a woman got too close to you she would know about these evil sexual fantasies."

"Yes, and then expose me for what I am. A depraved and evil man."

"So when you've tried previous diets you immediately became fearful of it working. Being fat is safer than being thin, even if you're dying."

Jeff pondered my words. "I never consciously experienced fear although you might be right. I just found I was unable to lose any weight for more than a month or two."

"What would happen during your dieting?"

"I'm not exactly certain but I believe that I masturbated more when I dieted. I finally felt so bad that I needed to eat to stop becoming more depressed. Then I would really shovel food into my mouth. I never lost more than ten or fifteen pounds on any diet I ever tried. And I gained the weight back in a very short time. I just came to believe that my family background prevented me from losing weight."

"Do you believe that now?" I asked.

"I'm not sure," he responded. "I'm feeling confused. Maybe my evil sex life is involved in my eating so much."

The picture had become clearer. Early in adolescence Jeff began to develop his own sexual fantasies for masturbating. The compulsion to masturbate and create more bizarre fantasies intensified as he got older leading to intense guilt and the symptom of feeling evil. His preoccupation with his sexual thoughts made contact with women impossible for fear of disclosure. He felt his obesity would prevent anyone from being attracted to him. It was important to know what happened when he began his latest period of rapid weight gain.

"Jeff, I'd like you to think back to that time about four or five months ago when this current binging began and see if anything may have set it off."

"I know exactly what happened now that I realize that my sex life is somehow involved with my fatness," he immediately replied. "On a very foolish impulse I decided to take a few of my sexual stories to work so that I could masturbate that night. I had intended to sleep over on a cot in the lab to continue working on a new project that I'm developing.

"Stupidly, I placed them in a drawer of my desk and forgot them. I asked one of my assistants, a young woman, to get me some papers from my desk. When she didn't return, I went to look for them myself and found her reading the stories. I was shocked. She turned to me and in an angry voice, at least I thought she was angry, blurted out, 'The guy who wrote these stories is really a sicko. Where did you get them?'

"Foolishly, I was so flustered that I told her that a friend gave them to me.

"She looked at me kind of funny and said that I had some weird friends. I tried to minimize the damage and said nothing further, but I really got scared that she would spread the stories around. I waited until she finished reading the last one and then merely said that the guy who wrote them would be upset if he thought I let anyone else see them. She caught on and told me that she wouldn't tell anybody about them."

What would have impelled him to take several of his written stories to his lab, I wondered? If he needed to masturbate there why didn't he just make up a fantasy?

"Jeff, is it customary to take your stories to your lab when you stay overnight?"

"No. As a matter of fact that was the only time I've done it."

"Do you recall why you took them?"

"No, I just remember that I wanted to do it."

The session came to a close and Jeff agreed to return for another meeting to tell me more about his background and also to learn about my diet program.

Jeff's early memories began when he was about three

with the birth of his brother, David. They began to fight almost as soon as his brother could talk. By the time Jeff started grade school he was quite fat and his anger at David was intensified when his brother called him "fatso." His rivalry with David increased until the third grade when Jeff was being increasingly fussed over for his amazing mental feats and it was clear that his brother was no rival in that area. His relationship with David gradually diminished and to this day they rarely speak to each other.

Though remaining skeptical about losing weight Jeff appeared willing to try my diet program. He immediately grasped the value and the method for using water, the scale and stabilization periods. I was aware that he refrained from commenting that he never gets far enough along in a diet to worry about a stabilization period. Though we discussed the value of exercise, I indicated that he should follow the guidelines of his primary physician in this area. Our objective was to find a way for him to rapidly lose weight.

In most circumstances I advise patients to keep their weight loss to four to eight pounds a month but I felt that a more drastic diet was called for during his first month of dieting. I advised Jeff to reduce his food intake by 1,250 calories a day for the coming month. That would guarantee him a loss of ten pounds of body fat and I assumed another ten pounds of body fluid. That would exceed his best monthly weight loss during past diets. I assumed that his rapid increase of thirty pounds in the past few months indicated a large accumulation of body fluid that would be eliminated through dieting and increased water intake. He needed a shot of success that would carry him into the stabilization month where, hopefully, he would discover that he could break the old pattern of immediately regaining his lost weight. Special imagery exercises were called for to overcome his belief that he was genetically incapable of losing weight.

Jeff showed his first enthusiastic reaction to starting the diet program when I told him that the use of mental imagery was a primary part of my diet program. He was already expert in the use of mental imagery. He informed me that he used imagery to explore his creative ideas and many of his discoveries came from the use of imagery. Jeff spent the remainder of the session describing how he used it in his scientific work.

Each morning on awakening he would lie down on the floor, close his eyes and sink into a deep trance. Visualizing aspects of his current projects helped him "weave" his theories together and find ways to prove them. He was on the path to help explain how the universe was filled with invisible dark matter and dark energy, the stuff that was propelling the universe to expand at an ever-increasing rate. The agility of his mind as he described dozens of ways to visualize dark energy and matter was astonishing.

He imagined infinitesimally tiny particles rushing toward outer space and carrying entire galaxies with them. He also visualized incredibly long fiber-like energy forms stretching in one direction and contracting in the opposite direction pulling galaxies forward and simultaneously pushing them to expand. It was the elaboration of these visualizations that pushed his thinking into new areas of science. Jeff's belief in imagery as a mental force was total.

His incredible imagination was now going to be put to use to help him overcome his obesity. Our time was up before I had described the imagery for his diet program. He was eager to schedule our next session and begin his journey into his mind using the power of mental imagery.

Jeff bounced into my office for his third session. Even before sitting down he proclaimed his positive mood with a hardy, "Let's get started."

"I've already decided that I can lick this binging and today I'm on a fast. I plan to fast every other day this entire month. By my calculations I should drop a minimum of three to four pounds a week plus any excess water that is excreted. No telling how much water will come out of me."

No question he was "high" on his new diet plans. Such a rapid mood change could quickly revert back to self-doubt, depression and overeating.

"Sounds like you've made a very positive step forward," I said encouragingly. "However, I need to caution you that such enthusiasm, though initially helpful, can backfire when resistance to dieting occurs."

"No need to worry," he assured me. "I think I'm on to something with you and I'm determined to succeed."

"Jeff, I'm glad you have taken this step. However, breaking long standing habits and compulsions don't just happen without laying the groundwork for permanent control."

"I agree. But what is wrong with my taking a more convincing and extreme step. After all, I must be one of the heaviest persons you ever treated and I have so much weight to lose I can't be around here for years doing it."

"Actually I'm pleased that you've decided to plunge into a program to overcome your obesity, once and for all," I said. "However, Jeff, certain pitfalls may occur by taking the steps you're planning. Many dieters have difficulty in losing that much weight quickly and get discouraged when they can't meet their goals. Also, I believe it's helpful for planning purposes to start your actual diet at the beginning of the month, which is still six days away. I had already extended your calorie reduction to 1,250 calories a day, which would cause a loss of two-and-a-half pounds a week. Mental control requires discipline, as you know from your work. Overcoming a tenacious weight problem is not easy and your motivation can fluctuate."

"Look, Doc," he interrupted. "I don't know why you have to put a damper on my ideas. I'm quite capable of following what I'm telling you. Also, I understand the advantage of starting on the first of the month, which I'll do after this first diet period."

"What happened to prevent you from dieting more than

a month or two in your previous attempts?" I asked.

"I never believed I could lose weight. I like your ideas and you have already convinced me that genetics won't interfere with my doing it."

I was now treading in precarious territory. I didn't want to interfere with his newfound motivation by creating doubt in his mind. I decided to gamble with Jeff's own instincts regarding the extent of his weight loss for this month. The stabilization period would be time enough to show him the need of a different form of discipline. I also felt that he would not be able to continue his alternate day fasting for long. I was to be proven wrong.

"All right," I acceded. "You certainly have reason to lose weight rapidly and trusting yourself to accomplish it is one of the keys to success."

As soon as I began explaining that he could create diet imagery that is directed at changing his belief systems and behavior that control his overeating, he slapped his fist into his hand and said, "Okay, I get the picture. First, I'd like you to give me a brief idea of the kinds of things you include in your diet imagery."

I inwardly smiled for I felt certain that Jeff's use and understanding of the power of imagery probably exceeded my own. I described how the imagery was directed to the areas of compulsive eating that needed to be changed. The purpose was to change negative belief systems. I gave examples of how to mentally block access to refrigerators, cupboards, dining tables, and markets. I briefly indicated how imagery is directed to one's physiology, emotional reactions to overeating, and to eating in general. When I described end-state imagery, he made his first comment. "I fully understand what you do. It all sounds helpful. However, I prefer to construct my own imagery."

I smiled and nodded in agreement. He would take the initiative in developing his own imagery, a practice I actively encouraged with all my patients.

"Good," I said. "Anything more you want from me at this point?"

"No. Just give me a few minutes to reflect on what you have told me."

After a brief delay Jeff proceeded to describe the imagery exercises he created to begin his diet program.

I'll enclose myself in a container that is impervious to any excess food. The container will have its own mind and know when I'm overeating. It will be very sensitive to any fats, candy, cake or excess sugars. It will know with great exactness when I have reached 1500 calories a day and then will not allow any additional food to pass it. I shall praise it highly knowing it will do its job. I shall also give it the power to stop any food from passing through it every other day for the entire first month I'm on the diet. I shall instruct my mind to absorb the power of the impervious container and it won't be long before the container and I are one.

I'll imagine I'm depressed and craving food. At the moment I feel like eating, a clown will appear and sweep away any food in sight and tell me a series of very funny jokes that will feed my mind and eliminate any need to feed my stomach. He'll repeat that overeating is like a joke and should only be laughed at.

I shall send into my body a specially developed bacterium modified to clean genes of all genetic factors that cause me to remain fat. Whatever genetic influences are in my body are going to be wiped out.

I shall battle my tendency to compulsively eat whenever there is any food near me. My urge to eat will immediately provoke an attack by a grotesque animal that will proceed to consume me for as long as my desire to eat continues. He'll start with my hand and, if I still feel hungry, will continue to eat me alive. I'll be terrified of dying and this will quickly eliminate any hunger. As soon as I do, my body will be repaired. If I still feel hunger I'll end up dead. He laughed when he described this exercise saying how true that belief is. He must stop eating to remain alive.

Whenever I have a sex fantasy I will see my stomach filled by a balloon totally eliminating any hunger so it is disconnected from eating. I will accept my sex fantasies as good for me, very nourishing and wholesome.

I will also see myself as increasingly desirable to women despite having sex fantasies. I'll incorporate into my imagery one of my fantasies that I think makes me an abomination and instead see myself surrounded by women who clamor to be with me and want to be part of my fantasy.

Naturally, I'll end my imagery exercises with seeing myself thin and handsome and very attractive to women and also to men. Everyone will be drawn to me as a highly desirable person to be with. I will be admired for my body as well as my mind.

In a few minutes Jeff had come up with seven insightful and targeted imagery exercises that would attempt to correct many of his belief systems that impacted on his diet. I would soon learn that these preliminary imagery exercises would be relegated to a secondary role in changing his thinking patterns.

During his first diet period Jeff alternated a day of fasting with a day of regular dieting. At the end of the five weeks he had lost twenty-two pounds. He weighed 353.

I had been seeing him weekly since his third visit. As he modified and expanded his imagery exercises he became more and more enthused at the empowerment he felt as his mind battled his compulsive eating. He rarely mentioned anything personal and he had not mentioned his sexual fantasies again. In the middle of his stabilization month he suddenly announced it was time to tell me more about why he felt evil. He wanted to use imagery to overcome the guilt over his fantasies.

"When I was a teenager I used nude pictures from Playboy and other nudie magazines for my fantasies. My imagination had no limits and anything was possible. My fantasies included intercourse, oral sex, anal sex, S and M, bondage, and submission-domination scenes. I imagined myself as a giant in control of countless women who begged for my sexual favors.

"About six or seven years ago another element entered my fantasies. The women not only became sexually excited by my enormous cock, they began to look on it as a toy to be played with. The women gave it nicknames and kissed it not just to arouse me but with affection. I found my sexual excitement stronger than ever and my orgasms overwhelming. I began to imagine that I was not creating the fantasies. They had become part of my real life."

Jeff now paused and looked closely at me. I sat there quietly and waited. So far I found nothing unusual about his sexual fantasies even having his sex partners give his penis pet names. What could have made him believe he was evil? I noted that when he described his fantasies he made it appear that the other subjects spoke with their own voice and were not merely representations of his own thoughts. But giving such fantasies a sense of reality was also not uncommon. It was like directing and being an actor in your own movie.

Jeff looked away from me and then continued. "It seemed as though my thoughts were being taken over by others and my fantasies began to change without any conscious effort on my part. For the most part I ignored this since my sexual pleasure was greater than ever. Then a few years ago when I no longer felt that I had any control over my fantasies a major change occurred that first astonished me and then terrified me. It happened spontaneously and I felt I had no control over it. It happened each time I decided to masturbate."

Jeff again paused. "I wanted to stop fantasizing but I couldn't. I began to see myself growing smaller, everything except my cock. The transition took several months. At first I was more astonished than scared. But when my image in the fantasies began to truly shrink in size and my efforts to stop it failed I began to think I was losing my mind. I only had to think of masturbation and a fantasy would appear. I tried not to think of doing it but my need to have an orgasm was stronger than my resolve to stop."

Jeff's breathing became heavier. He looked at the floor. He had stopped talking.

"Jeff, I'm aware that whatever was happening to you was terrifying. But there is a reason for this to occur. But it's still not clear to me why this series of fantasies made you feel evil."

"It's because of what the adults did to the baby."

"What baby?" I asked.

"The baby I had become in the fantasies."

"How old did you feel the baby was?"

"I stopped shrinking in age and size when I was about two, although sometimes I even appeared younger, maybe one."

"Once you reached that age did you remain there?"

"Yes, I've been that age for several years. Sometimes I think I'm insane and being controlled by these fantasies."

Jeff was very aware that his out-of-control sexual fantasies were abnormal. He made it clear that he had attempted to stop them but had been powerless to do so. I was convinced that he was not suffering from a typical delusional system. Rather some part of his mind had assumed control of his sexual life in a most unusual way. I had a strong suspicion that some childhood crisis or trauma had contributed to his mental state.

During the next few sessions Jeff finally revealed why he felt depraved and evil. The baby was undergoing all the sexual experiences that he did as an adult. He cringed at watching adult men and women use the baby for their sexual purposes. Despite his wish to stop masturbating, he was unable to do so. Each fantasy brought forth gratification followed immediately by a terrible feeling of self-loathing. At times he came close to suicide.

"I felt like a pedophile, a horrible person who abuses children. There's nothing more abominable in my mind than that. Can't you understand why I feel evil and don't deserve to live?"

"Jeff, something in you has created this delusion-like condition. It's like a foreign body inside you. Your intense guilt makes it clear that these fantasies are serving several purposes. One is obviously for gratification. The other is for suffering. Why your fantasies took the turn they did is not clear at this point. In general, sexual fantasies are always enjoyed. When they're not, we tend to find a repetition of an early traumatic experience that a child was unable to understand or deal with psychologically."

"I don't agree with you," Jeff retorted strongly. "I'm guilty because what I'm doing is abominable."

"But you're acting under a compulsion that acts without your conscious intent."

"What's the difference? Those thoughts come from me. You can't deny that."

"Jeff would you condemn someone who was plagued by hallucinations or delusions and did something heinous as a result?"

"I'm not dealing with a delusion or hallucination. These thoughts spring from me. I see them and hate them but they're from me."

"Unlike the person with delusions, you recognize the irrationality and compulsive nature of your symptoms. This is why you suffer so much. If your symptoms took the form of a delusion what would you think of yourself?"

"How would I know?"

"Most likely you would feel intense anger at whoever you thought had put those thoughts in you, but you would not be guilty. You would not blame yourself for what you believed had been done to you. We need to try to understand where these persistent sexual ideas come from, just as we would if they were delusions."

Jeff stared at me. "Okay," he grunted. The session ended. Further understanding of his sexual fantasies was temporarily postponed.

Do sexual fantasies of children stem from sexual abuse in childhood? Frequently, but not always. Such fantasies may derive from other early trauma or conflicts and become displaced to sexuality. At times abuse in later childhood and even adolescence could lead to conflicts being played out through sexual fantasies.

No evidence of sexual abuse or mistreatment appeared in his memories. From the time his brother was born he recalled sibling rivalry but nothing that would appear to cause the kinds of conflicts that might result in his excessive eating or his sexual fantasies. Although envious of his brother's thin body, Jeff's brilliance in and out of school, plus his popularity seemed to have insulated him against the times some students taunted him about his obesity.

Several months would pass before an incident in his life would open the door to the use of guided imagery and an indepth look into his childhood.

Meanwhile Jeff was assiduously modifying and creating

new imagery exercises that were tantamount to waging war against part of himself.

> He visualized taking a sharp knife and slicing off a layer of fat from his face to his feet. "It's my way of molting, like a snake who sheds the top layer of his skin. I'm deliberately eradicating my top layer of skin, which I see as my total body fat. Underneath my fat is my real self. I am declaring that what I cut off is no longer part of my body. I am actively disowning it. I then say 'Fat you are gone for good. I am free of you. I shall live without being fat.'"

> A second imagery exercise involved sexual relations with countless women who sought him for his body. "I see woman after woman coming to me and admiring my body and touching and caressing me and then seducing me into great sex. There is no evidence of anything infantile in this imagery. After each sexual experience I talk to my body and tell it how happy it's made me. My body responds by becoming available to yet another woman desiring sex."

At the end of the stabilization period Jeff weighed 351. His regulation of his body weight was exemplary. For his second diet month he stopped his fasting and instead reduced his food intake by 1,000 calories a day. In that month he lost another eleven pounds, which he maintained during his second stabilization month. His weekly visits continued and although I learned more about his work he seemed reluctant to probe into his past.

It was during his fifth month, a diet month that he lost control and binged for two straight days gaining eight pounds. He started the special extra-water diet the day after the binging ended. Eight pounds of weight gain required twelve additional glasses of water and on that day he drank all day. The following day he had lost five pounds and lost the remaining three pounds one day later.

"What occurred before the binging started?" I asked.

"The day before I binged a close friend, actually a colleague was killed in an auto accident. Really tragic. She was just beginning to come into her own as a researcher. But I can't imagine why that should have made me binge, although I certainly felt sad," he replied.

"Sometimes an event can set in motion a temporary relapse by linking to some memory in you. Perhaps the death of your friend triggered something."

Jeff didn't think so, but he felt uneasy. Something had stirred in his memory. Attempts to find some link to the past proved fruitless. On his next visit I decided to return to his early childhood using guided imagery. He was already familiar with the technique and needed no prompting to begin. We decided to probe into his early childhood to a period where his memories were sparse.

"Jeff, imagine you are back in your home in the same room with your mother a few months before David was born," I said

"Mother seems sad," he responded.

Jeff, what did you call your mother then?"

"Mommy."

"Use that name, for that is where your emotions lie."

Jeff inexplicably began to cry. He seemed unable to speak although he made a few attempts. Finally he whispered, "Mommy."

His mother did not appear to notice him.

"Mommy," he again whispered.

His crying became more intense. His body heaved and his breaths were tortured.

"Jeff, go to your mommy and hold her," I suggested.

"She doesn't seem to notice me," he said. "She seems so sad."

"Ask her why she is sad."

"Mommy, why are you sad? Mommy, I love you." Jeff was crying and held out his real arms as he inwardly reached for his mother.

His mother remained mute and unmoving.

"Jeff, go back to an even earlier period of your childhood, back before your mother was pregnant with David. "You will again be in the same room with her."

"I can't find her," he said startled. "She's not here. Mommy, Mommy, where are you?" he screamed. The depth of his suffering struck me deeply.

"Jeff, your mommy is around somewhere. Look around the rest of the house until you find her."

Frantically, little Jeff ran through the house screaming, "Mommy, Mommy, Mommy."

His mother had disappeared. Why had she disappeared from his unconscious mind? Was he just unable to see her? In guided imagery, such an absence is almost always real. Not finding his mother strongly implied she wasn't with him then.

Jeff's grief was unbearable. Nothing seemed to matter except the absence of his mother.

"Jeff, I know how you're suffering but we need to find your mother. You know where she is, even though she is not at home. Try to relax a few moments." I waited while his crying diminished.

"Remain in the same age period," I said. "Now go to wherever your mommy is. You will now find her."

I watched as Jeff's eyes darted from side to side under his closed lids. Then his eyes stopped moving and a look of abject fear appeared on his face. "Mommy," he screamed. "Where are you?" Jeff seemed to curl up into a little ball despite his immense size. He began to rock back and forth.

"Jeff, where are you?"

He gave no hint that he heard my voice.

"Jeff, I know you're frightened, but try to describe what

is happening."

Jeff began to moan while his body writhed in torment. I felt no link between us. I waited. Jeff needed time to assimilate whatever he had discovered as he searched for his mother. The moaning continued and he seemed unaware of my presence.

"Jeff, tell me if you want to continue?"

By now I was becoming alarmed. Something highly disturbing had happened back in his early childhood. It was clearly related to the disappearance of his mother, or at least some separation from her. His anguish was overwhelming. He needed to come back to this reality.

I spoke decisively. "Jeff, I am going to count to five. On the count of five you will open your eyes. You will remember whatever you have experienced."

Jeff did not react, although I felt that he had heard me.

"Jeff," I said very loudly. "You hear my voice. You now know that you lost your mother when you were a baby. You are afraid to face your feelings about her leaving you. You need to know what happened. When I clap my hands you will open you eyes."

With those words I clapped and Jeff stopped moaning for a few moments. But he remained steadfastly behind his wall. He was too frightened to reappear. I was now running out of options. I hesitated to wake him by physically shaking him. There was no way of knowing if he'd awaken in a fury or in a state of apathy. Rather than wait until he awakened naturally, I decided to enter his world. But would he accept me there?

I took the role of his mother.

"Jeff, my baby, I'm here. Look at me Jeff. I'm now here with you." My voice was warm and inviting.

Jeff slowly stopped crying, His face softened and he seemed intent at looking at something on his visual screen.

"Yes, darling, it's me. Mommy. I've come back."

Jeff started to cry as he became animated and whispered.

"Mommy, I was afraid you had gone away."

"I know, Jeff, darling. I know how frightened you must have been. What did you think had happened to me?"

"I don't know, Mommy, but I was all alone. I was so afraid."

"Wasn't daddy here with you?"

"No."

"Who fed you?"

"Nanny, but she never talks to me."

"But Nanny was supposed to take care of you."

"She doesn't like me. She doesn't take care of me. She only wants to be with daddy."

"I'm so sorry you felt so alone. I love you and I want you to be happy."

"Are you going to stay with me now?"

"I may have to go away again for a little while but I'll be back."

A scream of terror shattered the dialogue I was having with Jeff. "No, No, you can't leave me again. I need you. Mommy, don't leave me, don't leave me."

Jeff's anguish poured out again. What could have happened to his mother? What had happened to him?

"Jeff, I won't be gone long but you have someone new to take care of you. When you open your eyes you will see Dr. Berenson who will always be here for you. He won't let anything happen to you. You won't be alone anymore."

"No, Mommy, you can't leave me. I won't let you." With those words Jeff rose from his chair trying to reach something he saw in his mind's eye. He was experiencing his imagery as though it were real. I felt my heart racing as I searched for a way to resolve this.

"Jeff, I'm here. You can see me. I'm not leaving you. Now go back to your seat. I'll hold your hand."

Slowly, again encumbered by his massive weight, Jeff sat down heavily. His breathing quieted. He held my hand tightly. I must find a way to transform his mother into me.

He can't be alone.

"Jeff, do you feel better now?" I asked warmly. "I want you to feel safe."

"Yes, Mommy."

"What will make you feel safe, Jeff, darling?"

"Only if you stay with me."

"Jeff, you know that with your eyes closed you have made me come alive like I was when you were a little boy. You do understand that, Jeff?"

Silence.

"Jeff, you can tell me what you're thinking."

"I don't want to open my eyes. Then you'll go away."

"I know that frightens you, but you can always bring me back. All you have to do is imagine that I am with you. But now you must allow Dr. Berenson to be with you. He is the one who helped you find me and he can do it again."

I felt his trembling through my body; he still held my hand. He had become silent again.

"Jeff, you suffered when I went away and you're afraid I'll leave you again. But now you need to open your eyes. You know that you can always bring me back."

"Can I really bring you back?"

"Yes, whenever you wish and someday I'll come back and stay with you forever. I'll be able to give you all the things you never had as a baby."

Jeff opened his eyes and saw the tears in my own eyes. He let go of my hand and slowly rose. Standing unsteadily, he reached out to me. We held each other and cried together.

From that day Jeff's world changed.

During the next month we made other excursions into Jeff's past with the same results. If his imagery was correct then his mother had been absent from his life from the ages of one to two and a half. There were no memories about why she disappeared or how she returned. One day his mother just appeared at home already pregnant. She was distant and rarely spent time with him. Jeff's deprivation was extreme.

His desperate need for love remained unfulfilled.

His father interacted little with his son. He seemed pre-occupied and spent his time with Martha, the housekeeper, who also served as Jeff's nanny. Several guided imagery attempts to have him interact with his father proved fruitless. His father was always unresponsive. However, Jeff easily visualized his father and Martha disappearing into her bedroom. It was clear that Jeff lived in a desolate world prior to the birth of David.

Jeff decided to visit his parents in Chicago and confront them with his memories. It was time to ascertain the truth about what had happened to him in his early childhood.

When Jeff entered the office following the visit I knew the meeting with his parents had not been a happy one. He immediately began. "It was not easy to get my mother to tell me what happened then. My father essentially avoided me until the last day when I refused to be ignored by him.

"Apparently the courtship of my parents was rather stormy and they got married when she had become pregnant. Shortly after the wedding she had a spontaneous miscarriage but soon became pregnant with me. My mother inferred that the relationship had been more about passion than love. During her pregnancy and after my birth my father grew distant, causing her much fear and anger. When I was about a year old my mother had a nervous breakdown and apparently became suicidal and mute. She was sent away to a mental hospital. A year and a half later she returned home. She was pregnant by someone she had met in the hospital. To avoid a scandal, my father claimed the baby as his own. To this day David does not know this.

"Both my parents said that they felt it was better that I did not see my mother during her hospitalization because she talked funny or just wouldn't talk. My father said she had been diagnosed as schizophrenic. When I spoke to my father alone he reluctantly admitted that he had carried on an affair with the housekeeper both before and after my mother was sent to the hospital.

"The most terrible thing I learned was from my mother." Jeff stopped and cried. Several minutes passed before he was able to go on. "She told me that after my birth she didn't want to know me or even want me. That entire year after my birth she suffered in silence, hating the day she ever met my father."

How does one ever assimilate such news as hearing that your mother didn't want you? I now understood that Jeff's sense of aloneness was all he knew from birth. He came into this world with all the normal needs of an infant and found the world empty and rejecting. During his early years he had been alone. The time when an infant is normally filled with his mother's love Jeff had been abandoned. There could be no doubt that his enormous eating needs and some aspects of his strange sexual fantasies stemmed from this overwhelming deprivation. Would he be able to overcome such a deficit?

"After David's birth, mother seemed to improve and she and my father agreed to try to live together and raise us. My father was away much of the time busy with his growing medical practice. My mother became absorbed with David and me. As I grew older my needs became so enormous that my mother spent more and more time with me. She gave to me by supporting my many interests."

Jeff stopped and seemed deep in thought. He finally said. "Now that I know that the imagery was correct and I was alone the first three years of my life, what do I do with this information?"

"Jeff, that's our next task," I said. "I have no doubt that what you have discovered has played a major part in your obesity and sexual fantasies. I believe we should just continue our work and focus on this new information."

"I can certainly understand how my suffering as a small child has carried into my adult life," Jeff responded. "I not only want to lose all this weight but I want to live a normal life. I still can't stop those sexual fantasies and I still feel guilty when I use them to masturbate."

During the remainder of the session Jeff examined his feelings about growing up. He realized that he had distorted many of his memories to fit into a picture of an idyllic childhood. Jeff's life had seemed happy and productive. As he grew older he had became immersed in his widespread social and intellectual activities. He had suppressed knowledge of the lack of affection or closeness between his parents and ignored how little he had shared with his brother.

In the following few months, using guided imagery, Jeff returned to his early childhood and worked though many of his feelings of loneliness, isolation, and abandonment. His underlying anger was still unexpressed, although he often cried with pain when he sought to find comfort where none existed. His sexual fantasies were lessening in frequency though not in their compulsive urgency.

He intensified his exercise program and was able to increase his food intake while still maintaining a weight loss of two pounds per week. At the end of one year Jeff had lost sixty-five pounds and weighed 310. He agreed to continue losing no more than eight pounds a month for his second year of dieting. The advantage of slow weight loss and the benefit of the stabilization period were well established in his mind.

His health had markedly improved. His blood pressure was easily regulated by medication and the rapid fluctuation of his blood sugar and the potential of developing Type 2 diabetes had diminished. He no longer audibly wheezed. His increased stamina attested to a marked improvement in his cardiac efficiency.

Early in his second year of treatment Jeff had another breakthrough during a guided imagery session. We were once again delving into his early childhood when Jeff suddenly became silent. Although his silences were rare they were not unknown. I waited. Finally he spoke. "I'm seeing a black wall. Nothing else."

"Try to break through the black wall. Use a weapon or instrument if necessary."

"It's impervious. Nothing I use against it seems to make any difference. I just tried a large hammer and something wrenched it from my hands."

"Okay. Something's preventing you from going deeper. Let's try to by-pass the wall," I said. "Move away from it. Look around you. What do you see?"

"A large space like a cave."

"Is the black wall visible?"

"It's at the far end of the cave and is blocking my seeing anything beyond it."

"Look carefully and you will notice a small opening on the left side of the wall."

"I see it."

"Enter the opening which extends into a tunnel. This tunnel will take you through the black wall to the other side. Do you want to move into the tunnel?"

"Yes. I'm going now. I have to stoop to get through the opening. It's rocky and getting smaller. I'm crawling. My God, there are rats in here brushing against me. Get away. Get away. There's slimy, sticky stuff all over the ground and it's getting on me. I don't know if I can go any further."

"Jeff, it's up to you. Whatever exists behind that black wall is very frightening. All the obstacles suggest something terrible awaits you. What do you want to do?"

"I'm not stopping now. This may be my one chance to find out what has made me into a monster." Jeff grimaced, as he fought the impulse to turn back. "I mustn't stop. Out of the way, you damn rats. Ugh, this sticky stuff is getting on my face. The ground is rough. I'm bleeding. Go on, damn you," he screamed at himself.

He was determined. The passage became almost impassable. Without warning the tunnel ended.

"My God, I almost fell in. I'm at the edge of a hole. It's

like an abyss. I can't see any bottom. Something is pulling me toward it. My God. God help me, I'm falling." A terrified scream broke from Jeff's mouth. The scream seemed endless. His face contorted with horror. "I'm going to die. I'm going to die."

"Jeff, listen to me," I said. "You are now entering some terrifying part of your past. Something you need to face. Something you have been searching for. You are not going to die."

"I've reached the bottom," he said, the terror fading. "It's so dark here I can't see anything. What should I do?"

"Just stay there and let your eyes get used to the dark. You've entered a frightening time from your early childhood. Every little child has fantasies and fears that seem real. You're entering such a time when you were alone and frightened."

"I hear something moving."

"Can you see anything?"

"No. It's still too dark. Something just touched me. It feels slimy. I can't stay here much longer. I think something terrible is going to happen."

"Jeff, remember that everything is coming from your mind. You're behind that black wall. You need to face whatever happened when you were a small child."

"Why am I so afraid? I should be able to face anything inside me."

"You're reconnecting with very early and very frightening feelings and experiencing them as though you are a child. It's very similar to when we experience a nightmare. Something has broken through into consciousness that is usually hidden. What are you doing now?"

"Nothing. I'm just waiting. But I hear something moving. I wish I could see."

"Then imagine you have a flashlight. Remember you're finally facing something you have been unaware of as far as we know."

"I'm afraid. I don't want to see what's here."

"Jeff, you've struggled hard to go back to this early period. If you left now you might not be able to return easily. What you discover may help you finally overcome your eating compulsion as well as help you understand the meaning of your sexual life."

"I'm turning on my flashlight," he said tentatively. "My God, what are you?" He screamed. "Don't come near me."

"Jeff, what are you seeing?" I interrupted.

"It's a huge animal with an enormous mouth. Some slimy stuff is dripping from its mouth. Its eyes are red and bulging. The mouth is so big it could easily swallow me. It's just sitting there looking at me. It's horrible."

"You're looking at part of yourself as an infant," I said. "Now is the time to face this part of you. Talk to it."

"I think if I move it will swallow me."

"Jeff, this is the time to gain control over this greedy, insatiable part of yourself. The big mouth is you. It's what you were like when your mother left you. It's taken this form because of your feelings during that period. You can face it now and try to diminish its effect and possibly even eliminate it."

"What do I do?"

"Speak to it in the voice of your child self. Have it answer you. Above all try not to run away."

For several minutes Jeff remained silent. Unlike a night dream, which disguises early conflicts so they remain out of awareness, Jeff was about to face his infant self directly. He was about to experience an awake nightmare.

"Who are you?" he asked timidly.

"I'm hungry," the mouth screamed. I was startled by the raucous screeching that Jeff gave voice to as he reacted to his inner voraciously hungry self.

Jeff struggled for composure as he faced his insatiable self. "What do you want to eat?"

"I'm hungry," the mouth screamed.

"I know. I want to feed you."

A hysterical laugh broke from his lips. "You feed me.

You, who's been starving all his life and gorging on food, want to feed me."

"You're me," Jeff shouted. "When I say I'll feed you, it means I'll feed you."

And inexplicably Jeff began to cry. Torrents of tears poured from his eyes. I felt his pain but did not intervene. I waited for him to talk.

Finally I asked, "Jeff, what happened? Try to continue."

He remained silent. I wasn't even certain he heard me. Had he again disconnected from me?

"Jeff, try it one word at a time."

"I'm starving. I'm starving. I'm going to die." Jeff was inconsolable. These words came from Jeff and not the mouth.

"Jeff, you realize the mouth is speaking for you. When you were an infant you were starved. Starved for love that was not given to you. You remained hungry no matter how much food was eaten. You were dying for lack of love."

As I watched with rising apprehension, Jeff slid off his chair onto the floor. As I was about to go to him, he rolled on his side and drew his feet toward his chest and began to suck his thumb. My heart ached as I watched this huge man curl up into the position of a small baby and cry. I knew he felt completely alone. I was torn by what I was seeing. What should I do? I could feel his desperate longing for love. No matter how much food he had eaten he had never felt filled. Food was unable to fill his emptiness. He needed love. Do I go over and hold him? Does he know that I am crying too? I knew that I had to speak to him.

"Jeff, you are doing what you have to do. Love yourself. Love yourself as much as you can. Suck your thumb. Feed yourself. You have been starving all your life. Feel your hunger deeply. In the future you will love yourself and receive love from others. You will no longer need food in place of love."

Did Jeff hear anything I said? I thought of the intense

suffering that Jeff had gone through all his life. Not to be loved and wanted as a child leaves immutable scars. No one fully overcomes such deprivation.

A few more minutes passed as I watched and waited. But now it was time for him to return to his adult self.

"Jeff, do you hear me?" I asked softly.

Silence.

"Jeff, what are you seeing now?" His body shifted slightly. He had heard me.

"Jeff, what…"

In a voice so low I strained to hear, Jeff spoke. "I'm inside my mouth. I want my mouth to swallow me and it won't."

"You want to eat yourself?"

"Yes. I want to give myself all the love I never had. I need to love myself. It's my only chance to live." Tears ran down his face. "I'm a good person. I was a good baby. How could my mommy not love me?"

"You were a good and lovable baby. Your mother was unable to love anyone, even herself. You have blamed yourself for her not loving you, but it wasn't you. You were and are a lovable baby and man."

"Yes, I am a lovable baby and man," he said softly.

"Now, Jeff, tell the mouth, your baby self that you will love him, that you will be the one to fill yourself with love. The mouth can now swallow you and keep you inside. He will take in your loving self."

Gradually a look of peace came over Jeff as he lay quietly on the floor. His tears continued but no longer were they tears of anguish.

"I'm inside myself," he whispered. "How wonderful I am. I'll never leave again."

I resisted the urge to have him describe what he saw. His uninterrupted experience of being in a new place within his mind was paramount. Jeff was savoring feeling safe and peaceful in a newfound world. This was another of the pivotal steps that Jeff would make on his way to health.

In the following session Jeff created a number of striking imagery exercises to fortify his new insight.

> He visualized a huge mouth, attached to an enormous body, floating in space and swallowing everything in sight. Birds, butterflies, bees, falling leaves. Then the mouth swooped down and ate bugs, squirrels, snakes, even rats. The mouth's appetite was voracious and endless. Without warning it swallowed Jeff in a single gulp. Jeff was deep within the body of the floating mouth. The huge body began to shrink. It got smaller and smaller until it was finally a normal sized man with a normal sized mouth. He had become a new person. He ended by saying, "I love who I am. I love myself and will nourish myself forever."

> He visualized himself as a tiny magical figure entering his own body through his mouth. He goes into every organ in his body, including his brain. With a pure white light he rids his body of every vestige of childhood fear, feelings of badness, self-hate and feeling unloved. He leaves his body knowing he has been healed by his own efforts. Once more he ends saying, "I love who I am. I love myself and will nourish myself forever."

> He visualized an endless number of people coming to him and saying how much they loved him. Each would say how wonderful and loving he was. In this imagery he saw himself in his current body and he knew that he was loved for himself.

> He visualized returning to his early childhood and

being held by his mother. He said how much he loved her and she responded by saying she loved him too. She stated that she had never intended to hurt him and that he is a good and loving baby and she will always love him.

During the next three months Jeff returned many times to his early childhood and faced issues involving his mother, father, and his infant self. Slowly the horror of that period faded; and Jeff began to focus on his sexuality. He explored his fear and distrust of women until he believed that he had severed the connection between his mother and other women. His masturbation fantasies continued although with less frequency. He still shied away from dating and believed he was unattractive to women. I suggested a new imagery exercise to see if Jeff could grow up sexually.

He would visualize having the infant in his imagery exercise grow one year at a time. Each change in age would be transferred to the actual masturbation fantasy. The real test would be his ability to masturbate at his new age and size for a period of two weeks without relapsing. When accomplished he would move to the next age. Jeff liked the idea and immediately implemented it.

He decided to start the imagery as well as continue his sexual fantasies seeing himself at the age of three, rather than two. The imagery exercises proved more successful than anticipated. In a number of body changes he would move to the next level in a week or even less. At the end of three months he had reached the age of twelve where he stalled. Entering adolescence when his real sexual desires would have started proved to offer resistance to his growth.

He talked about his adolescence.

"I remember going up to a girl when I was in the tenth grade to ask her to go to the library with me. Our teacher had just given us a special assignment that required the use of the library and I thought I could impress her with how well I got around in the library. I really liked her but I had never even said hello. She just looked at me and without saying a single word turned and walked away. I never asked another girl to do anything with me after that."

"Why do you think she did it?"

"Because I looked like a fat slob."

"How much did you weigh then?"

"I think it was around 275 pounds. I remember that in the last two years of high school I really ballooned out. By the end of high school I weighed almost 325 pounds."

"Why do you think you can't get beyond twelve in your sexual fantasies?"

"When I was a teenager I used to really get horny and imagined screwing every girl in school. But the idea of approaching one for just a movie date was impossible."

"But you've told me that everyone liked you, including many girls and that you could take good natured ribbing."

"That's true. They liked me because I told good jokes and I was the editor of the school newspaper and one of the smartest kids in the school. But that's not the same as wanting to go out with me. I did go to parties that didn't require a date. Dating meant sex and that was out as far as I was concerned. No one knew what I felt and no one ever asked."

"What did you feel?"

"I went through a period of self-flagellation," he said without hesitation. "It wasn't like my current fantasies. Instead, I would beat myself up or have women do it to me. I was burned, cut up, flayed and beaten to a pulp. Any torture I could think of I tried. I masturbated using those fantasies and always got off. There was no real sex, no oral sex or intercourse. Only being brutalized. And I always felt better after doing it. So what more does that tell you about me?" He grinned.

I laughed. "Actually nothing. As you know we've already established your need for punishment and how self-hate gave you fulfillment since self-love wasn't available to you at that time. The question we're facing is why you can't continue to grow into normal sexuality now that you've reached puberty in your imagery exercises."

"I think I know the answer," Jeff replied. "I need to take that first step and ask a real live girl out for a date. That's what I would have done in adolescence if I felt that I would have been accepted."

"I think you have a good point," I said encouragingly. "Sometimes real change occurs by actively changing your behavior rather that getting some new insight or even working with imagery. Do you feel up to it?"

"I think so. The worst that can happen is they say no and that won't devastate me. I feel too good about myself for anyone to change that."

Jeff plunged into his new social life. He asked female colleagues out for dinner and to the movies. Some accepted. Some did not. He made no attempt to limit himself to one woman and never went beyond a friendly interaction. The newfound warmth from women who found him entertaining and "a perfect gentleman" reinforced his growing self-esteem.

By the end of the third year of his therapy and diet program he had lost almost 150 pounds. He weighed 227 pounds and now set his goal for what he considered his ideal weight at 175 pounds that he hoped to reach in a year and a half.

Although his age in his sexual fantasies had now reached into his early twenties he remained a virgin. But now it was by choice, for several women made it clear that they would welcome having a sexual relationship with him. Just as he was beginning his fourth year with me he met Joanna, a woman who fulfilled his dream for romance and a soul mate. Jeff was now thirty years old and for the first time in his life was falling in love.

His first comments to me after meeting Joanna said it all. "I met a woman who is so tuned into me and me into her that when we spoke we almost felt we had already heard each other's words before we said them."

By their third date they already felt a deep commitment to each other. Although they had not yet made love, Joanna had broached the subject of sexual fantasies by remarking that many lovers never know each other sexually because they govern their sex life through fantasies. "Instead of making love to your partner," she had said, "you make love to someone in your fantasy. How sad that so many people never fully know the beauty and wonders of making love to the actual person they are with."

"She had touched on a subject that frightens me," Jeff continued. "I'm afraid that I may not be able to see and feel Joanna in my arms when we finally make love. All my sex partners come from magazines or movies. I've never been able to imagine sex with a real woman. I tried imagining it with Joanna the night before we met for our third date, but I was unable to visualize her in one of my fantasies. I was also guilty of trying to use her that way. I imagined she read my mind when she brought the subject up. Talking about sex with her was embarrassing."

"Are you referring to sex in general or about your fantasies?" I asked.

"Both, I think," he responded. "I doubt that I would ever want to tell her about my fantasies. I also think she's right that people shouldn't have to use them when they're making love, although I know that many people do."

"Agreed. But now that you want to make love to someone you like, why use them?"

"I still somehow think I'm a dirty person and shouldn't have sex with someone I care for. Sex with someone I don't know is different."

"Jeff, that's a carry over of feelings from your past. Making love with Joanna will help you understand that she is the one who is arousing you. You have to trust yourself that you won't need fantasies. Your love making would truly be between the two of you."

"She wouldn't know that I was doing it. After all, it would still be sex between us and we would both enjoy it."

"Jeff, you would still not be making love with Joanna. Something else is bothering you?"

For just a moment Jeff hesitated. "I'm afraid I won't be able to get it up unless I have sex the same way that I do in my fantasies. I expect certain kinds of stimulation that I get by controlling the women. Even when they act aggressively it's because I wish it. When I'm utterly passive, the women take an aggressive approach. When I'm aggressive the women succumb and even beg me to do more to them. The women have no real say in what I want or do. I do things to them I would never dream of doing to Joanna. I don't think I can have sex any other way."

"Jeff, having sex with Joanna using your fantasies would be holding on to something that still bothers you. I believe you can change this."

"I want to change. I feel there's still something inside me that I can't control. Believe me I've tried. I thought when I grew up physically in my fantasies that what I did would change. And it hasn't. I can't get aroused unless I use one of them."

His desire to form a real loving relationship with Joanna became the impetus to finally end his dependence on his sexual fantasizes. We decided that Jeff would return to his early childhood using guided imagery and try to find out what else may have happened that influenced his sexual life. The last remaining obstacle to getting well was about to be overcome.

Jeff closed his eyes and went into a state of relaxation. Unknown to either of us he was about to enter a place in his past that had previously eluded him.

"Go back in time to your earliest memories of having sexual feelings," I directed him.

Instead of images and words flowing into his mind Jeff grimaced before responding. "Strange, but I only see grayness, like a gray curtain is hung over my eyes."

"Stay focused on it until some image becomes clear to you."

"I see something moving near me. I'm in a crib and I feel hungry. I'm starting to cry. I hear other noises. Someone's talking but not to me. I can hear other voices, maybe two other people. I'm not sure. And it's still quite dark."

Jeff became increasingly restless and he stopped speaking for a few moments. "I feel funny, like I don't belong here. Yet everything is familiar. Like it's the same crib I've been in many times before." Jeff began to cry, softly at first, then louder. "I'm hungry." He began to scream and held his hands over his abdomen. "There's a man in the room and he seems angry. The other person is Nanny and she's trying to soothe him. I'm hungry." Again a scream. Jeff was mentally in his childhood at a time when he still used his crib.

"Everything is hazy," he said. "I can't see the people but I know their voices. The man is my daddy. Daddy, I'm hungry. Nanny, I'm hungry. Nanny, Nanny, I'm hungry."

Jeff was in the throes of deep pain. Something was unfolding and he was now beginning to feel frightened.

"Get the kid and bring him here and get him to shut up. You knew I was coming here. Didn't you feed him?" Jeff had taken on the deep gruff voice of his father. "My nanny is picking me up and taking me into her bed. My daddy's there too. They have no clothes on. I'm hungry."

"Get the kid to stop screaming, will you?" he ordered.

Jeff could hardly talk as he felt what now took place. "My nanny is rubbing me down there. It feels good. I don't feel hungry anymore." A peaceful look came over Jeff.

"Don't stop," Jeff screamed again. "She's doing it some more. I like it. I want more. More."

As I watched Jeff groped toward his genitals.

"What's going on here?" A new voice rose out of Jeff. A voice of anger and terror. "My God, what are you doing to my child, you terrible woman? Roger, what are you doing here with Martha? What have you done to my baby?" A piercing scream filled the air. Jeff rolled to the floor of my office and rocked back and forth. The screaming slowly diminished.

I waited many minutes until he was quiet. His rocking continued. "What is happening now?" I asked cautiously. "I believe you have discovered the beginning of your sexual fantasies and it can help you become free."

"No, you don't understand," Jeff wailed. "You don't understand."

"What is it, Jeff?"

"That's when my mommy left me. That was the last time I remember seeing her until she came home. I've been trying to see her and I can't. She's gone."

The final piece of the puzzle had been identified. In a brief moment, Jeff experienced the quieting and pleasurable effect of having his penis rubbed, his mother's horror at discovering her husband's infidelity, and her disappearance from his life. Becoming an infant in his sexual fantasies was now understandable. He had been compulsively repeating a very traumatic episode from early childhood.

In his sexual fantasies he had repeatedly experienced arousal as an infant, alternating between being passive with something sexual being done to him and being aggressive, by forcing himself on women. He used various forbidden sexual acts. He often hurt women much as his father had hurt his mother. The unrelenting compulsion to continue the fantasies was tied to the loss of his mother. Such a loss is almost too difficult to fathom at his age. The incident had happened shortly before he was one year old.

Can imagery take one so far back in time? The answer is yes. Imagery is the way an infant's mind is formed. The memories are then fused to words from a later period. Usually such images and words remain unconscious. Bringing these memories into consciousness allowed Jeff to arrive at the insight that would lead to his being able to enter into an adult relationship with Joanna.

Although he had grown up physically in his fantasies, the underlying fixation had remained steadfast. He had not consciously known the one remaining critical element needed to give up his childhood sexuality. To assimilate the terrible loss of his mother he needed to remain in part fixated to the time just before she disappeared. He was eventually able to learn that all the women in his fantasies represented his early memories of his mother. To be able to fully engage in an intimate and loving relationship with a woman he had to finally give up needing his mother. He had been ready to do this and meeting Joanna became the stimulus to undo this remaining conflict from his past.

Shortly after the experience in guided imagery, he made love with Joanna. He did not use a fantasy. I was deeply moved when he described his first lovemaking. "When we entered her bedroom I was nervous. We had planned this evening knowing we would be making love. The room was filled with flowers and candles. As she lit them, I was thinking that some wonderful God had brought her into my life. She put on some of our favorite piano music.

"When we laid down on the bed we were still fully clothed. When I took her in my arms to kiss her I felt her body melt into mine. I can't describe what I felt. At that moment I knew that I loved her, loved her with all my heart. For many minutes we just kissed. I caressed her face and told her that I loved her. Tears came to her eyes and we cried together. Her words that she loved me too entered my entire being. I knew beyond any doubt that my love and desire for her were real. I knew I was finally free. Doctor, can you understand what I felt as we made love together. I was in love and loving Joanna alone."

Jeff reached his desired weight of 175 pounds about a year after he met Joanna. I continued to work with him for another year beyond that. Why did he need additional therapy? Jeff was a man imbued with the desire to leave no stone unturned in his efforts to become well. He set high goals for himself. When a goal was reached he discovered other areas in his life that were not completely satisfying and he sought to resolve whatever conflicts prevented his feeling fulfilled.

Did he want something that was unattainable? Not at all. He wanted freedom to live as fully as possible. He wanted to fully believe in himself. He wanted to know that he was a lovable and good person and that he could love without restrictions. Meeting Joanna helped spur him to an even greater search for self-awareness.

Two years after Jeff had completed his therapy they were married. I received a beautiful letter from Joanna written during their honeymoon in Hawaii.

"I write for Jeff and myself. He is standing next to me. Outside a glorious sunset fills the sky and a warm breeze surrounds us. We want you to know that we feel our life together is blessed. Even though we have never met, I often think of you. Jeff says that he'll always remember you as his real mother. I want you to know that I love him as much as you did."

APPENDIX 1

SUMMARY

THE FIVE KEYS TO
PERMANENT WEIGHT CONTROL

The Essential Guide for Achieving Your Ideal Weight

For those unfamiliar with my diet book, *The Five Keys to Permanent Weight Control,* I am presenting this brief summary to help you understand the specific references to the *Five Keys* diet that are part of each of the real life stories presented in *The Stranger in My Bed.*

The Five Keys to Permanent Weight Control represents a breakthrough in the field of dieting and weight control. Rather than focusing on specific foods to eat or specific combinations of carbohydrates, proteins and fats, the emphasis is on changing thinking and beliefs about eating.

There are five specific factors that comprise *The Five Keys to Permanent Weight Control.* They are:

1. How to use water to reduce food cravings and control appetite. Water is used to reduce appetite by filling the stomach at all meals and snacks. Each dieter will take a glass of water on awakening and a glass before each meal and at least one additional glass during meals. Also a half glass of water accompanies any snacks, no matter how small.

2. How to use the bathroom scale as a psychological assistant to reduce guilt over weight gain and how to initiate a special one-day water diet. Each dieter is encouraged to eliminate any negative feel-

ings about the daily use of the bathroom scale. The
scale provides accurate information about weight loss
and weight gain on a daily basis. Since the actual
gaining of just one pound of body weight requires
3500 additional calories of food it is unlikely that
those who gain two to five pounds in a single day
have done so by eating excess calories. Such weight
gain is almost always due to excess salt intake and its
related water retention. How salt excretion removes
the extra weight within one day or at the most two
days is described. A special one-day water diet is pre-
scribed to quickly reduce the extra weight. Daily use
of the scale is required to use this special technique
for weight control.

**3. The use of exercise to facilitate weight control
and improve overall physical and mental health is
recommended by most diet programs, including
this one.** Although weight control is strictly a matter
of calorie input and calorie utilization, exercise tends
to decrease body fat and increase muscle mass. Mus-
cles use over twice the amount of calories in a resting
state than fat and thus aid weight control. Exercise
improves mental functioning, self-esteem and the
capacity for all physical activities. The metabolic rate
is raised by exercise, especially aerobic exercise, when
the heart rate is elevated for a prolonged period of
time. The metabolic rate remains elevated for as long
as 12 hours after exercising, burning additional calo-
ries during this period.

**4. The stabilization period should be an essential
part of all diets.** Diet periods last one month at a
time followed by a one month period of stabiliza-
tion. During the stabilization period the dieter
strives to maintain the weight loss that occurs during

each period of dieting, but does not attempt to lose additional weight. The use of the stabilization period will prevent any reduction of the basal metabolic rate, which frequently occurs in prolonged diets. By adjusting to the slow and gradual weight loss that occurs on alternate months, dieters learn weight control.

In addition to allowing dieters to adapt to a relatively small monthly decrease in body weight, the stabilization period also offers them an opportunity to reflect on what makes them overeat and what difficulties they have in maintaining weight control. By the time their ideal weight is reached dieters have gained confidence in their ability to never regain lost weight. The use of the stabilization period also means that dieters will lose the same amount of weight for the same calorie reduction throughout their entire diet program. They will not reach that period when "they can't lose the last ten pounds."

5. Learning to use the power of mental imagery to change the thinking and behavior that has contributed to becoming overweight. By changing negative belief systems related to overeating, dieters learn to overcome their compulsive need to eat. To gain weight control, dieters learn to modify their thinking and subsequently their behavior using powerful visualization techniques. Most common situations that contribute to overeating are described in the *Five Keys* diet book and various imagery exercises are suggested to control them. The detailed examples of imagery provide a basis for dieters' creative efforts to produce imagery that fit their specific problems.

For example, if a person mainly binges by raiding the refrigerator the imagery exercises address that issue. If binging occurs only after a visit to the market that becomes the focus. If a preoccupation with body size causes depression and overeating then the imagery addresses that issue.

Here are three sample imagery exercises.

1. The dieter visualizes seeing the refrigerator completely locked by heavy chains.

2. The dieter opens the refrigerator and a ferocious animal leaps out and attacks him for attempting to binge.

3. The dieter looks into the refrigerator and sees the food as completely inedible.

These three examples, though simple in construction, are helpful if practiced daily. A positive statement follows each visualization like "I'll never use food from the refrigerator to binge again."

Imagery exercises can include great detail and be very specific to an individual's circumstances and problems.

In the eight case histories you will find many examples of how imagery is used by actual patients during their dieting and stabilization periods.

Mental imagery tends to be more effective when done in a relaxed manner. I suggest the use of a simple, but highly effective technique, which I call the **rag doll technique**. The dieter visualizes him or herself as a rag doll. After a slow inhalation the dieter slowly exhales and imagines becoming the rag doll. The inhalation and exhalation are repeated a second time allowing the dieter to quickly move into a state of heightened auto-suggestibility. During this relaxed state the dieter does the imagery exercises. Learning how to use imagery for dieting also opens up its use to overcome other difficulties and to foster personal growth.

Since the process of losing weight and learning weight control is primarily designed to enhance good health, it is important that all dieters strive to improve the quality of their diet. The *Five Keys* diet does not require that specific foods be eaten. However, a healthy diet is described and encouraged in the book. Overall health, longevity, reduction of various illnesses, including many cancers, depends on a well balanced diet. The *Five Keys* diet follows the guidelines of the USDA that consists of 55-65% daily calorie requirements from carbohydrates, 25-30% calories from fat, and 10-15% calories from protein. The diet is simple to follow and involves a 20 to 40% reduction of normal calorie needs in order to reduce weight by 4 to 8 pounds a month. During the non-diet month the calorie intake is usually increased to prevent further weight loss. The book includes a discussion of various other popular diets to provide some understanding of how the *Five Keys* diet differs from them.

There is a discussion of body size, body image, and how an "ideal" body size differs from one that is "idealized." A method to assess your body configuration and your level of body fat is described. Other subjects covered in the book include genetics, diabetes, binge eating, dietary problems in PMS and the influence of emotions on body weight and dieting.

Finally, in the chapters on **relapse** and the use of a **journal** there are discussions of ways to overcome any tendency to stop the diet program. They explain why dieters feel discouraged or have difficulty in maintaining their motivation to continue dieting. A list of questions that dieters can ask themselves about resistances to dieting helps them focus on underlying causes of relapse. Relapse is never seen as a reason or excuse to stop dieting.

The journal provides a safe place for self-exploration of conflicts about the diet program or other resistances to dieting. The many questions posed in the journal chapter on developing self-awareness help dieters face various personal issues that are frequently stirred up by dieting. The journal is seen as a personal confidant to assist dieters in their successful pursuit of permanent weight control.

APPENDIX 2

GUIDED IMAGERY THERAPY

Guided imagery, a visualization technique, has sometimes been called "waking dream" therapy. It delves into the unconscious mind and uses dream mechanisms, such as symbolic representation, whereby an object may take the place of a person or one person replaces another. Many times the dreamer readily interprets the visualizations. At other times the imagery therapist makes the interpretations.

Patients enter into a state of relaxation and keep their eyes closed during the guided imagery period. The therapist suggests an imagery setting to start the guided imagery. Such settings could include entering a cave, going underwater or into an empty house. Other settings can include going back to a specific time in one's past or to a situation where there is a confrontation with certain individuals, such as parents, siblings, etc.

Once the setting is established, the patient describes the changing imagery as fully as possible. The therapist follows the visualizations of the patient, as well as changing the setting when indicated. The patient will not only describe the changing scenes, but also will say whatever is spoken by anyone in the imagery. Since all imagery is a reflection of what is within one's unconscious mind, different parts of the person are expressed. By understanding the interaction of these internal figures, a new and often profound understanding of one's conflicts becomes possible.

Due to the use of visualization it is often possible to return to very early periods of childhood, even as early as the first year of life. All sensory impressions are recorded by the infant. Thus images, sounds, smells, and emotions can be reconstructed and experienced from this early period. For example, a one-year-old baby is very aware of his environment

and records experiences with great detail. Later if these ex-
periences are reproduced and described in the words of an
older person they can be extremely revealing. This is well il-
lustrated in the case study of Jeffrey.

When going back in time to one's childhood the emo-
tional content of the imagery can be intense. Often the pa-
tient will use the sounds and words of a still young, though
verbal, child. Frequently the patient will change voices as dif-
ferent characters enter the images. At times the patient as-
sumes a totally different body that symbolizes feelings experi-
enced during an earlier age. Occasionally the patient or other
persons from his life assume non-human forms that symbol-
ize attitudes or conflicts about the self or another person.

It is important to carefully evaluate a patient's readiness
when considering the use of guided imagery. I tend to use it
when a patient is struggling with a problem that has reached
a major barrier that is preventing needed insight. In all cases
the patient is aware of the process of the imagery and can
stop it at any time by opening his eyes and coming back into
current reality. The benefit comes from allowing the uncon-
scious self to be expressed and giving the adult ego an oppor-
tunity to correct the negative effects of the past.

Unlike more conventional therapy, guided imagery al-
lows a therapist to quickly by-pass resistances and reach into
the unconscious to hidden areas of conflict and trauma.
Therapists must carefully assess what they hear and guide
their patients into those areas of conflict that will offer a truly
corrective emotional experience. Guided imagery is a tech-
nique that offers an in-depth view of one's past and provides
solutions to working through forgotten experiences. The
eight case histories illustrate how certain patients faced the
unknown and, through the technique of guided imagery,
found new insights and ways to change their lives.

ABOUT THE AUTHOR

Marvin H. Berenson, M.D. is Clinical Professor of Psychiatry and Behavioral Sciences at the University of Southern California School of Medicine and specializes in the use of mental imagery for the treatment of psychosomatic disorders, addictions, compulsive disorders, and weight control problems. He uses a diverse array of psychological techniques in his general clinical work that include psychoanalysis, behavioral and cognitive therapy, as well as guided imagery therapy.

He has created a series of mental imagery techniques and exercises that he uses to enhance creativity, improve artistic and literary skills, help athletes maximize their performances and treat various physical and emotional problems. He has written *The Five Keys to Permanent Weight Control* and is co-author of *Think Yourself Smokeless* and the audiotape program, *Change Your Mind, Change Your Life*.